WARFARE BENEATH
THE WAVES

WARFARE BENEATH THE WAVES

GERMAN U-BOAT BATTLES WITH ALLIED CONVOYS

1940, 1943 & 1945

Axel Niestlé

Greenhill Books

Warfare Beneath the Waves

First published in Germany in 2021 by
Edition Erich Gröner

This revised edition first published in 2025 by
Greenhill Books,
c/o Pen & Sword Books Ltd,
George House, Unit 12 & 13,
Beevor Street, Off Pontefract Road,
Barnsley, South Yorkshire s71 1HN

www.greenhillbooks.com
contact@greenhillbooks.com

ISBN: 978-1-80500-073-0

Copyright © Axel Niestlé 2021

All rights reserved.

The right of Axel Niestlé to be identified as author
of this work has been asserted in accordance with
Section 77 of the Copyrights, Designs and Patents Act 1988.

CIP data records for this title are available from the British Library

Edited and designed by Donald Sommerville
Typeset in Arno Pro Small Text 12.25/15 pt

Printed and bound in India by Parksons Graphics Pvt. Ltd.

Page ii: The rear part of the conning tower of Otto Kretschmer's *U 99* with seven victory pennants hanging from the attack periscope. Unlike other commanding officers Kretschmer had no tonnage figures painted on his pennants, but simply the horseshoe emblem of the boat. Harbour details of the western Scorff bank at the Lorient base in the background have been carefully painted over by a censor for security reasons.

Contents

	List of Maps and Diagrams, Photo Credits	vi
	Preface	vii
	Introduction	1
1.	**The Night of the Long Knives** *Convoy SC 7 – October 1940*	18
2.	**Five Days in Mid-Atlantic** *Convoy SC 118 – February 1943*	82
3.	**The Final Convoy Battle** *JW 66 & RA 66 – April/May 1945*	198
	Appendices	
1.	Allied Day and Night Convoy Escort Positions	242
2.	U-boat Officers Deployed against Convoy SC 7	243
3.	U-boat Officers Deployed against Convoy SC 118	244
4.	U-boat Officers Deployed against JW 66 & RA 66	246
5.	Torpedo Attacks on SC 7	248
6.	Attacks on U-boats near SC 7	250
7.	Torpedo Attacks on SC 118	252
8.	Torpedo Attacks on JW 66 & RA 66	254
9.	Attacks on U-boats near SC 118	256
10.	Attacks on U-boats near JW 66 & RA 66	258
11.	Details of Air Cover for SC 118	260
	Ranks and Abbreviations	261
	Index	262

Maps and Diagrams

Fig. 1	SC 7 route map, Oct. 1940.	page 20
Fig. 2	*U 48* and SC 7, 17 Oct.	26
Fig. 3	*U 38* and SC 7, 18 Oct.	33
Fig. 4	Battle map. SC 7, 18/19 Oct.	39
Fig. 5	*U 46* and *U 101* vs. SC 7, 18 Oct.	42
Fig. 6	SC 118 route map, Jan.–Feb. 1943.	83
Fig. 7	Groups Haudegen and Pfeil.	84
Fig. 8	U-boats near SC 118, 4 Feb. 1940.	98
Fig. 9	Action around SC 118, 4–5 Feb.	105
Fig. 10	U-boats near SC 118, 5 Feb.	116
Fig. 11	Action around SC 118, 5–6 Feb.	128
Fig. 12	U-boats near SC 118, 6 Feb.	132
Fig. 13	Action around SC 118, 6–7 Feb.	148
Fig. 14	U-boats near SC 118, 7 Feb.	150
Fig. 15	Action around SC 118, 7–9 Feb.	174
Fig. 16	U-boats near SC 118, 8 Feb.	180
Fig. 17	Group Faust, from 21 Apr. 1945.	207
Fig. 18	JW 66 route map, Apr. 1945.	212
Fig. 19	Group Faust, from 26 Apr.	215
Fig. 20	Action near RA 66, 29/30 Apr.	222
Fig. 21	RA 66 route map, Apr./May 1945.	227

Photo Credits

The author and publishers would like to thank the following agencies for supplying illustrations on the pages noted.

Bibliothek für Zeitgeschichte: 2, 3, 15, 25, 27, 32, 41, 43, 48, 49, 51, 52–3, 56–7, 60–1, 62, 68, 77, 88–9, 100–1, 108–9, 119, 120, 124–5, 131, 138, 144, 155, 156, 160, 165, 179, 198–9, 219, 224, 233

Braeuer Collection: 31, 58, 67, 102, 110, 112, 141, 143, 146, 152, 158, 162, 166, 188, 190

Neelsen Collection: 39
Skjolt Collection: 12, 234

Images from the Imperial War Museum (IWM) and US National Archives (USNA) are individually acknowledged in captions.

All other images are from the author's collection.

Preface

SINCE THE LAST DECADES OF THE 20TH CENTURY, there has been a tendency to dismiss unjustly many of the earlier, but previously praised works describing the combat history of military actions of World War Two. Jürgen Rohwer's *The Critical Convoy Battles in March 1943*, first published in Germany in 1975, stands out as a superb operational history of the U-boat war between the Kriegsmarine and the Allied navies. Ever since its publication I have constantly referred to this book, with its unemotional but detailed narrative style, enriched by an abundance of tables, graphics and situation maps, and it has inspired me in my own research. Comparable German-language publications about the events of the U-boat war have largely been absent ever since. Fortunately, combat history, often embedded in a broader, much more differentiating perspective, has undergone a renaissance in recent years. In combination with modern approach methods, this will hopefully lead to a deeper understanding of wars as breaches of taboos in civilisation.

The basis for the three main parts of this publication describing the history of selected convoy battles arose during the last twenty or so years in the course of my research on the history of Germany's U-boats. However, for some parts of the story, the transition from bits and pieces of records, wedged between document folders, to a fully documented version was still missing. Taking a broader and deeper view, the descriptions of the individual battles around convoys SC 7, SC 118 and RA 66 suggest reflections on both strategic and tactical developments during the whole course of the Battle of the Atlantic between 1939 and 1945. The twists and turns of the fighting were characterised by triumph and defeat on both sides, linked by rays of hope and often by parity between the opponents. The individual battles are therefore joined by an invisible thread of developments. A special challenge in the work about just these three convoy battles was that, despite several attempts, previous scholars had been unsuccessful in creating a consistent and comprehensive narrative setting out the details of the action. This work is intended to close these gaps and, in many cases, correct earlier published information about the attacks and the causes of the losses on both sides.

With the end of secrecy embargoes, most of the military and technical documents dating back to World War Two have now become freely accessible for research. Also, the increasing availability on the internet of online catalogues of the important archives in all the combatant countries, as well as many of the records themselves, means that there are now almost no limits to the opportunities for detailed analysis and reconstruction of wartime events through careful research and examination. In this connection, the author is proud to thank the many unnamed, but always helpful, members of staff at the German Bundesarchiv/Militärarchiv in Freiburg and the British National Archives in London. In addition, many long-time friends and fellow researchers have offered their help over the years and I am most grateful for their support and willingness to participate in critical discussions about many controversial questions. My sincere thanks go especially to Walter Cloots, Frans Beckers, Eric Zimmermann, Malcolm Llewellyn-Jones, David Sibley†, Thomas Weis, Ragnar Ragnarsson†, and Jerry Mason. Special thanks also go to Derek Waller, who kindly gave me valuable help in editing the English text version. Greatly appreciated also was the support from Karl Heinz Jockel, who produced the original German layout.

This project, like all the others in my past and hopefully many more in future, would have been impossible without the support of my family. A deep thanks therefore goes to my wife Katrin and to Friederike, Erik, Lennart, Lasse and Bosse for their acceptance of my repeated temporary absence from our family life while investigating and writing up the stories of these tragic actions that took place so many decades ago.

Introduction

AFTER THE DEFEAT OF IMPERIAL GERMANY in the First World War and the subsequent ban on U-boats for the Reichsmarine in accordance with the requirements of the 1919 Versailles Peace Treaty, Germany was once again allowed to possess U-boats after the signing of the Anglo-German Naval Agreement in June 1935. The newly appointed Flag Officer U-boats, Kapitän zur See (KptzS) Karl Dönitz, soon developed the necessary operational plan for the use of his numerically small, but well trained and elite branch within the strategic concepts of the German Navy. Dönitz considered that the chances of success of the available U-boat types against warships were poor due to their relatively slow surfaced and submerged speeds and the alleged ability of the Royal Navy's ultrasonic detection device (Asdic) to

Small talk among U-boat aces aboard *U 100* at Lorient on 12 October 1940.
From left Kptlt Günther Prien of *U 47* (famous for sinking the battleship HMS *Royal Oak*), Kptlt Joachim Schepke and the commander of 2nd U-boat Flotilla, KKpt Heinz Fischer.

The British steamer *Creekirk,* here photographed in January 1939 off Montevideo in Uruguay, had had a varied history since its construction in 1912, before it was torpedoed by *U 99* on 18 October 1940. Owing to its heavy cargo of iron ore *Creekirk* went under in less than 30 seconds with all hands. This was a common fate of such heavily laden old ships.

locate submerged U-boats. With a military conflict against Britain a definite possibility from 1938 on, he soon concentrated his thoughts on the prospects for commercial warfare by his U-boats. Based on the tactical knowledge gained during World War One, when Dönitz had served as the commander of *UB-68,* he created, among other ideas, the basics of the so-called pack tactic. This relied on several boats working together against escorted merchant ship convoys, whose area-wide reintroduction in case of war Dönitz took for granted. By deploying a centrally led mass of U-boats he hoped this pack tactic would solve both the problem of finding the convoys in the vastness of the oceans and of overcoming the escorts in the course of any attacks on the merchant ships themselves. Following the commissioning of the first ocean-going Type VII and IX U-boats, large-scale exercises were carried out during the spring manoeuvres in the North Sea and the Atlantic off the Bay of Biscay in the pre-war years 1938 and 1939 to test the practicability of the pack tactic, and proof of its utility was established. Contrary to the expectation of foreign navies, Flag Officer U-boats counted especially on the nearly complete invisibility of a surfaced U-boat by night due to its low silhouette, which made optical detection by usually higher placed lookouts difficult. The attacking U-boat was to break through the enemy escort screen at high speed in a torpedo-boat style, retreating in the same way after a successful attack in order to escape from an expected counter-attack by the warships. As long as the enemy escorts had to rely on optical methods to detect attacking U-boats in the hours of darkness, Dönitz believed his own U-boats to be superior to the enemy's defences despite much scepticism about this even within the Kriegsmarine.

After the beginning of hostilities with France and Great Britain on 3 September 1939, the nominal strength of the U-boat arm proved to be totally insufficient for the task of merchant warfare against the Allies

HMS *Bluebell* was among the first Flower-class corvettes to join the Royal Navy. Commissioned on 19 July 1940, the ship had its first encounter with U-boats during the battle around SC 7. The photograph shows *Bluebell* later in the war after it was fitted with Type 271 radar.

and the British Royal Navy as the world's largest fleet. At that time Dönitz, as newly appointed Befehlshaber der Unterseeboote (BdU), had only 57 U-boats in commission, with only 27 belonging to the ocean-going Types I, VII and IX, whose range of operations allowed their use in the seas west of the British Isles. Moreover, out of the total number, only 45, including 22 ocean-going boats, were available for immediate front-line use with the rest undergoing tests, work-ups or being used for operational training. Operational losses during the first months of the war, temporary assignments to other tasks and necessary yard overhaul periods, as well as long transfer times between the combat zones and the U-boat bases in the North Sea and Baltic made it almost impossible until the summer of 1940 to plan and execute pack operations by the U-boats against Allied convoys west of Britain. Instead the U-boats mainly operated individually during these

Kptlt Otto Kretschmer (*centre*) on the conning tower of his boat *U 99*. In contrast to most other U-boat commanders Kretschmer preferred wearing a black boat cap instead of the usual officer's cap with its white cover. In front of the handrail on the side of the conning tower a golden coloured horseshoe is fixed as the emblem of the boat.

early months of the war within assigned areas along the known or expected traffic routes.

Results achieved at this time in the tonnage war against Allied merchant fleets nevertheless exceeded German expectations and caused heavy damage to the Allied war effort. However, from the perspective of the U-boat arm, German successes during the first year of the war were paid for dearly by heavy losses. Out of a total of 71 boats temporarily or permanently used in front-line operations during that period, no fewer than 29 were lost, mostly to Allied surface ships employed in the anti-submarine (A/S) role and to mines. The majority of these boats sank with all hands and the few survivors mostly went into British captivity. During the same time, German U-boat building yards delivered just 28 new boats, keeping the Kriegsmarine after one year of U-boat warfare nominally at almost the same strength as in September 1939. Still worse, the number of ocean-going boats ready for front-line service had dropped to just 16 with the total number of front-line boats at 22. The blood-letting for the U-boat arm in well-trained pre-war personnel was especially high and caused major problems in the following build-up phase of the U-boat arm, after the increased building programme ordered in October 1939 had got going properly.

Kptlt Heinrich Liebe of *U 38*, here shown in ordinary working dress before leaving on patrol, preferred the cap with blue cover instead of the more common 'captain's' white cover.

Following the successful land campaign against France in May/June 1940, operational prospects for the U-boats changed drastically. With the availability of layover and yard locations along the French Biscay coast as from July 1940 for crew resting and repairs or fitting

The US Coast Guard Cutter *Ingham* (WPG-35) in heavy North Atlantic weather. The cutter was part of the ocean escort group for the convoy SC 118 and played a vital part in the battle despite a defective sonar set. On the morning of 7 February 1943, the *Ingham* assisted in the rescue of survivors from the torpedoed American troop transport *Henry R. Mallory*. (USNA)

Lt-Cdr Richard Been Stannard, VC, RNR, on the bridge of the destroyer *Vimy*. Stannard was awarded the Victoria Cross for his service commanding the trawler *Arab* off Norway in April–May 1940. He was appointed to *Vimy* in late 1942 and played a notable part in defending SC 118, including in the destruction of *U 187*, the first convoy shadower. (*IWM A 15013*)

out, there was no need for the former long in- and out-bound transits around the north of the British Isles. Consequently, the total number of sea days being spent within the operational area increased considerably despite the still very small number of front-line boats. However, the necessity to detach a larger number of U-boats for training purposes and to cover the demand for officers and crews to man new constructions led to a continuing decrease in the number of active front-line U-boats during the second half of 1940, reaching an absolute low point with just 20 (ocean-going) boats at the turn of the year 1940/41. Despite this, Dönitz started a new attempt in August 1940 to carry out pack operations against any reported Allied convoys under the different combat conditions, profiting also from a temporary numerical weakness of the Royal Navy after its heavy losses off Norway and in the retreat from France. Following initial success with group operations, termed 'wolf packs' in the propaganda language of the day, against convoys SC 2 and HX 72, sinking or damaging numerous merchant ships, the month of October 1940 was to bring a temporary high point in the fight against

Allied merchant ship convoys. The detailed examination of the fight around the eastbound convoy SC 7, covered in the first chapter of the book, exemplifies this phase of the U-boat campaign between August 1940 and March 1941, often referred to as 'The Happy Times' by the U-boat men. Tactical combat conditions at that time favoured the good results achieved. Correspondingly the personnel and tactical deficiencies in the Royal Navy were highlighted and subsequent improvements and new developments suggested.

The years 1941 and 1942 saw a constant build-up of the U-boat arm. With comparatively low casualty rates, and despite the loss of several of the most successful and prominent U-boat commanders in March 1941, the U-boats became the only effective offensive naval weapon against Great Britain after German surface battle units played no further role following the loss of the battleship *Bismarck* in May 1941. The numerical increase of British A/S forces by new construction and the transfer of 50 old destroyers from the officially still neutral United States, improved training methods and an increasing use of aircraft for escort and A/S work soon strengthened the Allied position. Achievements by the Royal Navy and the British Naval Intelligence Department in capturing and deciphering the highly secret U-boat radio codes used between shore command and the boats at sea led to a sharp decrease in merchant ship sinkings during the second half of 1941. This process was further accelerated by orders from Adolf Hitler and the German Naval Staff to detach numerous U-boats to side-show theatres such as the Mediterranean and Arctic Sea. To make matters even worse, monthly losses in December 1941 reached for the first time a temporary high of ten boats with four of them lost in a single convoy battle against the well-defended convoy HG 76 running on the Gibraltar–Britain route.

Despite numerous clues and much evidence, especially for the deep break into the operational radio circuits, Dönitz and his relatively small operations staff at BdU Headquarters remained generally in the dark about results and developments on the British and Allied side. This applied especially to the technological advances in radar to locate surfaced U-boats from ships and aircraft and the use of ship-based High Frequency Direction Finding equipment to pinpoint

U-boat transmissions. Due to increased use of these new means, the U-boats soon lost their previous tactical advantage of invisibility at night and in bad weather. The chances for a successful torpedo attack against escorted merchant ships by existing U-boats, which were technologically submersibles rather than true underwater vessels owing to their dependence on batteries to drive their electric motors when submerged, became ever smaller after mid-1941. The absence of German aerial reconnaissance over the eastern Atlantic along the convoy routes to and from Great Britain also turned out to be a serious disadvantage for the U-boat arm in finding and keeping contact with Allied convoys.

The interlude of renewed U-boat successes in the first half of 1942 following the entry of the United States of America into the war deceived the U-boat Command about the apparent trend in the tonnage contest. Results in this period were mainly achieved by individually operating U-boats against unescorted merchant ships off the US East Coast and in the Caribbean, because the US Navy was neither numerically, tactically nor technologically at par with the British Royal Navy, and the C-in-C of the US Navy stubbornly resisted the introduction of convoys for coastal shipping traffic. Following the gradual introduction of convoys in Northern and Central American coastal waters after May 1942, the U-boats were able to compensate for poorer results in these waters by shifting into less controlled waters off South America, West Africa and South Africa during the following months. The option to replenish fuel, torpedoes and provisions at sea from supply U-boats newly introduced in spring/summer 1942 was most helpful in the full exploitation of the available number of U-boats. Parallel to the southerly shift of operational areas, in July 1942 the U-boats returned to the North Atlantic battlefield to combat the transatlantic convoys, which had been left mostly unmolested since January 1942 in favour of the better chances in American coastal waters. The number of front-line boats, which had continuously risen since the end of 1941, helped to keep the sinking figure at a high level, although encounters with the increasingly better trained and equipped escorts and aircraft led to rising losses among the U-boat fleet.

Due to the rapid increase from mid-1942 in new merchant ship tonnage, especially by the numbers of Liberty-type standard ships from the huge American shipyards, the strategic tonnage war as a means of defeating Britain had failed by the autumn of 1942 despite substantial sinking figures. Faced with the statistical evidence, the German Naval Staff was forced to turn the tonnage war concept into a campaign against the steadily rising supply of goods and war material to Great Britain to prevent an expected Allied invasion of the continent from there. Hence the Europe-bound convoys running on the transatlantic routes became a prime target for the BdU. The battle around convoy SC 118, sailing from America to Britain in early 1943, is covered in the second part of the book as an example

The Flower-class corvette HMS *Abelia*, showing the wear and tear of the Atlantic weather, on entering harbour with the off-watch crew on the forecastle. At the beginning of 1943 the small, but highly seaworthy corvettes still made up the majority of vessels in the convoy escort groups. (*IWM A 7312*)

U 187 entering the ice-covered port of Farsund in southern Norway in the afternoon of 14 January 1943. This is the last known photograph of the boat, which, after a short stop, sailed again on the following day on its first and only patrol in the North Atlantic, where it was sunk on 4 February 1943 shortly after the first sighting of convoy SC 118.

of the combat conditions in the North Atlantic during this phase of the war. Dönitz himself recalled this convoy battle in his post-war memoirs as probably the fiercest during the whole conflict. Both sides still considered themselves at this point as likely to come out on the winning side in the war, although recent German defeats on land in Russia and North Africa and the effects of terror air attacks against the German homeland revealed a steady weakening of the German strategic position.

The increasing inexperience of U-boat crews as the war proceeded is another important factor in any examination of the operational results of the U-boat war. For the whole period of the war the German Navy's Manning Department only coped with the high demand for additional personnel to man newly constructed U-boats or to be front-line replacements by drafting in inexperienced officers and men from other service branches in the Kriegsmarine. Even the provision of sufficient numbers of U-boat commanding officers with front-line U-boat experience proved impossible at times. U-boats newly assigned for front-line service from 1942 onwards normally carried only a few crewmen with previous combat experience, and this contributed to the high percentage of boats lost on their first patrol. Increased loss rates from July 1942 onwards after the renewal of anti-convoy operations in the North Atlantic led to a constant drain of experienced front-line personnel, exacerbating the manning problems in the U-boat arm during the following months.

On 24 May 1943, owing to recent heavy losses, operations against Allied convoys in the North Atlantic were temporarily stopped on orders from Grand Admiral Dönitz, now promoted to C-in-C of the Kriegsmarine but still also serving as BdU. Thereafter the focal point of the U-boat campaign shifted southwards into the Mid- and South Atlantic for the next months without any substantial change in the loss figures. A renewed attempt during the autumn and winter months of 1943/44 to revive the anti-convoy campaign in the North Atlantic theatre with the existing U-boat types but new weapons also failed, with heavy losses among the boats and crews. The now almost complete surveillance by shore- and ship-based aircraft, a steady increase in the number of modern escorts, further technological advances in weapons and detection techniques, and good cooperation between Allied departments made convoy ship losses to U-boats the exception and kept Allied transport across the Atlantic almost unaffected. Thanks to the frequent deciphering of the German operational radio traffic, which happened almost in real time owing to the use of electro-mechanical decryption machines, Allied air and sea forces gained increasing opportunities to use this information tactically against individual U-boats. Following the utter failure of several more anti-convoy operations U-boat Command eventually abandoned all centrally controlled group operations against transatlantic convoys in March 1944. The remaining U-boats then continued either to operate individually or they returned to their French bases to become available after overhaul for use in reaction to the expected Allied invasion of France.

The installation of the new schnorkel device starting in early 1944, which allowed unlimited submerged transits by the use of diesel engines at periscope depth and also recharging of the batteries while submerged, initially made the otherwise technologically outdated U-boats of the Kriegsmarine relatively immune against air attacks. However, it provided only a limited increase in combat efficiency due to the much slower cruising speed and other disadvantages. Owing to bottlenecks in production, transport and shipyard capacities, the refits of front-line U-boats were much delayed, so that even in mid-1944 some boats sailed for the North Atlantic without schnorkel equipment.

The introduction of the schnorkel opened the final chapter in the U-boat campaign, now termed 'Total Underwater Warfare'. Starting in June 1944 with operations against the Allied invasion forces in the Channel, it later transformed into a full-scale inshore campaign, mainly within British or American coastal waters. In subsidiary theatres like the Arctic, the installation of the schnorkel equipment on U-boats was often delayed well into 1945. This forced the Flag Officer U-boats Arctic Sea to continue centrally controlled pack operations against the supply convoys passing through his command area towards the Soviet ports of Archangel and Murmansk until March 1945.

But even the use of the schnorkel left the old U-boat types still very vulnerable to Allied escorts. Once located, their slow underwater speed made it extremely difficult for them to escape from experienced and skilfully led groups of escort ships, especially in shallow waters. Sophisticated sonar sets and powerful A/S weapons like the Squid depth-charge thrower aboard the latest British Loch- and Castle-class escorts achieved much higher kill ratios than previous sensors and weapons. Despite some limited U-boat successes during the winter months of 1944/45, by the end of the first quarter of 1945 the Allied A/S forces had again gained a firm upper hand against the old-type schnorkel U-boats. When the BdU at the end of March 1945 finally became aware of the high loss rates during the previous months,

INTRODUCTION

The ships of the Loch class represented the highpoint in the development of A/S vessels for the Royal Navy at the end of World War Two. On the evening of 29 April 1945 HMS *Loch Shin*, as a member of 19th Escort Group, took part in the destruction of *U 307* and *U 286* prior to the departure of convoy RA 66.

the old-type schnorkel U-boats were then mostly withdrawn from inshore operational areas to more distant regions west of Britain. With the new U-boat Types XXI and XXIII coming too late to have any significant effect on the U-boat war, the Allies had achieved a full victory against the U-boats by the time that hostilities in Europe ended in May 1945.

The last convoy battle during the war around the Arctic double-convoy JW 66/RA 66 in late April and early May 1945, covered in the third chapter, stands out as an example of the failure of the U-boat war pursued with the outdated and old-fashioned submersible types. It also marks the end of the campaign for superiority on the oceanic lifelines of the Allies, which lasted for 69 months. For the second time in the 20th century the feared German 'hunters of the oceans' had been beaten by Allied naval forces under the leadership of the British Royal Navy and the US Navy. The German strategy to undermine the world-wide dominance of the two leading naval powers by the use of a relatively small military branch and the pursuit of economic warfare turned out from the beginning to be a hopeless attempt to change the military

U 481 under Kptlt Klaus Andersen was an ex-Group Faust schnorkel U-boat which was intercepted off Norway and is shown here while being escorted to surrender at a British port by the 9th Escort Group. The boat is fitted with armoured boxes on both sides of the bridge, often temporarily installed during 1943–44 to shelter the lookouts and gunners from machine-gun fire during air attacks. (*IWM A 28903*)

The crew of *U 286* on deck after the commissioning ceremony of the boat at Vegesacker Werft of Bremen on 5 June 1943. In the first row the officers (*with or without officer's sash, left to right*): Engineer Officer Lt Ing Ulrich Hemken, commander ObltzS (KO) Willi Dietrich, 1st Watch Officer LtzS Jürgen Kriegshammer and 2nd Watch Officer Oberfähnrich zur See Rolf Skukies. Extreme right is Warrant Quartermaster Rudolf Kärgelein. Only Kriegshammer survived the war.

situation. More than 30,000 U-boat men killed in action during World War Two paid the highest price for their loyalty to a criminal regime and to their Commander-in-Chief, who served it in blind obedience. Although the figures of victims on both sides in the campaign can seems overshadowed by the massive daily loss rates on the land fronts, the endless lists of the names of those killed on the various memorials to the war at sea in Germany, Great Britain and elsewhere remind us to pause for a moment to remember. As their legacy, the millions of dead place a commitment on future generations to live together in peace in order to avoid a repeat of the deadly mistakes of the past.

1.
The Night of the Long Knives
Convoy SC 7 – October 1940

Prelude to Battle

ONE OF THE MOST OFTEN CITED CONVOY BATTLES in the opening phase of the Battle of the Atlantic is the one around convoy SC 7 in October 1940. Ranking high among the worst Allied convoy disasters in the entire war, the battle is often referred to as the full start of the

U 99 on the River Scorff shortly before making fast at Lorient on 22 October 1940. While the officers have assembled on the conning tower, the men of the sea watch have already put out the fenders for the mooring manoeuvre and the off-watch crew are lined up behind the conning tower.

Convoy Cruising Order of SC 7 on 5 October 1940

14 *Valparaiso* (Swe) Tyne	13 *Carsbreck* (Br) Grimsby	12 *Flynderborg* (Br) Medway	11 *Beatus* (Br) Tyne
24 *Trevisa* (Br) Grangemouth	23 *Languedoc* (Br) Clyde	22 *Convallaria* (Swe) Medway	21 *Corinthic* (Br) Hull
34 *Winona* (Br) Glasgow	33 *Gunborg* (Swe) Medway	32 *Soesterberg* (Neth) Hull	31 *Blairspey* (Br) Grangemouth
44 *Inger Elisabeth* (Nor) Methil	43 *Trident* (Br) Barry	42 *Botusk* (Br) Hull	41 *Scoresby* (Br) Sunderland
54 *Empire Brigade* (Br) Tyne	53 *Havorn* (Nor) Mersey	52 *Snefjeld* (Nor) London	51 *Assyrian* (Br) Liverpool
64 *Eaglescliffe Hall* (Br) Preston	63 *Thoroy* (Nor) Mersey	62 *Fiscus* (Br) Clyde	61 *Clintonia* (Br) Manchester
74 *Aenos* (Gre) Manchester	73 *Niritos* (Gre) Mersey	72 *Thalia* (Gre) Mersey	71 *Sedgepool* (Br) Manchester
	83 *Somersby* (Br) Leith	82 *Dioni* (Gre) Belfast	81 *Empire Miniver* (Br) Newport
94 *Sneland* (Nor) Newport	93 *Boekelo* (Neth) London	92 *Karlander* (Nor) Sharpness	91 *Creekirk* (Br) Cardiff

Ownership and destination of each vessel shown.   *General direction of travel.* →

U-boat pack tactics planned since pre-war days. Instead of attacking submerged at daylight or in night-time submerged manoeuvres as expected by the British Admiralty, the U-boat Command under Konteradmiral Karl Dönitz, advocated surface night attack tactics, if possible, even from inside the convoy screen. The low and small silhouette of a surfaced U-boat facilitated the unseen approach. Likewise, the U-boat could easily retreat at high speed after launching an attack and avoid long and exhausting submerged withdrawals under the threat of possible counter-attacks by the convoy escorts. The high hopes in Admiralty circles that the pre-war development of the highly secret Asdic equipment for detecting and maintaining contact with submerged submarines would reduce their effectiveness so that they would never become a fatal menace again, as they had been during World War I, were far from realistic. The result of the surface U-boat

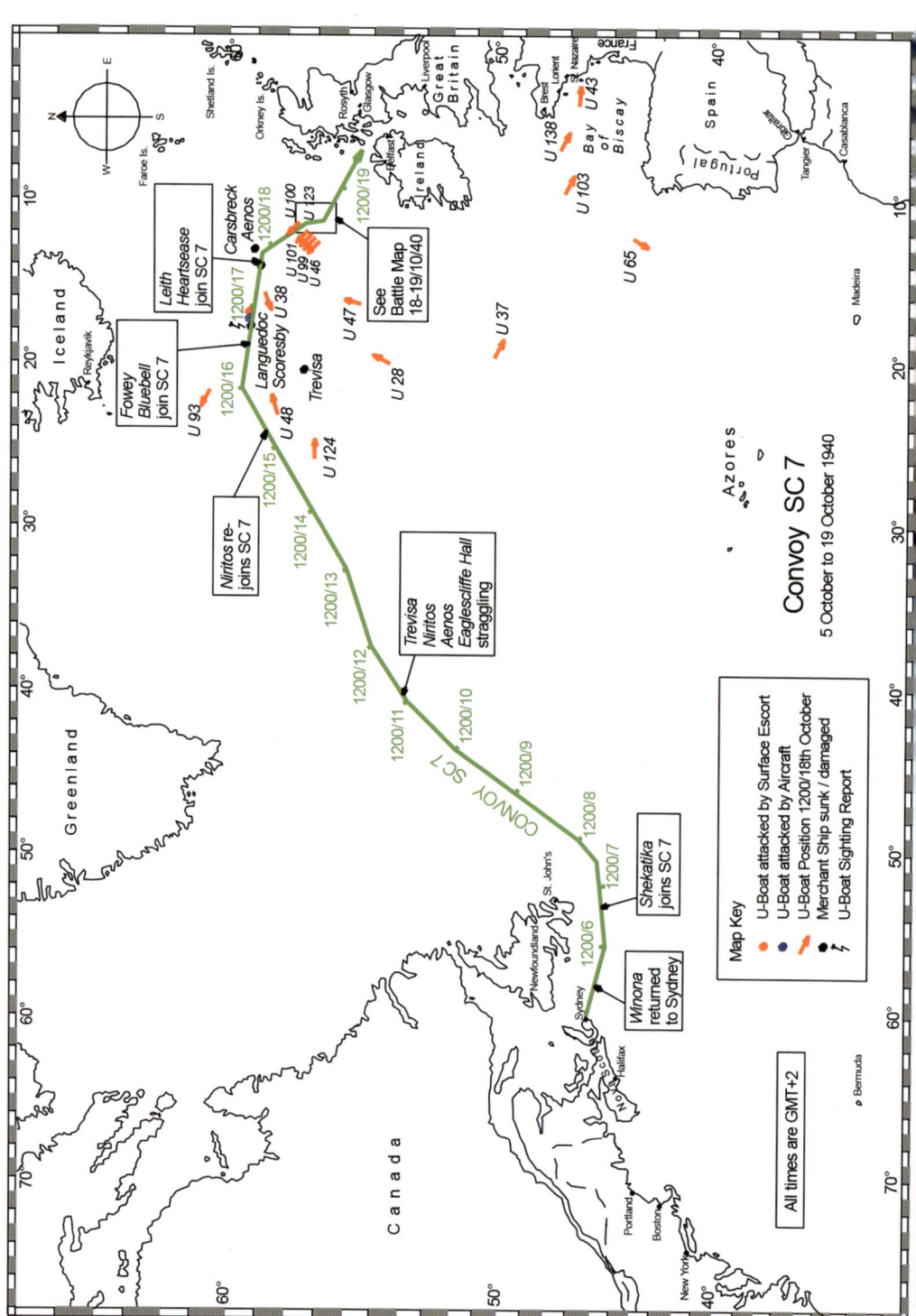

attack tactic was that the Asdic was practically useless. Hydrophones, which hitherto had often been relied on at night or during bad weather also offered no help in the vicinity of a convoy. Thus, the only practical means of detecting a surfaced U-boat at night were visual, which reduced the chances of sighting to a minimum. Without assistance from radar, which was yet to come, the Allied convoy escorts, insufficient in number and often also incapable of successfully pursuing a surfaced U-boat owing to their lack of speed, were virtually helpless against the aggressive U-boat attacks.[1] The period of autumn/winter 1940/41, when the men of the U-boats for the first time felt entirely equal to the enemy defences, is generally known as the 'Happy Time' for the U-boat arm.

Ironically, the British Admiralty was already aware of this new tactical situation. An analysis of U-boat attacks on ships actually in convoy, carried out by the Director of Anti-Submarine Warfare (DASW), showed that during August 1940 ten convoys were attacked, seven by night and three by day. Figures for September 1940 were nine convoys attacked, seven by night and two by day. In only four out of fourteen night attacks was any Asdic contact made by escorting ships. These figures did not include attacks on stragglers. From the evidence available, DASW concluded that the U-boats probably closed on the surface, preferably on the bow of the convoy, relying on their small silhouettes to escape detection and high surface speed to effect retreat. U-boats in other words were being used as torpedo boats. Attacks were believed to be pressed as close as considered safe, but the possibility of the use of long-range slow-speed torpedoes was also taken into consideration. DASW reported his analysis of recent U-boat attack tactics, which was remarkably correct, to the Admiralty on 14 October 1940.[2]

At this time convoy SC 7 had already been at sea for nine days on its way to Britain and unknown to the ships and crews, this convoy was to endure the full extent of the new U-boat tactics in the following days.

For the senior officer of the escort or the convoy commodore it was often impossible to record the correct train of events amidst the

Fig. 1 (left): Course map of Convoy SC 7, 5–19 October 1940.

confusing situation in the heat of a night-time battle. Escorts and merchant ships often became engaged in rescue work, thus dropping behind the convoy and losing touch with the situation ahead of them. Even after the termination of the battle, conflicting reports and testimonies sometimes made it impossible to find the truth. After the war, historians and authors tended not to care too much about an exact analysis of the battle but concentrated on various other human or technical topics.[3] Thus, it is not surprising that more than 80 years after the events, and even after the full set of the contemporary records of both sides became available to researchers, no exact assessment for the battle around convoy SC 7 has been made.[4] Thus, for the first time, a detailed analysis of the events based on British and German documents

U 46 on entering Kiel-Tirpitzhafen on 29 October 1940 just before making fast. Right of the periscope stands Kptlt Richard Zapp, embarked for one patrol as supernumerary commander under training. At the front of the conning tower the first three painted numbers of 158,381 grt, the boat's total claimed tonnage sunk by then, are visible.

HMS *Scarborough* was one of the first sloops built for the Royal Navy after World War One, completed in 1930. From February 1940, *Scarborough* was part of the 1st Escort Vessel Division based at Liverpool and was initially the only escort vessel attached to Convoy SC 7.

is offered, especially for the most intense period of the attacks against convoy SC 7 during the night of 18/19 October 1940. All times are given in German Summer Time (= GMT+2) maintained aboard all U-boats throughout the action, unless stated otherwise. Allied ships variously kept either GMT, British Summer Time (BST = GMT+1) or in rare cases individual ship times.

The 35 ships of convoy SC 7 left Sydney, Newfoundland, at 1300 on 5 October 1940. A single warship, the British sloop HMS *Scarborough* (Cdr N. V. Dickinson) provided escort for the crossing of the western part of the North Atlantic. The Admiralty envisaged reinforcing the escort when the convoy reached 21° West. During the first night at sea the British steamer *Winona* had to return to Sydney when its dynamo broke down. On 7 October the British steamer *Shekatika* joined the convoy after being unable to keep up with its original convoy HX 78 owing to low quality coal received in Canada. The following days were

The Type IX B *U 124* entering Lorient on 13 November 1940, displaying its pennants in the wind. Kptlt Wilhelm Schulz oversees the mooring manoeuvre, standing on a step in the conning tower. The 'weather frog' painted on the conning tower symbolizes *U 124*'s temporary detachment as a weather-reporting boat during the previous patrol, a task that was thoroughly disliked by all U-boat crews.

The Greek *Aenos*, which lost contact with SC 7 on 11 October 1940 in a storm, subsequently fell victim to *U 38* on the straggler route. Built in 1910, the vessel here displays its unusual bow design.

uneventful, but in a heavy storm during the night of 10 October four ships lost contact with the convoy and began straggling. Only the Greek vessel *Niritos* was able to rejoin the convoy on 15 October while the Great Lakes' steamer *Eaglescliffe Hall* finally reached the Clyde on 19 October after an independent passage.

The two other stragglers were less lucky as both were sunk by U-boats operating along their track to a British port. The Canadian *Trevisa*, also a former Great Lakes' steamer, loaded with 460 standards of lumber, was sighted by *U 124* (Kptlt Wilhelm Schulz) at 1500 on 15 October. A torpedo fired at 1729 in a submerged daylight attack missed unobserved by the crew of the *Trevisa*. *U 124* pursued the ship and at 0350 on 16 October fired a second torpedo in a night-time submerged attack.[5] The *Trevisa* was hit in the stern and sank soon afterwards with the loss of seven of its crew. The destroyer HMS *Keppel* (Lt R.J. Hanson), returning independently to Liverpool after escorting the troop convoy OL 7 until

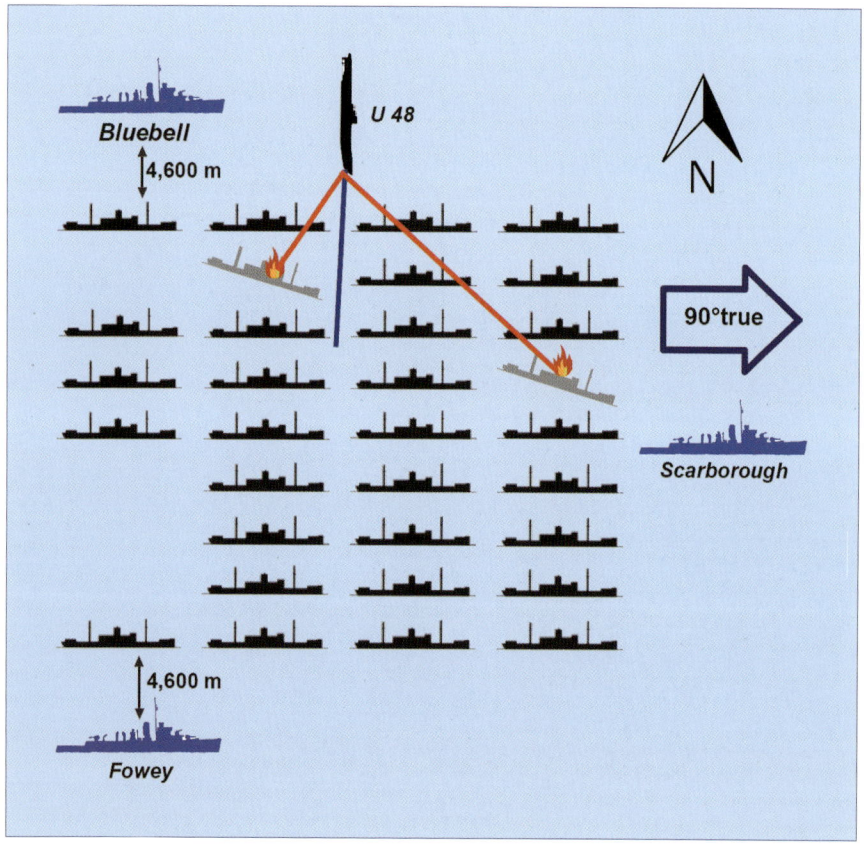

Fig. 2: Situation during the attack of *U 48* on SC 7 at 0553 on 17 Oct. 1940.

16 October to its mid-ocean dispersal point, rescued fourteen survivors at daylight. The Greek steamer *Aenos*, carrying 6,276 tons of wheat, was found by *U 38* (Kptlt Heinrich Liebe) at 0907 on 17 October in a position well ahead of its original convoy. A single torpedo fired at 0951 in a daylight submerged attack missed the ship by the bow. Following the miss, *U 38* surfaced near the ship and opened fire with its 10.5-cm deck gun. After many hits the *Aenos* finally sank at 1052.[6] Four of the crew were killed in the action, while the *Eaglescliffe Hall*, led to the scene by an RAF Coastal Command aircraft, picked up the remaining 25 survivors several hours later.

On the evening of 16 October, the lone escort of SC 7 was joined by the sloop HMS *Fowey* (Lt C. G. de L. Bush) and the Flower-class corvette HMS *Bluebell* (Lt-Cdr R. E. Sherwood), which had previously escorted the outbound convoy OA 228 as far as its mid-ocean dispersal point. During the following night *U 48* (Kptlt Heinrich Bleichrodt) sighted the convoy at 0300 about 500 nautical miles north-west of the North Channel and reported it to the BdU. At this time the convoy was steering a mean course of 090° at 7 knots and was carrying out zig-zag pattern No. 17. The escorts were stationed as shown opposite and were zig-zagging independently. To gain a better position for an attack, *U 48* crossed ahead of the convoy to be down-moon before attacking on the surface. Evading *Bluebell* on the port beam, at 0553 the boat fired three single torpedoes at different targets at long range from outside the convoy. First the ex-French but now requisitioned British tanker *Languedoc* in convoy position No. 23 was hit about 150 feet from the bow by the last torpedo after a run-time of 160 seconds (= 2,470 metres). The first torpedo exploded in No. 3 hold of the British steamer *Scoresby*, then the lead ship of the fourth column, after a run-

The *Scoresby* was owned by Headlam & Son of Whitby and was sunk by *U 48* on 17 October. All 39 crew members were rescued by the corvette *Bluebell*. This photo was taken at Cape Town before the war.

Kptlt Heinrich Bleichrodt following the award of the Knight's Cross of the Iron Cross on 24 October 1940 as commander of *U 48*. After two successful patrols with that boat he took command of the Type IX C boats *U 67* and *U 109* and eventually received the Oak Leaves on 23 September 1942 after further successes. From 1943 onwards he held shore appointments at home, where he finished the war as commander of the 34th U-boat Flotilla.

time of 371 seconds (= 5,725 metres). Both ships were hit on the port side. The second torpedo missed its target in the third convoy column, although *U 48* mistakenly assumed a hit when a faint detonation was heard inside the boat after a run-time of 265 seconds.[7] Right after the torpedo detonations the convoy commodore ordered an emergency turn of 40 degrees to starboard, altering back to the mean course of 90° at 0625.

In reaction to the attack, *Scarborough* immediately increased speed and turned down the port flank of the convoy, stationing *Bluebell* one mile on its beam. The two escorts searched without success for the U-boat, believed to be submerged, until two miles astern of the

U 99 at anchor off the Île de Groix on the approach to Lorient in the early morning of 22 October 1940 while waiting for *U 37* with its more senior commanding officer to enter the port first. The photograph demonstrates the low silhouette of a Type VII B U-boat and its successor Type VII C, which made optical detection by enemy lookouts at night highly difficult.

torpedoed ships. In fact, *U 48* remained on the surface throughout, but was forced to retreat to the north-east by the searching escorts, losing contact with the convoy. At 0640 *Fowey*, which had unsuccessfully called up the other escorts by W/T before cutting across the convoy to investigate, replaced *Bluebell* with the latter detached to pick up survivors. *Scarborough* and *Fowey* then continued to search along the flank of the convoy. The *Scoresby*, carrying 1,685 fathoms of pit-props, sank within thirty minutes. The *Languedoc*, filled with 13,700 tons of Admiralty fuel oil, was abandoned by its crew immediately after the hit but the ship remained afloat until 1230 when the derelict was sunk by gunfire from *Bluebell*. The corvette picked up the complete crews of

ObltzS Engelbert Endraß on the conning tower of *U 46* on arrival at Bergen, Norway, on 4 August 1940. Right the 1st Watch Officer ObltzS Heinz Uphoff, behind left is the 2nd Watch Officer LtzS Hans-Jürgen Hellriegel. In the centre behind Endraß stands the Engineer Officer, Lt Ing Heinz Engemann. All four were killed later in the war.

both ships.⁸ By 0900 *Scarborough* and *Fowey* had resumed their stations with the convoy. Meanwhile *U 48* had regained contact with the convoy at 0735 and continued to shadow, but was sighted at 0915 on the surface by Sunderland flying boat H of 210 Squadron RAF, piloted by Fl Lt E. R. Baker. The aircraft attacked immediately, but the two depth charges dropped at 0917 from 50 feet exploded harmlessly in the wake of the crash-diving boat. Two minutes later two 250-lb A/S bombs were dropped 30 yards ahead of the first attack position without any result.⁹ The Sunderland, however, signalled the attack and the last known position of the U-boat to *Scarborough*, which proceeded at full speed to the spot and obtained Asdic contact at 0957. With *Fowey* ordered to join, *Scarborough* carried out five depth-charge attacks between 1020 and 1204 without result.

The commander of *U 123*, Kptlt Karl-Heinz Moehle, following the award of the Knight's Cross on 26 February 1941 aboard his boat at Lorient. He was an old hand, having joined the U-boat arm in March 1936. On 16 June 1941, he was appointed to command the 5th U-boat Flotilla at Kiel, responsible for fitting out hundreds of newly trained U-boats before their departure on front-line operations.

While *Scarborough* continued the search until the afternoon, *Fowey* and *Bluebell* were ordered to re-join the convoy, which was sailing without any escort at that time. *Fowey* reached the convoy at 1515, but *Bluebell* only arrived at 2100 after being delayed by the scuttling of the *Languedoc*. *U 48* stayed submerged until 1520, but with *Scarborough* still searching in the area, it had to dive again and eventually gave up the chase of SC 7 at 1710. Two minutes later Bleichrodt radioed to BdU his loss of contact with the convoy, giving its last known position at 0930 as 59°27′N, 06°36′W on a course of 100° True, 8 knots.

Based on its plot of U-boat positions at midnight on 17 October 1940, the BdU quickly assessed the chances of intercepting the convoy on its likely course towards the North Channel. Out of fourteen boats then at sea to the west of Britain in addition to *U 48*, four were on return to base, two were operating against the outbound convoy OB 228 and three more were standing too far to the west or south to reach SC 7 in time. Hence, on receipt of *U 48*'s sighting report early on 17 October, the BdU directed only the five nearest boats to operate against the convoy along a general direction of advance of 120° True, 8 knots. The U-boats detailed to operate against SC 7 were *U 46*, *U 99*, *U 100*, *U 101* and *U 123*.

However, after the attack by *U 48*, convoy SC 7 continued on its general course of 90° True until the following afternoon. Then ahead of time for its fixed rendezvous off the North Channel, the convoy commodore ordered a short leg northward before the convoy turned onto its new general course of 130° True later in the day. In the absence of aerial reconnaissance to relocate the convoy, the BdU was unaware of

The British steamer *Carsbreck*, built in 1936 by the Ayrshire Dockyard Co. at Irvine in Scotland, survived a torpedo hit from *U 38* in the morning of 18 October thanks to its timber load.

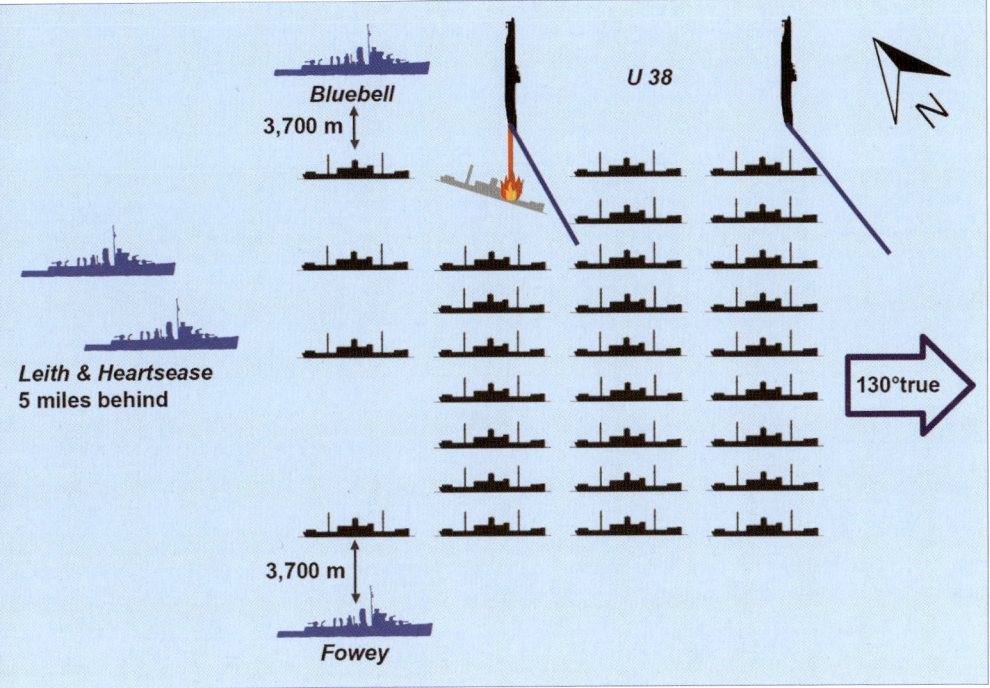

Fig. 3: The attack of *U 38* on SC 7 at 0204 and 0227 on 18 October.

the actual position of SC 7 and waited eagerly for new sighting reports from the boats before the coming darkness. Responding to questioning at 2043, *U 48* corrected the last observed position of the convoy as of 0930 to even further north than hitherto reported, which added more confusion. To clear the obscure situation, at 0040 on 18 October the BdU ordered a patrol line of six boats just east of Rockall Bank by 0800 on the following morning to relocate the convoy. The search line with *U 100* (Kptlt Joachim Schepke), *U 28* (Kptlt Günter Kuhnke), *U 123* (Kptlt Karl-Heinz Moehle), *U 101* (Kptlt Fritz Frauenheim), *U 99* (Kptlt Otto Kretschmer) and *U 46* (ObltzS Engelbert Endraß) stretched some 60 miles at right angles across the assumed convoy route. *U 28* was unable to comply with the order as it was still too far to the south at that time. Likewise, *U 99* reached its assigned position only at 1028. All boats were led by experienced officers, mostly in command of U-boats since pre-war times after intensive peacetime training in U-boat tactics. Except Moehle in *U 123*, all commanding officers were already decorated with the coveted Knight's Cross of the Iron Cross. The BdU expected that the convoy would pass the new patrol line during the daylight hours of 18 October.

In the meantime, the two escorts remaining with the convoy took station two miles on the starboard and port beams respectively during the night of 17/18 October. After an uneventful passage during

U 38 arriving at Lorient on 24 October 1940. Kptlt Heinrich Liebe (*extreme left*) supervises the manoeuvre, while the other officers watch from the flak platform. On the conning tower side is the emblem of the boat, designed in late 1939 by its then 2nd Watch Officer ObltzS Alfred Hanschel, showing Cupid with bow and arrow riding on a torpedo warhead.

HMS *Leith* was another pre-war sloop taking part in the battle around SC 7. The Grimsby-class design's long endurance of more than 6,500 miles at 10 knots made the vessel extremely useful for escort work.

the first part of the night, the U-boats suddenly struck again shortly after midnight. *U 38*, now also operating independently against SC 7 following the reports from *U 48* and the sinking of the *Aenos* the previous day, gained a bearing on it during a routine underwater listening search at 0040. Half an hour later the ships of the convoy came into sight, then zig-zagging at 6 knots around a mean course of 130°. Diving for a night-time submerged attack because the full moon made a surface attack unfavourable, the boat fired a double-spread at 0204 from the port side of the convoy on a 6,000-ton freighter. Only one torpedo was observed to hit the target. Actually, the British steamer *Carsbreck*, convoy No. 13, was hit port side in Number 2 hold. The other torpedo missed the target unseen. A further attack on a second steamer became impossible when the target turned towards the boat. The *Carsbreck* remained afloat on its cargo of lumber despite a large hole in its side and was still able to proceed at 6 knots. None of the crew were lost or seriously injured by the torpedo hit. However, no signal was received from the ship to indicate that it had been torpedoed and the convoy continued on its original course.

Fearing a concentrated attack, the Admiralty had also detached the sloop HMS *Leith* (Cdr R. C. Allen) and the Flower-class corvette HMS *Heartsease* (Lt-Cdr E. J. R. North) on 17 October from the outbound convoy OB 228 to join SC 7. At the time of the attack by *U 38*, the two warships were still five miles astern of the convoy. Just before the two ships joined, the British steamer *Beatus*, convoy No. 11, reported a torpedo crossing its bow, which was later sighted also by the *Blairspey*, convoy No. 31. This torpedo was probably the one fired by *U 38* at 0227, which also missed the target. On receiving this information, the convoy commodore ordered an emergency turn to starboard at 0235. After half an hour the convoy resumed its original mean course. The commanding officer of *Leith* took over as senior officer escort from Cdr Dickinson on *Scarborough*, which was still

The Shoreham-class sloop HMS *Fowey*, like its many early sister ships, was originally designed and used for overseas service. With the outbreak of war the A/S role became paramount and the sloops with their excellent accommodation were often used as convoy escorts.

behind at that time after its search for *U 48*. At 0245 *Leith*, on seeing the convoy making an emergency turn to starboard while itself being still astern of the convoy to starboard, believed a ship to have been torpedoed and cut across the convoy's wake to the port side, ordering *Heartsease* to take station one mile on its port beam. Both ships searched 3,000 yards along the port side of the convoy's wake for *U 38*. *Fowey* and *Bluebell* started a sweep for the attacking U-boat along the port flank of the convoy at 0305, later joined by *Leith* and *Heartsease*, but obtained no contacts. The presence of the escorts, however, forced *U 38* to stay submerged until 0530. By then the convoy was already out of sight and *U 38* gave up the chase because contact could not be re-established before daylight when aircraft cover was to be expected according to a report from *U 48*.[10] Rather inexplicably, Kptlt Liebe of *U 38* saw no immediate need to inform BdU about his encounter with the convoy and simply turned south-west towards his former operational area.

Meanwhile, at 0345 *Heartsease* was detailed to stand by the damaged *Carsbreck* and escort it into port. The *Carsbreck* eventually arrived at Kames Bay off Great Cumbrae in the Clyde on 21 October 1940 under its own power. The other escorts went after the convoy and resumed their stations. Although by then four ships including the two stragglers had already been sunk and one more damaged, this was only the prelude to the main battle.

When *U 38* belatedly reported at 1250 on 18 October about its sighting of the convoy that morning again to the north of the revised line of advance, BdU feared that the convoy would skirt around the patrol line to the north. Therefore, at 1455 he ordered *U 46*, *U 101*, *U 123* and *U 100* to operate in a north-easterly direction in accordance with *U 38*'s report, giving the position of the convoy at 1400 hours as about 58°20′N, 11°10′W, based on dead reckoning. *U 28* and *U 99* were not included in the order as the BdU considered them to have not yet reached the former patrol line. During this redeployment the U-boats again made contact with SC 7.

Night Battle – Part 1
(18 October evening until midnight)

The first out of the pack of five boats to sight the convoy was *U 101* at 1732. Seventeen minutes later *U 99* also sighted the forward escort of the convoy, soon followed by the rest of the ships. However, the first victim this evening was a ship apparently steaming independently on an easterly course about ten miles to the south-east of the convoy. The ship was first sighted by *U 123* at 1601, but was later also observed by *U 101* and *U 99*. All three prepared for a submerged attack, but Moehle on *U 123* was quickest to score, recording the action in his war diary:

> 1601 Steamer in sight bearing 120° True, distance 20,000 m, course about 250° True. Large modern freighter. Changed course soon to 180° and later 140°. Approaching at the limit of sight. At 1700 hours the steamer suddenly reversed course. We followed and submerged at 1803 hours. Previously I had gathered from radio traffic that this ship was waiting for a convoy to pilot it in. Radio tuning o.k. Approached submerged at high speed.
> 2021 Ship stopped zig-zagging at twilight, considering itself safe, and then stopped. One electric torpedo fired from bow at 1,100 m, hit amidships. Name and insignia illegible in the gathering darkness. Very large modern freight ship, apparently Type Tuscan

CONVOY SC 7 – OCTOBER 1940

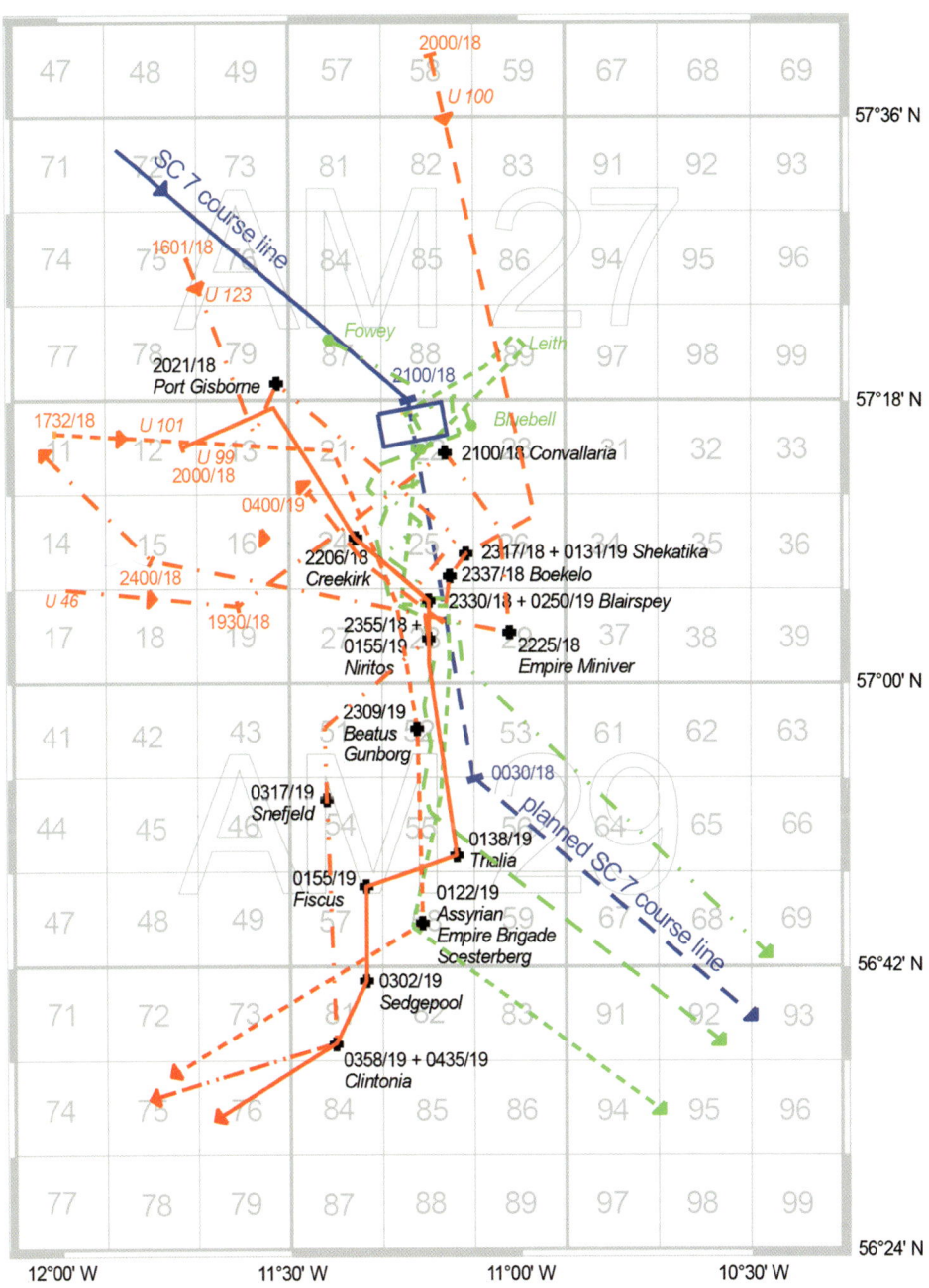

Fig. 4: Battle map. Convoy SC 7 on 18/19 October 1940. The grid used here and throughout this book is based on German naval map 1843G: *Quadratkarte – Nordatlantik von Island bis Kanarische Inseln und Mittelmeer, Westlicher Teil, 1940.*

Star (11,400 tons). Minor effect despite large explosion cloud. Remained on even keel.

2028 Second torpedo at same target. Hit underneath the bridge. Again, small effect. Seems to have very good bulkhead arrangement.

2030 Surfaced. Suddenly a U-boat surfaced 300 m in front of me. *U 99*, which was very angry because he was five minutes too late with his torpedo.

2046 Fired third torpedo as the steamer still showed no sign of sinking. Steamer started to settle deeper. Therefore went across to the opposite side of the steamer. When we had him abeam on our starboard side, he started to sink quickly. Sunk.

2143 After following the flickering lights of his rafts suddenly saw light signals and star shells to port in a position ahead, illuminating brightly a large convoy. Owing to a convoy escort closing the position of the sinking, left to the west until 2150 hours, then operated against the convoy.[11]

The torpedo hits were observed by both *U 99* and *U 101*, which then turned away and began chasing after the convoy. For a long time, the identity of the independent ship sunk by *U 123* was something of a mystery. Neither Lloyd's Shipping Loss Register nor the Admiralty List of British Ships lost in World War Two gave any clue about its identity as no vessel was reported sunk or missing at the time of attack. However, Moehle had the ship in sight for a full four hours, describing it as a modern refrigerated-cargo motor ship of the *Tuscan Star* type. This type of vessel was comparatively rare. From detailed research it seems very likely that *U 123* had in fact encountered the floating derelict hull of the British motor ship *Port Gisborne*, which had been hit near the bridge by one torpedo from *U 48* late on 11 October while sailing in convoy HX 77. The crew abandoned ship in three lifeboats in gale force conditions. The abandoned wreck was believed to have sunk later in position 57°02′N, 17°24′W, but apparently stayed afloat and drifted with the prevailing wind and current some 190 miles eastward in the following days until encountered and finally sunk by *U 123*.[12]

Meanwhile *U 46* had also made visual contact with the convoy at 2000 and worked itself into an attacking position ahead of the port column. Without knowing of the presence of *U 46*, at 2100 the convoy started to alter its mean course to starboard in a succession of moves from 130° to 170° as an evasive measure. It had been intended to resume the previous course at 0030 the next day. With *Scarborough* still behind, the three available escorts at that time were *Leith* zig-zagging ahead of the convoy, *Bluebell* zig-zagging 3,000 yards on the starboard bow and *Fowey* sent five miles astern at dusk. The weather was favourable for the U-boats with very slight wind and a calm sea, allowing visibility up to several miles. The moon was to rise through the clouds at 2145. When *U 46* was about to fire its torpedoes, *Leith* was just on the starboard leg of its zig-zag. Thus, the port flank of the convoy was wide open for an attack. Endraß fired four single torpedoes between 2058 and 2104

The fate of the modern British refrigerator ship *Port Gisborne*, built in 1927 by Swan Hunter & Wigham Richardson Ltd at Wallsend, has only recently been clarified. Originally torpedoed by *U 48* on 11 October 1940 while sailing in Convoy HX 77, the abandoned wreck was sunk seven days later by three *coup-de-grâce* torpedoes from *U 123* ahead of the courseline of SC 7.

at four different ships. The first missed its mark, but the remaining three were all believed to have hit their targets.[13] Observation of the results was certainly made difficult by the fact that *U 46* had fired its torpedoes at long range from between 1,500 and 3,600 metres. Allied reports recorded only one ship torpedoed at that time. This was the Swedish steamer *Convallaria*, convoy No. 22, which was hit at 2100 on the port side by No. 4 hatch, sinking fifteen minutes later.

Only minutes after the attack by *U 46* from the port side, *U 101* approached the convoy from the starboard bow. During the run-in *Leith*, correctly identified by the lookouts as a sloop, was observed to port with its bow on at a distance of 2,500 metres, forcing Frauenheim to fire his three torpedoes at 2112 from a greater distance than anticipated.

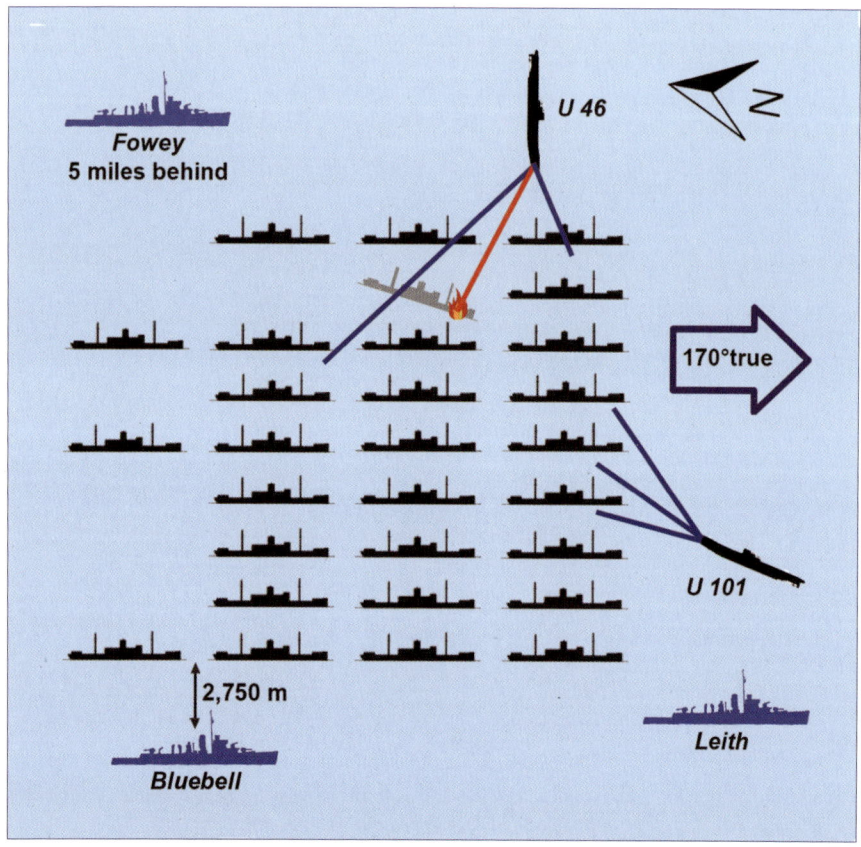

Fig. 5: Situation during the attacks of *U 46* and *U 101* against SC 7 at 2054 and 2112 on 18 October 1940.

The British steamer *Assyrian*, which was built by Blohm & Voss at Hamburg in 1914 and surrendered to Britain in 1920 as war reparations. Due to its passenger installation the convoy commodore, Vice-Admiral Lachlan D. I. Mackinnon, RN, and his staff were embarked for SC 7. The *Assyrian* sank after a torpedo hit from *U 101*. The master, the commodore, three naval staff members, 20 crew members and nine passengers were picked up by the sloop *Leith*. The *Assyrian* is shown here passing under the Clifton Suspension Bridge on the way up the Avon Gorge into Bristol.

Immediately afterwards high-speed evasive manoeuvres were necessary to keep his distance from *Leith*. With observation hampered during the evasive action, *U 101* believed it had hit two ships of 6,000 and 5,000 gross tons respectively after torpedo run times equalling a distance of some 3,700 metres. Both ships were considered sunk.[14] However, because no other ship except the *Convallaria* is recorded as hit or sunk around the time of attack, it is evident that *U 101*'s claim was based on a mis-observation due to the circumstances. Times given for the torpedo hit on the *Convallaria* in the various reports vary between 1950 and 2020. The latter would also fit with the attack of *U 101*, but all

its torpedoes were fired with bearings between 33° and 73.5° True, thus making it impossible to hit the *Convallaria* on its port side while it was steering a southerly course. *Bluebell* reported hearing first a single distant, faint explosion, probably coming from a position several miles away on the port quarter of the convoy. Some time later two more very faint explosions were heard which also seemed to come from the port side of the convoy. It appears that the first explosion was the hit on

Left & above: Two triumphant U-boats at Lorient. *U 37* (*front*) and *U 99* alongside on the River Scorff after entering on 22 October 1940. Both boats display various sinking pennants from the extended attack periscope mast, while the conning tower of *U 99* carries camouflage nets against aerial reconnaissance.

the *Convallaria*, while the two later ones probably marked end-of-run explosions of two torpedoes fired by *U 101*, wrongly assumed as hits by that boat. While *U 101* retreated from the scene to a forward position, *Leith* heard the explosion on the *Convallaria* on its Asdic and turned to port, increasing speed to 16 knots, to proceed across to the unescorted

A view of the forward wooden deck of *U 123*. In contrast to the slim lines of the smaller Type VIIs, the Type IX boats had a wide upper deck with integrated pressure-proof tubes at each side to carry additional reserve torpedoes. Nevertheless, the Type IX also displayed the low silhouette typical for all U-boats.

flank of the convoy. Firing star shells, *Leith* failed, however, to locate the nearby *U 101*. *Leith* ran ten miles on this course, and then turned back towards the torpedoed ship. On this last leg *Leith* sighted *Fowey* at 2230, which had just picked up survivors from *Convallaria* while trying to catch up with its original port beam position after seeing the star shells. *Leith* stationed *Fowey* 3,000 yards abeam to port and both ships set course towards the convoy, which was then some ten miles ahead. *Bluebell*, off the starboard bow of the convoy at the time of the attacks by *U 46* and *U 101*, turned around after the hit on the *Convallaria* and ran down that side of the convoy before returning to its position. After hearing two more explosions on the port side of the convoy, *Bluebell* proceeded across the convoy's track to that side. Searching without result to a point two miles east of the convoy's position at the time of the first attack, *Bluebell* later set course to return to its convoy position. *U 46* noted the presence of several destroyer-type escorts in its war diary, but noted that none of them saw the surfaced boat even at close range.

By about 2200 the manoeuvres of the three escorts after the attacks by *U 46* and *U 101* inevitably led to a concentration of all escort ships on the port side astern of the convoy. At the same time the convoy became somewhat disorganised after repeated emergency turns at irregular intervals and in addition all ships were zig-zagging independently. That was the situation when *U 99* entered the scene. Having watched the torpedoing of the *Port Gisborne* by *U 123*, Kretschmer gained contact with the convoy at 2110. His position was then ahead on the starboard bow. To avoid the leading destroyer, actually *Leith* then on the starboard leg of its zig-zag, he dropped back onto the starboard beam. *U 101* observed a U-boat approaching the convoy at 2130; this was probably *U 99*. Now attacking the outer starboard column, Kretschmer fired a single bow torpedo at 2202 but missed the target. Four minutes later he fired his stern torpedo at the same steamer, estimated at 6,500 gross tons, from a distance of 700 metres. A hit on the starboard side slightly forward of amidships caused it to disappear bow first within twenty seconds.[15] Without doubt the British steamer *Creekirk*, the lead ship of the outer starboard column, convoy No. 91, was hit at this time. The *Empire Miniver*, normally the lead ship of the eighth column, saw the

Two views of the British steamer *Beatus*, a typical tramp steamer of the type used between the two world wars. Built in 1925 by the Ropner Shipbuilding Co. Ltd of Stockton-on-Tees, the ship sank without loss among its crew following a torpedo hit by *U 101* shortly before midnight on 18 October 1940.

sinking. Due to its heavy cargo of 5,900 tons of iron ore the *Creekirk* went down rapidly.

U 99 then proceeded head on into the convoy and next fired a torpedo at 2230 at another steamer but missed the target. Within minutes of this miss, *U 99* was observed by a third steamer, which turned towards the U-boat apparently intending to ram. This was the commodore's ship, the British steamer *Assyrian*, which had noticed the U-boat four points on its port bow, 200 yards distant. Working up to ten knots, the *Assyrian* then chased *U 99* for about half an hour, but eventually lost sight of the U-boat on the starboard quarter of the convoy.[16]

While *U 99* had attacked the convoy from the starboard side and the escorts were still engaged in search operations astern on the port side, *U 46* attacked the convoy a second time, once more from the

The Swedish steamer *Gunborg* of the A/B Sylvia shipping company at Göteburg, whose vessels sailed under charter for the British Ministry of Transport during the war and were thus excluded from any protection arising from Swedish neutrality. A torpedo from *U 101* sealed the fate of this ship on the evening of 18 October 1940.

U 101 on the River Scorff before making fast at Lorient on 24 October 1940. Ten pennants indicate the claimed successes of the previous patrol. Just a few days later the veteran commanding officer Kptlt Fritz Frauenheim (*second from left*), who had been in command of U-boats uninterrupted since 1 October 1937, handed over *U 101* to his successor.

The honourable decision of the master of the Dutch steamer *Boekelo* to rescue the shipwrecked crew of the previously torpedoed steamer *Beatus* eventually led to the loss of his own ship, when it was torpedoed by *U 100*. Fortunately, the complete crew of the ship, sailing under British charter, was rescued thereafter by the sloop *Fowey*.

port beam. Again, Endraß fired from long distance, releasing a single torpedo at 2225 at a steamer estimated at 6,000 gross tons. A second torpedo did not leave the tube. Immediately after the failed launch, the first torpedo was observed to hit the target after a run time equalling 1,500 metres and before the stern tube could be fired. *U 46* then came under fire from another steamer and was forced to crash-dive at 2230.[17] The Dutch steamer *Soesterberg* in convoy position 32 reported seeing a submarine at 2330 BST on its port bow and fired one round at the spot where the U-boat dived. The time reported by the ship for the incident is possibly incorrect. No U-boat reported coming under fire from a merchant ship around that time.

From the time and the direction of the attack it is most probable that the torpedo from *U 46* hit the British steamer *Empire Miniver*. According to its master's report, the ship was torpedoed at about 2215 on the port side in the engine and boiler rooms. The master of the *Assyrian*, then on the port bow of the *Empire Miniver*, reported that the torpedo approached quite fast from the port quarter, missing his own ship's stem by about a foot before hitting the *Empire Miniver*. After twenty-five minutes the stricken ship went under when its boilers exploded. The survivors were later picked up by *Bluebell*.[18] Endraß quickly resurfaced after the incident but stopped chasing the convoy owing to continuous star-shell fire lighting up the area.

The next U-boat to fire at ships of the convoy was *U 123*. After sinking the derelict *Port Gisborne* before the beginning of the battle, Moehle had gained contact with the convoy at 2143, led to the scene by the star shells fired by the escorts after the first attack. Attacking the starboard beam side of the convoy, *U 123* fired three single torpedoes at short intervals from 2244 from a distance of 2,000 metres at a group of three ships. All torpedoes missed their targets when the ships turned away after firing, probably executing an emergency turn. Exactly the same happened when the boat fired another torpedo at 2320 against a single 5,000 gross tons steamer straggling behind the main body of the convoy. With two escorts in the area, closing as near as 300 metres at times, *U 123* was then forced to withdraw to the west to avoid being observed.[19] The two escorts must have been the two sloops *Leith* and *Fowey* trying to catch up with the convoy. The incident again proved the advantage of the U-boats' low profile during night-time surface actions in the pre-radar period.

With the remaining ships of the convoy still sailing unprotected by the escorts, *U 101* started a new

The Greek-flagged steamer *Niritos* survived the initial torpedo hit by *U 99*, but the drifting wreck was sunk by *U 123* only a short time later. This pre-war photograph shows the vessel off Montevideo in Uruguay, displaying the colours of its shipping company at the funnel.

attack after reloading its tubes. Having remained in a position ahead of the convoy after his first attack, Frauenheim attacked this time from the east. Fearing premature detection in the prevailing moderate weather conditions and with a full moon shining through the clouds, giving visibility up to 8,000 metres, he again fired his torpedoes at a long range of 3,600 to 5,100 metres. Four torpedoes were fired between 2308 and 2309 at four ships. *U 101* claimed to have observed two hits with a third detonation heard inside the boat after the same run time and afterwards turned ahead of the convoy to reload and attack again.[20] Assessment for this attack is difficult because of the conflicting information in the various reports. The most likely scenario is that the British steamer *Beatus* and the Swedish *Gunborg* were hit in this attack, both struck on the port side. The crew of the *Gunborg* left their ship in two lifeboats and soon watched it to go down. The *Beatus* took a hit between Nos. 4 and 5 holds and sank after thirty minutes. Survivors from both ships were later rescued by *Bluebell*.[21]

Just before *U 101* had attacked the convoy, *U 100*, the last of the pack ordered by BdU to attack SC 7, sighted the ships of the convoy.

Inspection prior to departure at Lorient before noon on 25 September 1940. Innermost is *U 100*, whose crew are standing to attention while the 1st Watch Officer reports to the captain. On the next boat, *U 65*, the crew are still forming up, while on the outer boat, *U 38*, all is still quiet.

Staying in a favourable position ahead, Schepke lost no time. At 2317 he fired a single torpedo at a medium-size steamer carrying a high deck load, scoring a hit. From monitoring the vessel's distress signal, it was identified as the British *Shekatika*. With several other ships in the vicinity and realising that his victim would not sink quickly, Schepke decided to attack another vessel and only later administer the *coup-de-grâce* to the first target.[22] The *Shekatika*, sailing as convoy No. 13, was hit on its starboard side abaft the main mast. The crew abandoned the ship about thirty minutes later. The *Shekatika* remained, however.[23]

Meanwhile *Leith* and *Fowey* were steaming up on the port quarter of the convoy to regain their stations. At 2305 two horizontal red lights were seen right ahead five to six miles distant. Five minutes later, an explosion was heard on the Asdic receivers aboard the ships, which probably resulted from one of the hits achieved by *U 101* in its attack on 2309. At 2320 a further explosion was heard, very probably resulting from the hit on the *Shekatika*. At that time Cdr Allen in *Leith* increased speed to 16 knots, drawing away from *Fowey*, which could only steam at 14 knots. Ten minutes later Allen ordered *Fowey* to investigate a damaged ship, identified as the *Shekatika*, while himself continuing towards the convoy. *Fowey* then closed the damaged merchant vessel and took its entire crew on board.

Following the skirmish with the *Assyrian* on the starboard flank of the convoy *U 99* quickly regained contact with the main body of ships, though these were now dispersed over a large area. This time Kretschmer attacked what he believed to be the right flank of the last formation. At 2330 he fired a single torpedo at a large steamer. Right after firing the target turned towards *U 99* causing the torpedo to pass ahead of it. However, the torpedo was then observed to hit an even larger ship of about 7,000 tons behind it abreast the foremast after a runtime equalling 1,740 metres. Allied reports record that the British steamer *Blairspey* was torpedoed at 2330 on its port side in No. 1 hold. The ship was hit just after changing its course hard to port, thus being hit on its port side. The vessel took only a slight list to port and then straightened up, but stopped due to a blowing steam pipe joint in the engine room. With the ship in no immediate danger of sinking, the crew remained on board while the engine-room personnel tried to repair the joint.[24] *U 99* instead believed the ship fatally damaged and did not wait for it to go down.

After his attack on the *Shekatika*, Schepke choose to attack a stopped steamer observed to be picking up the crew of another ship. A torpedo fired at 2337 hit the stern of the ship estimated at 3,500 tons, causing it to settle quickly. The vessel torpedoed on this occasion was certainly the Dutch *Boekelo* that had seen the hit by *U 101* on the *Beatus* while steaming one mile astern. On reaching the scene its master decided to stop and take the men aboard. The torpedo from *U 100* hit the

The British steamer *Sedgepool*, one of the largest ships in SC 7, became a prominent target. Following two misses, *U 99* achieved a hit at 0302 on 19 October 1940. Seven hours later the *Sedgepool* went under with its load of 8,720 tons of wheat.

Kptlt Joachim Schepke enjoying a coffee on the conning tower of his boat *U 100* after a strenuous convoy battle. He represented the ideal type of the good-looking and dashing U-boat commander for the propaganda newsreels of the Third Reich and was one of the tonnage kings during the first 'Happy Time' until his death on 17 March 1941 when *U 100* was sunk.

ship on the port side by No. 4 hold, causing an immediate list to port and the after rail was soon level with the water. Fearing that *Boekelo* would go down quickly, the crew left the ship in the lifeboats and set course for the Irish coast.[25] It is likely that the *Boekelo* went down soon afterwards. Luckily, *Fowey*'s captain, after taking the men from the *Shekatika* on board, decided to continue his rescue efforts instead of trying to regain the convoy as he believed he was now far astern. Thus, the boats of the *Boekelo* were soon found by *Fowey* and the men taken aboard the sloop.

On its way towards the convoy, *Leith* also heard the explosion caused by the torpedo hitting the *Boekelo* at 2337. Just three minutes later a U-boat was sighted straight ahead about two miles away. Picked up by its wash, the lookouts shortly thereafter saw the U-boat conning tower, stern on. A star shell faintly illuminated the U-boat which submerged a few seconds later. The U-boat was *U 100*, crash-diving before an approaching escort at 2347. The sloop obtained a contact at approximately 3,000 yards and held it until it was down to 800 yards, then lost it completely. At this time *Bluebell*, on its way to regain the convoy, appeared on the scene and was ordered to join *Leith* in the search. With *Bluebell* taking station one mile on *Leith*'s port beam, the two ships carried out a roughly circular search at 14 knots until 0040. They found no contacts, except from the ships which had been torpedoed nearby, and dropped no depth charges. By the conclusion of the search Cdr Allen in *Leith* was convinced that several U-boats were working together and, as the convoy was left unescorted, proceeded at full speed to rejoin. *Bluebell* was detailed to pick up survivors from nearby ships and lifeboats. The corvette also received instructions to report

The drawing of an attacking panther, initially in bright colours as shown here, but later in deep black, was the emblem of *U 100*, whose commanding officer happily greets the crowd assembled on departure.

the situation to the C-in-C Western Approaches, Admiral Dunbar-Naismith.

The final victim on 18 October was the Greek steamer *Niritos*. *U 99* recorded firing a bow torpedo at 2355 at a large freighter of some 6,000 tons at a range of 750 metres. The torpedo hit the ship on the starboard side abreast of the foremast. Immediately after the torpedo detonation, another explosion with a high column of flame extending from the bow to the bridge was observed. Smoke was seen to rise some 200 metres high and the ship continued to burn with a greenish flame. Allied records show the *Niritos* was hit at midnight. The torpedo detonation and the ensuing blast, described as a terrific flash like a petrol explosion, were also recorded by *Leith* during its search for *U 100*. The greenish flame certainly resulted from the cargo of 5,426

The Greek steamer *Thalia* was a typical vessel of the First World War period, in this case built in 1917 at the Japanese Kawasaki Dockyard Co. Ltd at Kobe. Just four members of its crew survived its loss following a torpedo hit by *U 99*.

tons of sulphur that had caught fire in the torpedo explosion. Because the ship kept floating despite the damage, the lifeboats remained nearby in case the ship could be re-boarded.[26] After torpedoing the *Niritos U 99* observed three destroyers approaching at 0015, seemingly searching the area in line abreast. Unknown to Kretschmer, *U 99* was neither detected by *Leith*, nor by *Bluebell* in fact searching for *U 100*, nor by *Fowey*, which was conducting rescue operations and not participating in the search.

Night Battle - Part 2
(19 October midnight until daybreak)

After midnight there was a short lull in the attacks. Of the four U-boats still operating against the convoy, only *U 123* attacked a steamer of 6,000 tons at the rear end of the convoy with one torpedo at 0021 but missed again. *U 100* was submerged to escape the search by *Leith* and *Bluebell* while *U 99* took evasive manoeuvres on the surface to the south-west to evade the escorts seen in the vicinity of its last victim. The first boat to score on 19 October was once more *U 101*, this time attacking again from the starboard side. Seeing 10 to 12 ships of the convoy, which was now completely scattered, Frauenheim fired his last four torpedoes. At 0122 he aimed three shots from the bow tubes at three vessels. Two minutes later he fired the stern torpedo at a 3,000-ton steamer. Three of the torpedoes found targets. First the commodore's ship *Assyrian* was hit in the stokehold on the starboard side. Just before that hit, *Assyrian*'s master saw a torpedo crossing his bow to port and said 'There goes my next-door neighbour,' which proved to be correct as the *Empire Brigade* was struck only a few seconds later on its starboard side beneath the bridge. Next was the Dutch steamer *Soesterberg*. The *Empire Brigade* went down after twenty minutes. Then the *Soesterberg* sank by the stern while close to the crippled *Assyrian*. At 0240 the *Assyrian* finally went down. Survivors from the three ships were later rescued by *Leith*.[27] It appears that the three ships, all struck in quick succession, were probably hit by the bow torpedoes with the stern torpedo missing its target. *U 101*, now out of torpedoes, started its return to Lorient in France.

Behind the main body of ships of the convoy, now dispersed over a wide area, *U 123* observed two shadows together with two escorts

The British steamer *Blairspey*, lying low in the water with a full load. In a similar condition the ship survived three torpedo hits from *U 99* and *U 100* on 18 and 19 October 1940 thanks to its timber load and was successfully salvaged by the ocean rescue tug *Salvonia* six days later.

some distance away from them. On closing, the shadows turned out to be two steamers lying stopped, apparently rescuing men believed to be from a tanker sunk shortly before in this position. Actually, one of the two ships must have been the *Shekatika*, which had been kept floating by its load of pit props following the first hit by *U 100*. The second vessel was the damaged Greek steamer *Niritos* with its two lifeboats waiting close by. *U 123* apparently mistook the large fireball following the hit on the *Niritos* as a hit on a tanker. The two escorts in the area were probably *Fowey* and *Leith*, which had joined at 0109 behind the convoy and set course, stationed one mile apart beam on, to catch up with main body of ships. Neither of the escorts, however, spotted the U-boat stalking the damaged ships. Assuming in the dim moonlight that the high deck load of the *Shekatika* was passenger accommodation, Moehle fired a torpedo from one of his stern tubes at 0131, hitting the ship amidships. Although *U 123* recorded that the vessel sank within four minutes, it must have taken somewhat longer. The torpedo firing and the subsequent explosion were heard close by on *U 100*, still submerged after the unsuccessful hunt by *Leith* and *Bluebell*. Surfacing at 0147, Schepke sighted a steamer sinking nearby, which must have been the *Shekatika*. The explosion was also seen by *Fowey* and *Leith*. Both ships altered course towards the location. On their way, however, they came across the *Blairspey* at 0200, still stopped after having been hit by *U 99* at 2330 but floating well on its timber load. The master was determined to get the ship into port, so *Leith* at first detailed *Fowey* to stand by, itself proceeding at 0216 to join the convoy at full speed. Because of the need for more escorts to stay with the convoy, *Leith* cancelled the order soon afterwards and told *Fowey* to re-join the convoy.

Meanwhile, at 0135 *U 123* had fired on the second shadow but missed the target because of a faulty torpedo. A second attack on the same target at 0155 proved more successful, this time hitting the *Niritos* in its machinery room. The explosion was also seen from the lifeboats, and the crew watched the ship go down after five minutes.[28]

Realising that the few escorts of the convoy, which had kept firing star shells throughout, had completely lost control of the tactical situation, Kretschmer now decided to attack the remaining ships from

U 99 makes fast at 1052 on 22 October 1940 alongside *U 37* which had entered the base at Lorient an hour earlier. In the background is the prominent Lorient–Lanester railway bridge.

a position astern of the convoy. *U 99*'s war diary recorded the firing of a bow torpedo at 0138 at a large heavily laden freighter of about 6,000 tons, lying low in the water. The vessel torpedoed in this attack must have been the Greek steamer *Thalia*, which was hit on the starboard side abreast the foremast and observed to sink in the explosion. Eyewitnesses from other ships later reported that there was a big flash followed by an explosion whereupon the *Thalia* sank immediately.[29]

Kretschmer attacked his next victim less than twenty minutes later. At 0155 he fired another bow torpedo at a similar vessel as before, estimated at 7,000 tons. After a run time equalling 975 metres distance, the torpedo hit on the starboard side abreast the foremast, sinking the ship within forty seconds. This time, the British steamer *Fiscus* had been hit. According to the report of the lone survivor, the ship sank within a minute of the explosion.[30] *U 99* continued its way through the scattered ships now sailing mostly independently towards the North Channel. At 0240 Kretschmer fired a single torpedo at one of the largest vessels of the convoy, identified as a *Glenapp*-class steamer of 9,500 tons, but missed. Another torpedo fired fifteen minutes later also missed the ship. Only the third torpedo, fired at 0302 from a range of 720 metres, hit the ship forward of the bridge. The British steamer *Sedgepool* is reported to have been hit at 0300 on its starboard side. Kretschmer did not wait to see the ship sink but continued to chase the others. The *Sedgepool* finally went down at 0955.[31]

The *Blairspey*, still stopped with its engineers repairing the damaged steam joint, was found at 0230 by *U 100*. Twenty minutes later Schepke fired a single torpedo as a *coup-de-grâce* into its starboard side between Nos. 1 and 2 holds but with very little effect due to the timber load. He accordingly fired a second torpedo at 0300, hitting the ship amidships on the port side. Schepke now considered the vessel beyond the possibility of salvage. However, the *Blairspey* was fated to survive. Found floating by the ocean salvage tug HMRT *Salvonia* (Temp. Lt G. M. M. Robinson) on the afternoon of 19 October, *Blairspey* was towed into the Clyde and beached in Kames Bay six days later. The repaired vessel returned to sea under a new name – *Empire Spey*.[32]

In the morning hours of 19 October, apart from *U 99* and *U 100*, only *U 123* was still pursuing the convoy. At 0244 lookouts spotted another shadow, soon identified as a steamer of some 5,500 tons lying stopped, with a high deck load of timber. At 0317 Moehle fired his last torpedo, hitting the target amidships. There is little doubt that this was the Norwegian steamer *Snefjeld* that was sunk in the reported action.[33]

Above: Like other captains in 1940, Kptlt Fritz Frauenheim of *U 101* had received a thorough peacetime training. After *U 101* he was assigned to various posts ashore, including commanding the 23rd and 29th U-boat Flotillas in the Mediterranean. In 1945 he was Chief of Staff with the Admiral of the Small Battle Unit Command.

Left: *U 48* after entering Heligoland at 0930 on 26 October 1940. After a short wait for the mine destructor vessel *Sperrbrecher 9* (ex-steamer *Lüneburg*) *U 48* left at 1145 on the same day for Brunsbüttel and passage to Kiel through the Kaiser-Wilhelm-Canal.

The Swedish steamer *Convalleria*, built in 1921 by Verschure & Co. at Amsterdam, was the first ship of SC 7 to be sunk in the course of the U-boat attacks during the night of 18/19 October 1940.

The British steamer *Clintonia* had watched the seemingly endless attacks on the convoy since the evening of 18 October. About midnight the master decided to leave the convoy and steamed off its track to the south-west for about ten miles and then turned back to the original route. Now sailing approximately parallel to the convoy, the master believed the ship to be clear of the enemy submarines. However, shortly before four o'clock a U-boat appeared on the port beam two ship-lengths away. This was again *U 99*, which at first missed the ship at 0356 with a torpedo. The next torpedo fired from the stern tube two minutes later hit the *Clintonia* on its port side between the engine

Right: U 48 alongside the quay at Kiel Tirpitzhafen on 27 October 1940. The triumphant return of the most successful U-boat during World War Two was celebrated with a great deal of propaganda output, while it also stands for the statistically most successful period of the U-boat campaign during this war.

U 48 just before making fast inside the lock at Kiel-Holtenau in the morning of 27 October 1940 after passage through the Kaiser-Wilhelm-Canal. The conning tower is painted with the claimed total sinking figure of 308,000 grt under its three commanding officers Schultze, Rösing and Bleichrodt, while the related pennants are flying from the extended attack periscope.

room and No. 3 hatch. Kretschmer, having used all his torpedoes, stayed nearby intending to finish *Clintonia* off by gunfire later in the day if necessary.

The floating ship was also spotted by *U 123* at 0435. Having also expended all of his torpedoes, Moehle lost no time and opened fire with his deck gun at 0500. After many hits the *Clintonia* finally went down at 0536. Some of the shells, however, landed very close to *U 99*, which

Right: Officers of *U 48* in front of the conning tower with the legendary Black Cat emblem of the boat on 29 October 1940, during a dockyard layover at Deutsche Werke in Kiel. In the centre is Kptlt Heinrich Bleichrodt with his newly awarded Knight's Cross. He was the third commanding officer of the boat to receive this prestigious award. Left is the 1st Watch Officer, ObltzS Reinhard Suhren, and right the Engineer Officer, Lt Ing Erich Zürn. Both officers were later also decorated with the Knight's Cross for their achievements aboard *U 48*.

Crew members of *U 48* display the front plate of its mechanical torpedo-data calculator on top of the breech block of the 88-mm deck gun, while the boat is lying at Kiel inside Tirpitzhafen. The names of all 48 steamers reported sunk up to then are written on the plate, together with their estimated total tonnage of 308,507 grt.

supposed them to come from a British destroyer, and accordingly left the area quickly. The crew of *U 99* only learned later that *U 123* was responsible, resulting in some recriminations. Both boats started their return to Lorient after the action. The survivors of the *Clintonia* were in two lifeboats and at daylight they set sail and made for land, but became separated. The chief officer's boat with 11 men was picked up by the salvage tug *Salvonia* the same day. The master's boat, originally with 23 men, was sighted by a Sunderland flying boat which dropped packets of food, medical supplies and cigarettes, and a chart giving the position of the lifeboat. The aircrew also sent a message saying they were very sorry they could not land and pick up the survivors, owing to the heavy swell. After 38 hours the destroyer HMS *Shikari* found the boat on 21 October, with the survivors being landed at Londonderry.[34]

Tactical Analysis of the Battle

The main battle around convoy SC 7 lasted from 2100 on 18 October until 0530 on the next morning. During this period of eight and a half hours, sixteen British, Norwegian, Dutch, Greek and Swedish ships were sunk and one more was damaged. The U-boats fired a total of 49 torpedoes, achieving 25 hits (51 per cent) and claimed 25 ships sunk totalling 143,500 tons.[35] Together with the four ships lost in the two days before, the actual tonnage sunk amounted to 79,592 gross tons excluding the wreck of the *Port Gisborne* sunk by *U 123* on the evening of 18 October.

The tactics employed by Otto Kretschmer in *U 99* were of note: he eventually penetrated right between the columns of the convoy to fire his torpedoes singly at point-blank range. It was later concluded by Allied analysts that this behaviour became a common tactic for U-boats during this early phase of the convoy battles in World War Two. However, analysis of the thirty torpedo firings carried out against ships of SC 7 while in convoy, excluding stragglers and shots fired as *coups-de-grâce*, reveals that the close-range attacks by *U 99* were rather the exception than the norm. While Kretschmer fired most of his torpedoes at a range of less than 1,000 metres, the average torpedo-firing distance during the battle around SC 7 was 2,425 m. This figure was, however, somewhat distorted by Frauenheim in *U 101*, who fired most of his eleven torpedoes at excessive range from outside the escort screen, resulting in his average firing distance being more than 3,000 metres. It appears that the decision to attack at close range was much more related to the individual capability and boldness of the commanding officer than any pre-formulated tactical instructions. With the majority of torpedoes being electrically driven, which made their tracks practically invisible, the cover of darkness during the night hours clearly favoured the more daring U-boat commanders.

At least 144 merchant seamen, naval gunners and other servicemen or passengers lost their lives in the attacks against ships of SC 7. More than 540 seamen were rescued, mostly by the escorting warships. However, at no time after the initial attacks by *U 46* and *U 101* on the evening of 18 October was any escort ship able to re-join its nominal

U 101 (right) and *U 38* moored in the Scorff shortly after entering port together at noon on 24 October 1940. Off-duty crew members enjoy a casual talk from conning tower to conning tower after the stressful weeks on the previous patrol.

night-time escort station in the convoy screen. Instead, all three escorts were constantly engaged in fruitless search operations or in rescue work. It is also open to question whether the number of ships torpedoed would have been smaller even if the escorts had concen-

trated more on protection of the convoy instead of picking up survivors. Both the numerical as well as the technical and tactical inferiority of the escorts against the attacking U-boats resulted in a minimal chance of successful protection of a convoy against determinedly led U-boats.

After another Allied convoy, the inbound HX 79, was also attacked by a pack of six boats during the very next night in the same manner, claiming 17 more ships totalling 113,000 tons (actually sinking 12 totalling 75,069 tons), Konteradmiral Dönitz, wrote in his war diary of 20 October the following summary of the two convoy operations:

a) The operations justify the principles on which U-boat tactics and training have been developed since 1935, i.e. that U-boats in packs should attack the convoys. Operations in pack formation were made possible by the development of radio communications since the First World War.

b) The execution of such tactics is possible only if the commanders and crews have been thoroughly trained in these tactics. This shows the need for comprehensive training in extensive sea areas, which would be impossible if we did not keep the Baltic free of enemy forces.

c) Such operations can only be carried out if there are sufficient boats in the operational area. This has happened only occasionally in the course of the war up to now.

d) There will be more of these operations as numbers in the operational area will increase, and there is more likelihood of intercepting convoys with the additional reconnaissance by larger numbers of boats.

e) Moreover, with more boats, the British shipping routes will not be left unoccupied after such attacks, as was the case today, when nearly all boats had to return to base for lack of torpedoes.

f) Successes as achieved in the above-mentioned operations cannot always be expected. Fog, bad weather, and other conditions may, from time to time, reduce the prospects to nil.

The capacity of the individual commanders will always govern the results.[36]

Dönitz was understandably proud of the success of his 'pack tactic' in combat. In October 1940, a total of 24 U-boats took part in front-line operations, spending a total of 374 days at sea. The average number of U-boats at sea was almost 12. In the same period 60 merchant ships totalling 342,204 gross tons were sunk by U-boats, resulting in an average daily sinking figure of 915 gross tons per boat, probably an all-time high in operating efficiency for submarines. In addition to inflicting heavy losses, the U-boats almost invariably escaped unscathed in this period; in October 1940 only one U-boat (*U 32*) was sunk in the Atlantic.[37]

The British steamer *Fiscus* disappeared within 40 seconds after the torpedo hit by *U 99* in the morning hours of 19 October 1940, leaving only Seaman E. S. King on a piece of wreckage from its 39-man crew. King was later picked up by a rescue boat from the Norwegian steamer *Snefjeld*.

However, the Royal Navy and the other Allied navies learned their lessons well. As an interim measure to tackle the problem of sighting surfaced U-boats at night, star-shell firing by the escorts was recommended until Snowflake illumination rockets were introduced in spring 1941. Snowflake rocket flares were fired from a projector and were able to turn night into day around a convoy. Each flare furnished some 300,000 candlepower for approximately 65 seconds starting at an altitude of 1,200 feet, where the flare ignition took place. The burning flare then descended by parachute at a rate of approximately 20 feet per second. Another stopgap measure was to open up the spacing of the convoy columns from about 600 yards to about 1,000 yards in order to reduce the chance of more than one ship being hit by a salvo. Escorts were stationed farther away from the convoy and new tactics were developed to search for a U-boat with illuminants following an

During its return to Germany for a dockyard refit after the battle around SC 7, *U 46* was lucky to survive an air attack by three Lockheed Hudson aircraft of 233 Squadron RAF shortly before noon on 25 October 1940 off the south Norwegian coast. The photograph shows the heavily damaged boat in a floating dock at the Germaniawerft dockyard at Kiel after entering port.

attack. To improve the tactical efficiency of the escorts, these ships were formed into permanent groups as far as possible. Likewise, the average number of hours flown monthly by RAF Coastal Command aircraft on anti-submarine duties was stepped up.[38]

Although the development of efficient radar and ship-borne high-frequency direction finding (HF/DF) sets was still in the early stages, their operational use and the introduction of long-range anti-submarine aircraft or escort carriers as well as improved or completely new, more sophisticated A/S weapons systems took less than a year. The increase in the total number of surface escorts, partly due to the

50 ex-US Navy destroyers negotiated for in 1940, also helped to make more time available for the A/S training of escorts and organising them into additional escort groups. In addition, improved tactical control of both the surface escort groups and the air escorts by the escort commander was facilitated by the fitting of voice radio (R/T) in addition to Morse (W/T) equipment. Together with the ever increasing A/S experience and close inter-service co-operation between RAF Coastal Command and the Admiralty, all this added much to the ships and crews engaged in combat. Last but not least, the benefits gained from signal intelligence (Ultra) and other sources of information proved to be of great value in the course of the battles yet to come. Thus, by the end of 1941 the situation in the Battle of the Atlantic had turned from desperate to hopeful for the Allies.

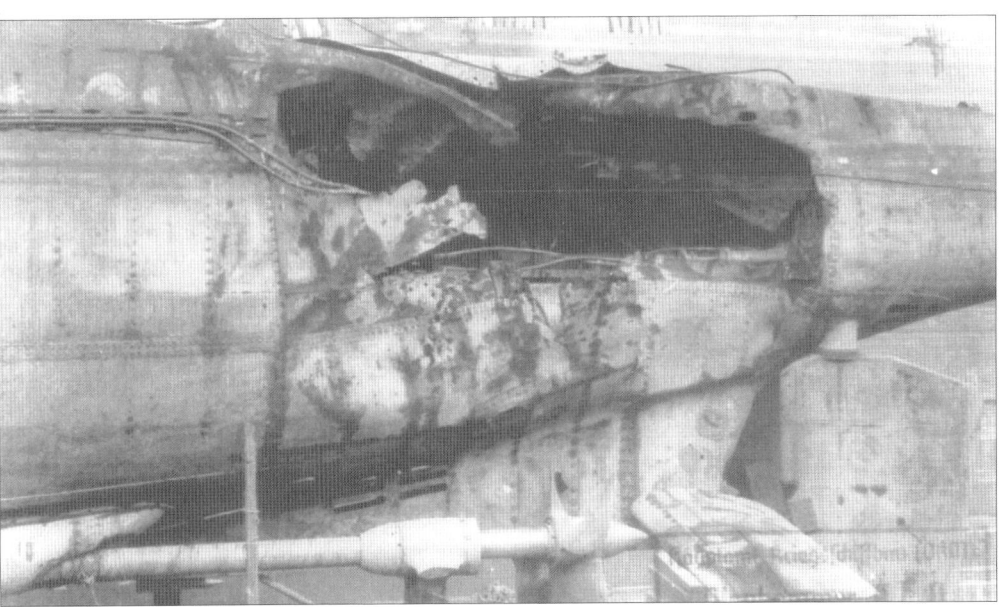

The Hudson E/233 (Plt Off. A. T. Maudsley, a/c captain, Plt Off. E. L. Baudoux, pilot) released a stick of ten 100-lb A/S bombs from 500 feet at the surfaced boat, hitting the stern of *U 46* at least once. The explosion caused widespread structural damage to the outer hull. During the attack Seaman Friedrich Hermann Plaep sustained a splinter wound in the abdomen; he died the next day in the sick berth of the minesweeper *M 18* in Kristiansand harbour.

Notes to Chapter 1

1. Grove, E. J., ed., *The Defeat of the Enemy Attack on Shipping*, Ashgate, 1998. [Revised edition of Barley & Waters' Naval Staff History.]
2. National Archives London (TNA), ADM 199/2215 Admiralty War Diary Summaries, 16–31 Oct. 1940, 14 Oct. 1940.
3. Lund, Paul, and Harry Ludlam, *Night of the U-boats*, London: W. Foulsham, 1973; Bezemer, K. W. L., *Geschiedenis van de Nederlandse Koopvaardij in de Tweede Wereldoorlog* [*The History of the Dutch Merchant Navy in the Second World War*], 3 vols., Amsterdam: Elsevier, 1987, 1:395–411.
4. Blair, Clay, *Hitler's U-boat War: The Hunters, 1939–1942*, New York: Random House, 1996, 199.
5. Bundesarchiv/Militärarchiv Freiburg (BA-MA) RM 98/331, Kriegstagebuch (KTB) *U 124*, 17 Oct. 1940.
6. BA-MA RM 98/38, KTB *U 38*, 17 Oct. 1940.
7. BA-MA RM 98/48, KTB *U 48*, 17 Oct. 1940.
8. TNA ADM 199/2134, 62f, Report of an interview with Captain L. Z. Weatherill, Master of SS *Scoresby*, 5 November 1940.
9. TNA, AIR 27/1298, ORB 210 Squadron RAF, 17 Oct. 1940.
10. BA-MA RM 98/38, KTB *U 38*, 17 Oct. 1940 and 18 Oct. 1940.
11. BA-MA RM 98/330, KTB *U 123*, 18 Oct. 1940.
12. BA-MA RM 98/330, KTB *U 123*, Torpedo-Schussmeldungen 18 Oct. 1940.
13. BA-MA RM 98/127, KTB *U 46*, 18 Oct. 1940.
14. BA-MA RM 98/101, KTB *U 101*, 18 Oct. 1940.
15. BA-MA RM 98/99, KTB *U 99*, 18 Oct. 1940.
16. TNA ADM 199/2134, 99f, Report of an interview with Captain R. S. Kearon, master of the SS *Assyrian*, 31 Oct. 1940; TNA ADM 199/1707, Submarine attacks on convoys, Report SS *Assyrian*.
17. BA-MA RM 98/127, KTB *U 46*, 18 Oct. 1940.
18. TNA ADM 199/2134, 91f, Report of an interview with Captain R. Smith, master of the SS *Empire Miniver*, 6 Dec. 1940; TNA ADM 199/1707, Submarine attacks on convoys, Report SS *Empire Miniver*.
19. BA-MA RM 98/330, KTB *U 123*, 18 Oct. 1940.
20. BA-MA RM 98/101, KTB *U 101*, 18 Oct. 1940.
21. TNA ADM 199/1707, Report Robert J. Woodgate, SS *Beatus*.
22. BA-MA RM 98/100, KTB *U 100*, 18 Oct. 1940.
23. TNA ADM 199/1707, Report Robert McInnes, SS *Shekatika*.
24. BA-MA RM 98/99, KTB *U 99*, 18 Oct. 1940. TNA ADM 199/1707, Report of an interview with Captain J. C. Walker, master of the SS *Blairspey*, 7 Nov., 1940; Report C. T. Hollingworth, SS *Blairspey*.
25. BA-MA RM 98/100, KTB *U 100*, 18 Oct. 1940. TNA ADM 199/2134, 105, Report of an interview with Captain J. de Groot, master of SS *Boekelo*, 24 Oct. 1940.
26. BA-MA RM 98/99, KTB *U 99*, 18 Oct. 1940. TNA ADM 199/1707, Submarine attacks on convoys, Report SS *Niritos*.

27. BA-MA RM 98/101, KTB *U 101*, 18 Oct. 1940. TNA ADM 199/2134, 99, Report of an interview with Captain R. S. Kearon, master of the SS *Assyrian*, 31 October, 1940; TNA ADM 199/1707, Submarine attacks on convoys, Reports SS *Assyrian*, SS *Empire Brigade* and SS *Soesterberg*.
28. BA-MA RM 98/330, KTB *U 123*, 19 Oct. 1940. TNA ADM 199/1707, Submarine attacks on convoys, Report SS *Niritos*.
29. BA-MA RM 98/99, KTB *U 99*, 19 Oct. 1940. http://www.warsailors.com/materials/norfleets1.html, report of DS *Snefjeld*. (DS = *Dampskip*, the Norwegian equivalent of SS/Steam Ship.)
30. BA/MA RM 98/99, KTB *U 99*, 19 Oct. 1940. TNA ADM 199/2134, 94, Deposition of Ordinary Seaman Edward Sidney King – SS *Fiscus*. http://www.warsailors.com/materials/norfleets1.html, report of DS *Snefjeld*.
31. BA/MA RM 98/99, KTB *U 99*, 19 Oct. 1940. TNA ADM 199/1707, Report on sinking of SS *Sedgepool* in convoy SC 7. TNA ADM 199/142, Report of survivors landed by HMRT *Salvonia*.
32. BA/MA RM 98/100, KTB *U 100*, 19 Oct. 1940. TNA ADM 199/1707, Report of an interview with Captain J. C. Walker, master of SS *Blairspey*, 7 Nov. 1940.
33. BA/MA RM 98/330, KTB *U 123*, 19 Oct. 1940. http://www.warsailors.com/materials/norfleets1.html, report of DS *Snefjeld*.
34. BA/MA RM 98/99, KTB *U 99*, 19 Oct. 1940. BA/MA RM 98/330, KTB *U 123*, 19 Oct. 1940. TNA ADM 199/2134, 6, Report of an interview with Captain T. H. Irvin, master of the SS *Clintonia*, 1 Nov. 1940; TNA ADM 199/2134 Survivor reports: Merchant vessels, Sept.–Nov. 1940; TNA ADM 199/2215, Admiralty war diary summaries, 16–31 Oct. 1940.
35. BA/MA RM 87/17, KTB BdU, 19 October 1940; Rohwer, Jürgen, *Axis Submarine Successes of World War Two*, Annapolis, Md: Naval Institute Press, 1999, 32–4.
36. BA/MA RM 87/17, KTB BdU, 20 October 1940, translation quoted from Hessler, Günter, *The U-boat War in the Atlantic 1939–1945*, London: HMSO, 1989, Vol. 1, 50.
37. Charles M. Sternhell and Alan M. Thorndike, *Antisubmarine Warfare in World War II*, Office of the Chief of Naval Operations, Navy Department, Washington, DC 1946, 9.
38. Sternhell and Thorndike, *Antisubmarine Warfare in World War II*, 11.

2.
Five Days in Mid-Atlantic
Convoy SC 118 – February 1943

Historical Significance and Prologue

AMONGST THE MANY CONVOY BATTLES in the long U-boat campaign in the North Atlantic during World War Two, the fight around Slow Convoy (SC) 118 between 4 and 8 February 1943 stands out as one of the longest and fiercest actions of its kind. The former Commanding Officer U-boats, Admiral Karl Dönitz wrote of it:

> It was perhaps the hardest convoy battle of the whole war. All honour is due to the commanding officers and crews of the U-boats, who fought these fierce convoy battles for days in the severe winter weather of the Atlantic. During the four nights of relentless fighting the commanding officers could not leave the bridges of their U-boats. The fate of their crews often depended on their lightning-fast decisions. It is hard to imagine the degree of determination and self-control required immediately after a depth-charge attack to give the order to surface, to close once more with the enemy and once more to penetrate the bristling circle of a convoy's inner defensive screen, with the full knowledge that the alternatives are success or destruction. The deeds of the U-boat commanders in these convoy battles must rank among the greatest achievements in the history of submarine warfare.[1]

The story of this convoy is therefore covered in varying detail in almost every history of the Battle of the Atlantic. In addition, several authors have published detailed battle summaries of the actions around SC 118, although from different perspectives.[2] American accounts

Fig. 6 (right): Course map of SC 118, 25 January–10 February 1943.

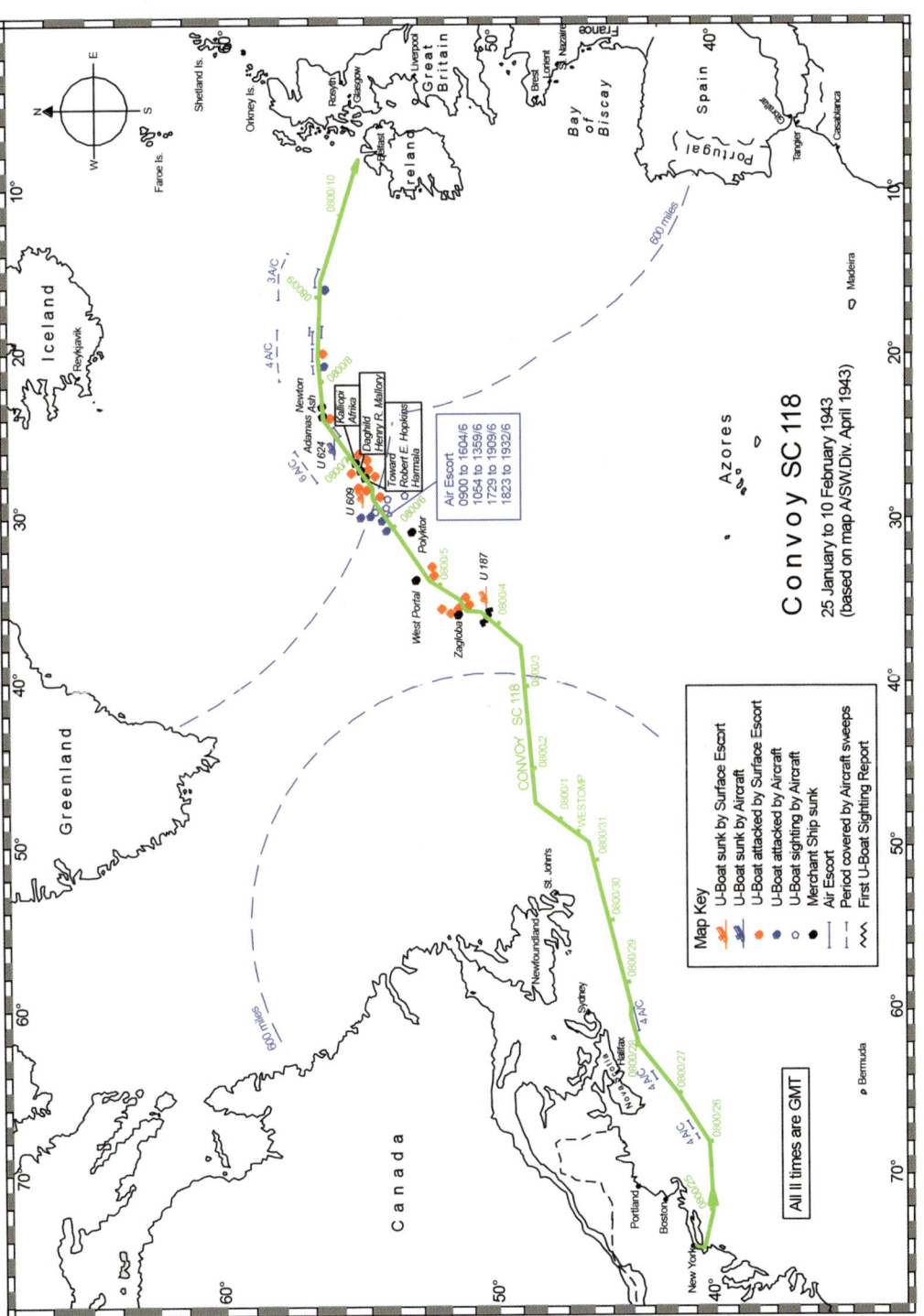

have often focused on the events leading to the sinking of the troop transport *Henry R. Mallory*, killing 272 of the 494 people on board.

Surprisingly, all accounts of the history of this convoy have so far failed to make full use of the available Allied and German documents recording the actions of the individual units in the course of the battle. Thus, their authors have made many mistaken assessments of individual actions by both sides. The present account gives a detailed step-by-step analysis of the operations during the five-day battle for the first time, resulting in many corrections to, and new assessments of, the actions conducted by both sides during the battle.

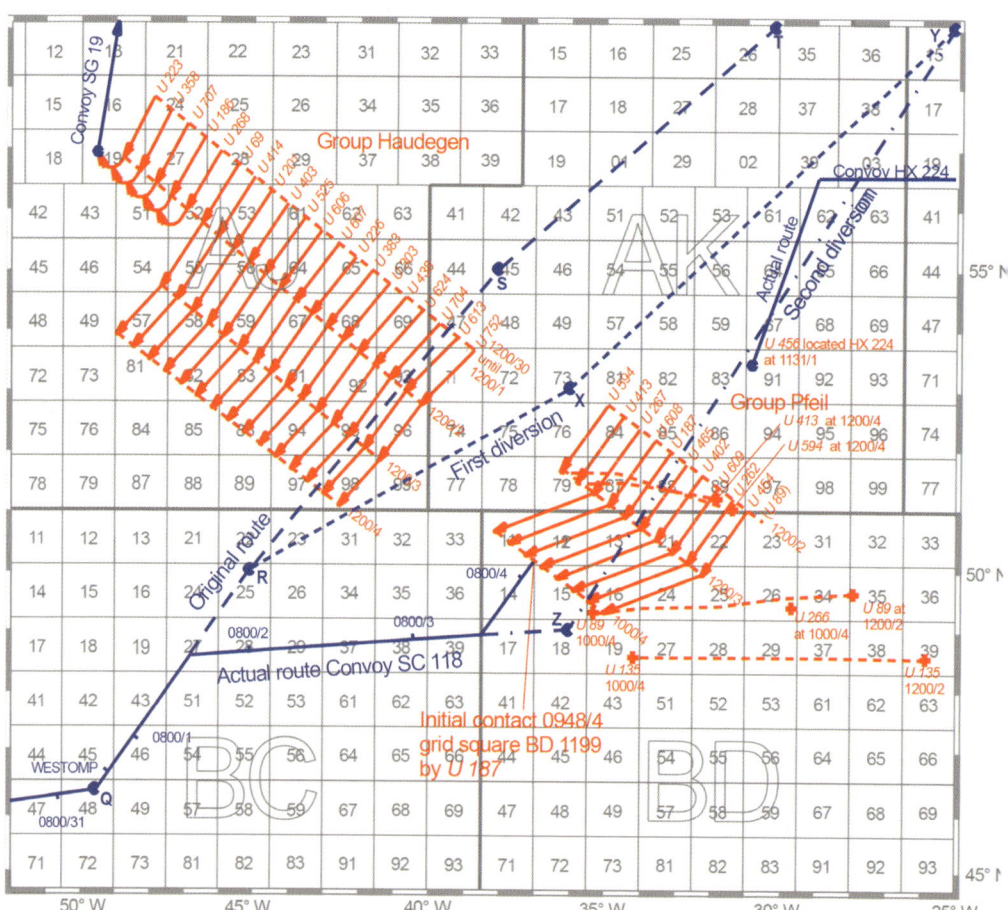

Fig. 7: Disposition of the U-boat Groups Haudegen and Pfeil against SC 118.

On 1 February 1943, U-boat Command had 416 boats in commission, with 178 of them earmarked for operations in the Atlantic. During the previous month, an average of 91 boats were at sea, including those in their operational area or on transfer to or from it. While this figure was still far from the 200 boats at sea demanded by Dönitz in 1939 for waging a successful U-boat campaign against Britain, the number of boats available enabled U-boat Command in mid-January 1943 for the first time in the war to build up two patrol lines in the western North Atlantic to cover most of the convoy routes across the central Atlantic towards Britain. The two groups, Jaguar and Haudegen, with 24 boats between them, nevertheless failed to locate convoy HX 223 and could establish only temporary contact with the following SC 117. Both eastbound convoys were routed around their patrol lines. Likewise, the two westbound convoys ON 160 and ON 161 evaded the U-boat groups by steering more southerly course lines. On 27 January 1943 Group Jaguar was dissolved and Group Haudegen was re-formed and moved further south-west towards Newfoundland to intercept convoy HX 224, which was expected to pass its line on 30 January. Again, this convoy successfully evaded the Haudegen patrol line, by steering on the southern Great Circle route.

At the beginning of February 1943, the U-boat Command, already deeply frustrated by the series of unsuccessful convoy operations during the previous month, was all too well aware of the serious defeat of the German Army at Stalingrad. A new victory in the tonnage campaign against Allied transatlantic convoys would certainly help to distract the German public from the depressing events on the Eastern Front. On the other hand, for the first time since February 1942, the Western Allies felt a certain relief when fresh Ultra signals intelligence, following the break of the latest U-boat cipher in December 1942, again repeatedly helped merchant ships to evade U-boat patrol lines built up across the original convoy routes. Together with abnormally bad weather in January 1943 with frequent low-pressure areas prevailing over the North Atlantic, often making offensive action on both sides impossible, this saved a great many ships and crews from destruction. Out of thirteen transatlantic convoys sailing in January 1943 in both directions, comprising about 520 merchant ships, U-boats made

Convoy Cruising Order of SC 118 on 31 January 1943

General direction of travel ↑

	12 Annik (Nor) Iceland	13 Lagarfoss (Ice) Iceland	
	22 Dettifoss (Ice) Iceland	23 Mana (Hon) Iceland	24 Yemassee (Pan) Iceland
31 Ann Skakel (US) Iceland	32 Daylight (US) Iceland	33 Henry R. Mallory (US) Iceland	34 Macedonia (Gre) Loch Ewe
41 Gogra (Br) Belfast	42 Liberty (Br) Loch Ewe	43 Redgate Empire (Br) Loch Ewe	44 Kalliopi (Gre) London
51 Baron Haig (Br) Loch Ewe	52 Vacuum (US) Clyde	53 Cetus (US) Clyde	54 Newton Ash (Br) Loch Ewe
61 Danby (Br) Loch Ewe	62 City of Khios (Br) Clyde	63 Samuel Huntington (US) Loch Ewe	64 Blairdevon (Br) Loch Ewe
71 Bestik (Nor) Clyde	72 Rodmanso (Swe) Loch Ewe	73 H.M. Flagler (Pan) Clyde	74 Harmala (Br) Loch Ewe
81 African Prince (Br) Liverpool	82 Dordrecht (Neth) Liverpool	83 Glarona (Nor) Clyde	84 Stad Arnhem (Neth) Liverpool
91 Sheaf Holme (Br) Liverpool	92 Baron Ramsay (Br) Barrow	93 Petter II (Nor) Liverpool	94 West Portal (Pan) Clyde
101 Dallington Court (Br) Belfast	102 Helder (Neth) Belfast	103 Gulf of Mexico (US) Belfast	104 Norbryn (Nor) Liverpool
111 Athelprince (Br) Liverpool	112 William Penn (US) Belfast	113 Sommerstad (Nor) Liverpool	114 Radport (Br) Loch Ewe
121 Gold Shell (Br) Belfast	122 Celtic Star (Br) Liverpool	123 Empire Gareth (Br) Belfast	124 Grey County (Nor) Belfast
131 Maud (Nor) Liverpool	132 Arizpa (US) Loch Ewe	133 Kiruna (Swe) Loch Ewe	134 Polyktor (Gre) Loch Ewe
141 New York City (Br) Clyde	142 King Stephen (Br) Loch Ewe	143 Danae II (Br) Larne	

45 Zagloba (Pol)	55 Ioannis Frangos (Gre) Belfast	65 Adamas (Gre) London
75 Tilemachos (Gre) Loch Ewe	85 Acme (US) Liverpool	95 Toward (Br) Clyde
105 Afrika (Br) Liverpool	115 Robert E. Hopkins (US) Loch Ewe	125 Deido (Br) Liverpool
135 Daghild (Nor) Liverpool		

Ownership and destination of each vessel shown where possible.

contact with only three, sinking just four ships of 31,865 gross tons plus a drifting wreck that had broken in half in heavy weather. The total sinkings by Axis submarines dropped to 307,196 gross tons in January 1943, the lowest figure since December 1941.[3]

Convoy SC 118, initially consisting of forty-four ships, sailed from New York at 0700 on 24 January 1943.[4] Two ships returned to New York soon afterwards because of technical defects. Protected by a Western Local Escort Group, made up of the corvettes HMCS *Fennel* (Senior Officer – SO), HMCS *Dunvegan*, HMCS *Mayflower* and the minesweepers HMCS *Cowichan* and HMCS *Truro*, it was routed well clear of the coast of Nova Scotia and Newfoundland towards the Western Ocean Meeting Point (WESTOMP) south-east of St John's. Arriving there on 31 January, the British mid-ocean B2 Escort Group, including the destroyers HMS *Vanessa*, HMS *Vimy*, HMS *Beverley* and the corvettes HMS *Mignonette*, HMS *Campanula*, HMS *Abelia* and HMS *Anemone*, as well as a number of additional merchant ships, rendezvoused with the convoy after having left St John's the day before in two divisions. At 1915 its SO, Acting Cdr F. B. Proudfoot, in *Vanessa* assumed command as Senior Officer Escort (SOE) for the crossing of the Atlantic. The command of Mid-Ocean Escort Group B2 had been temporarily handed over to Proudfoot, while its nominal senior officer, Captain D. F. G. W. MacIntyre, in the destroyer HMS *Hesperus* was at Liverpool repairing damage received in the ramming and sinking of *U 357* on 27 December 1942 while escorting convoy HX 219. The convoy now included sixty-two ships arranged in fourteen columns with three to five ships each. The convoy commodore, Rear Admiral H. C. C. Forsyth, sailed in the British steamer *African Prince*, designated as convoy No. 81. The Vice-Commodore was Captain J. Roberts, master of the British tanker *Athelprince*, convoy No. 111. The small converted British steamer *Toward* was attached to the convoy as a rescue ship, sailing nominally as convoy No. 95 in the rear centre part.

As usual, the British Admiralty had recommended a course for SC 118 to the Commander-in-Chief, US Navy (COMINCH) as early as 11 January 1943, which was duly accepted on the next day. According to this proposal SC 118 was to sail via the routing points R (50°02′N, 45°01′W), S (54°58′N, 37°59′W), T (59°05′N, 30°03′W),

The destroyer HMS *Vanessa* carried the SOE of the British Mid-Ocean Escort Group B2. Like its sister ship HMS *Vimy*, *Vanessa* was taken in hand for refit and conversion as a Long Range Escort by the Green and Silley Weir shipyard in London from September 1941 until June 1942.

The photograph shows the ship in its new guise with the Type 271 centimetric radar behind the open bridge, Hedgehog ahead-throwing mortar instead of the former A Gun and an increased number of depth-charge throwers astern.

U (58°57′N, 20°00′W), V (58°06′N, 13°08′W) to W (56°30′N, 08°29′W) with the Change of Operational Control (CHOP) from COMINCH to the Admiralty at 1000 on 4 February 1943. A straggler route was established some 50 nautical miles north of the convoy course. Probably based on the U-boat situation plot and a prediction of future German movements, at 1802 on 30 January 1943 the Admiralty nevertheless recommended to COMINCH to keep SC 118 west of 51°W until north of 55°N. In the afternoon on 31 January 1943 the Submarine Tracking Room at the Admiralty's Operational Intelligence Centre learned from signals intelligence about the BdU order to shift twenty-one U-boats of Group Haudegen to a new search line south-west of Greenland until 30 January 1943, which extended squarely across the original route envisaged for SC 118.[5] To avoid an encounter with Group Haudegen, COMINCH quickly diverted the convoy by a radio signal timed at 1707 on the same day to a new route (first diversion) around the south-eastern end of the U-boat search line. The convoy was now to sail from point R via the new points X (53°01′N, 36°02′W) and Y (59°02′N, 25°03′W) directly to U by omitting the previous points S, T and X. The straggler route was changed accordingly. The diversion route recommended by the Admiralty on the previous day had been changed on account of the weather situation north-east of Newfoundland. Fresh information from signals intelligence at noon on 1 February 1943 again indicated a likely encounter on the convoy's new route with a number of former Group Landsknecht U-boats redirected to a new assembly point north-east of Newfoundland. Allied reaction was quick again after the Admiralty had strongly recommended that COMINCH should keep the convoy south of 50°N until east of 40°W. Hence, COMINCH directed the SOE of SC 118 once again by a signal timed at 1521 on 1 February 1943 to alter course immediately to a more southerly course before turning north-east onto the northern Great Circle route (second diversion). The new convoy route ran via point Z (49°01′N, 36°02′W) directly to point Y by omitting X with the straggler route changed accordingly.[6] At 1805 convoy SC 118 eventually altered its course to 85° True to steer for point Z.

In addition, B2 Escort Group was reinforced during 1 February when the Coast Guard cutter USS *Bibb* joined it at 1340, followed at 1524 by the destroyer HMS *Witch* and the Free French corvette FFS *Lobelia*. All three ships had sailed from St John's the day before. The *Bibb* was to break off from the convoy on reaching the Iceland Ocean Meeting Point (ICOMP) to escort the Iceland portion of SC 118 to Reykjavik. The escort now included ten warships, which was a formidable force to oppose any U-boats waiting ahead in the so-called 'Black Gap' outside the effective range of the aircraft from Newfoundland, Iceland and the British Isles. All British and Free French ships were fitted with Type 271M centimetric radar sets. The American ships carried either centimetric Type SG-9 sets or the older metric Type SC-1 models. In addition, the *Toward* and *Bibb* were fitted with High Frequency/Direction Finding (HF/DF) equipment. However, Cdr Proudfoot considered the operators of *Bibb*'s newly installed HF/DF set as obviously still unfamiliar with their instrument.

Previously, on 29 January, the Coast Guard cutter USS *Ingham* and the destroyer USS *Leary*, attached to Task Force 24.6.1, also known as the Iceland Escort Unit, had been slated as further escorts for the Iceland portion from ICOMP to Iceland. Accordingly, the *Ingham* left Reykjavik at 1530 on 3 February to join SC 118 at sea, but *Leary* was held back by necessary repairs. Unable to complete the repairs in time, *Leary* was eventually replaced by its sister ship USS *Schenck*, which departed at 2130 on 4 February to augment the escort of SC 118.

U-boat Command was already waiting for SC 118 after the B-Dienst department of German Naval Intelligence had monitored its departure from New York on 24 January. Unknown to the Allies, during 1942/43 B-Dienst was able to provide excellent intelligence on Atlantic convoy cycles and at times on their routes after a deep break into the British 'Naval Cypher No. 3', used for radio communication and convoy coordination in the Atlantic. When *U 456*, one of the ex-Group Landsknecht boats on westward transit, reported a fast eastbound convoy at 1131 on 1 February on the northern Great Circle route, U-boat Command correctly attributed this convoy to the HX series (actually HX 224). Assuming the Allied intention to run the following SC convoy on the same general course as the HX convoy in the hope of evading the U-boats concentrating in the chase after the HX convoy, U-boat Command built up the new Group Pfeil late on 1 February

U 609 inside the lock at St-Nazaire before departure on 4 October 1942. Unlike many others, this boat carried no emblem or device on the conning tower. At left in the background, the sister boat *U 658*, which was lost with all hands on 30 October 1942.

from naval grid squares AK 8421 to BD 2316 across the likely route of the SC convoy.[7] Naval grid square AK 8421 converts to 52°45'N, 34°55'W, BD 2316 to 50°51'N, 30°35'W. Group Pfeil initially consisted of eleven boats. Of these, *U 267*, *U 608*, *U 187*, *U 465*, *U 402*, *U 609*, *U 262* and *U 454* had previously operated to the west of Ireland with Group Landsknecht, which was dissolved on 28 January. *U 594* and *U 413*, both low on fuel, had been patrolling in loose waiting positions to the south-west of Greenland after previous operations with Group Jaguar north-east of Newfoundland. The eleventh boat *U 89* came out fresh from France but was still too far behind to join the group in time. Therefore, on the next day *U 89*, together with *U 135*, also fresh outbound from France, were redirected to a waiting position in square BC 29, probably envisaged to join Group Haudegen after reaching this area. The centre of the naval grid square BC 29 converts to 48°45'N, 43°45'W. On 3 February *U 413* and *U 594* were recalled to France owing to their fuel situation, leaving eight Pfeil boats on station.

Due to a gap in deciphering German operational U-boat radio traffic, lasting from early on 2 February until the evening of 6 February 1943, the Submarine Tracking Room remained unaware of U-boat Command's latest disposition of Group Pfeil, which stretched squarely across the second diversion route ordered on 1 February 1943 for SC 118. This lack of signals intelligence during a crucial phase in the convoy's transatlantic transfer, when U-boat Command was eager to block all convoy exit routes into the North Atlantic by an almost continuous net of U-boat search lines, greatly raised the chances of an encounter between the two forces.[8] Even a final change of the route for SC 118, ordered by COMINCH at 1356 on 3 February following a recommendation by the Admiralty earlier that day, did not help to avoid disaster. Probably based more on intuition than hard facts, the U-boat Tracking Room ordered the SOE of SC 118 to alter the convoy course after dark at his estimated position 48°57′N, 37°40′W directly towards Y by omitting Z without change to the actual straggler route. The time for reaching the CHOP line was shifted to 0200 on 5 February. Therefore, SC 118 duly changed its course line in two steps at 2200 and 2300 on 3 February from 85° to 54° and finally 37° towards point Y.

In post-war publications it is often claimed that crucial information about the routing of SC 118 became available to U-boat Command by testimony from a survivor of the British tanker *Cordelia*.[9] Examination of the appropriate German documents, however, tells a different story. Separated from convoy HX 224, the tanker was torpedoed on the convoy's straggler route by *U 632* at 2054 on 3 February in position 56°37′N, 22°58′W and sank after a *coup-de-grâce* at 2124. At 2210 the chief engineer, Leslie Bingham, was picked out of the sea, eventually becoming the sole survivor. The remaining 46 crew of the *Cordelia*, including the master Captain Edward Marshall, all perished in the grim North Atlantic weather. Preliminary interrogation of the survivor aboard *U 632* disclosed that a large slow convoy from Halifax might follow the previous HX convoy on the same route to the North Channel. However, *U 632* reported this information to U-boat Command only a full 24 hours later when the convoy battle had already started. The radio signal from *U 632* carries the time group 2314 on 4 February 1943.

The signal was duly intercepted by Allied stations, but during its processing at Bletchley Park the decoded and translated version was assigned the date of the previous day by a typing error.[10] In consequence, any information provided by the survivor of the *Cordelia* was not instrumental in the operations of Group Pfeil against SC 118 or

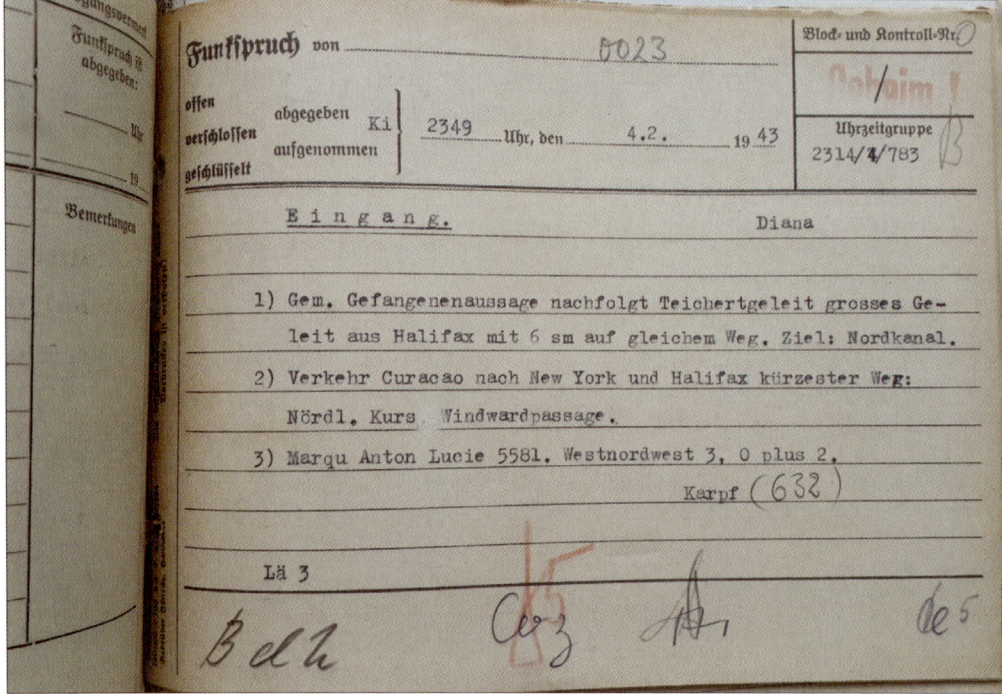

BdU copy of the radio signal from *U 632* of 4 February 1943 timed 2314 about the interrogation of the survivor from the British tanker *Cordelia*.

the subsequent location of the convoy. U-boat Command's eagerness to achieve a long-awaited success against an eastbound convoy was nevertheless raised when signal information produced by German Naval Intelligence led to the mistaken belief that various ships in the oncoming convoy were destined for onward routing to Murmansk in Northern Russia, carrying supplies for the Red Army on the Eastern Front. Therefore, U-boat Command considered the destruction of the convoy even more important. By then the general dispositions for the battle to follow were complete, with both sides confident of success.

Day One – 4 February 1943

The passage of SC 118 was uneventful until the morning of 4 February. Apart from a false alarm owing to a non-submarine Asdic contact by *Campanula* on 1 February and the usual problems with stragglers

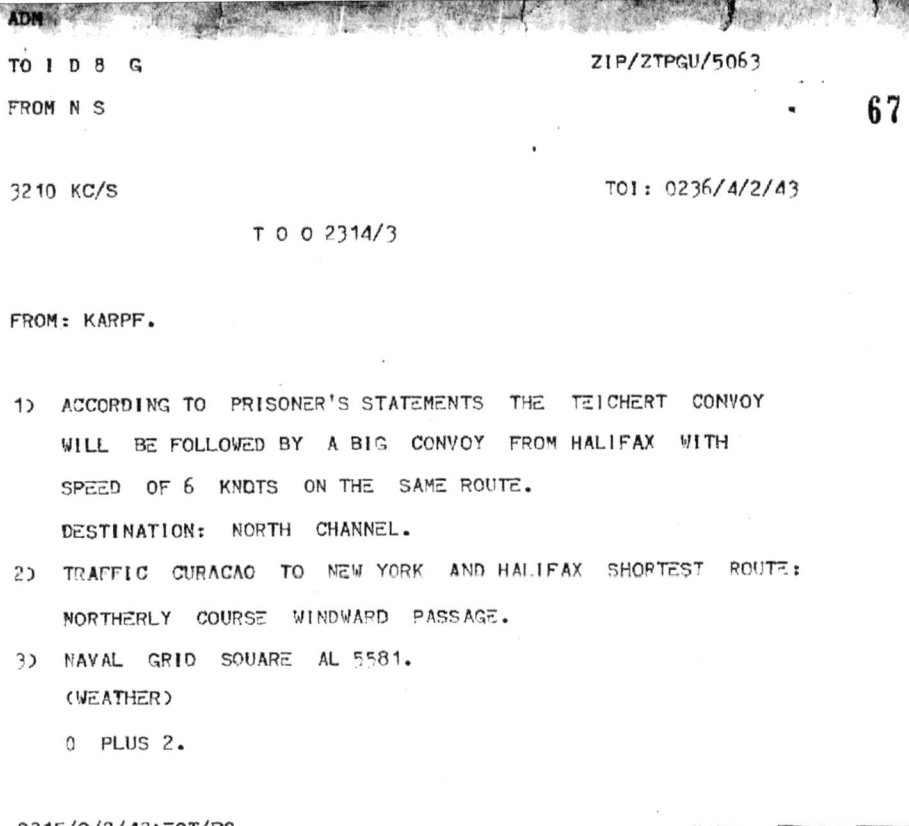

Decoded and translated version of the radio signal by *U 632* with the wrong dates for the time group 2314/3 for TOO (Time of Originator) and the time group 0236/4/2/43 for TOI (Time of Interception).
(TNA DEFE 3/710/ZTPGU 5063)

and excessive funnel smoke in the convoy, the only exciting incident occurred at noon on 3 February when a Snowflake illumination rocket was fired in error by a ship in the convoy. In broad daylight this bright

U 187, after yard overhaul and front-line fitting out, leaving Stettin (modern Szczecin) on 6 January 1943. Following a short stay at Swinemünde for anti-aircraft firing exercises and subsequent final fitting at Kiel, this Type IX C boat left on its first front-line patrol on 12 January 1943 together with five Type VII C boats.

light was clearly seen from *Beverley* 15 miles away and a signal to the Commodore asked him to warn ships to be more careful in future. Nevertheless, on the very next day it was just this kind of mistake which started the battle when the convoy was about to hit the centre of the patrol line. At 0854 on 4 February a Snowflake rocket was again fired in error, this time by the Norwegian steamer *Annik* sailing as No. 12. Both *U 187* and *U 402* observed its bright light. On investigating its origin *U 187* (Kptlt Ralph Münnich) made contact with SC 118 in naval grid square BD 1199 and quickly informed U-boat Command by a short signal timed 0948. At 1006 this was supplemented by a further report indicating a large convoy with a north-easterly course, speed 8 to 10 knots. SC 118 would probably have been detected anyway by

Group Pfeil even without the accidental firing of the Snowflake. At the time of initial contact, the convoy was still west of the patrol line and it seems unlikely that the fourteen-column convoy, extending several miles in width, would have slipped unseen through the line of U-boats spaced 15 miles apart in broad daylight.

U-boat Command's reaction to the long-awaited convoy sighting report was swift. At 1032 all eight boats of Group Pfeil, plus $U\,89$ and $U\,135$ approaching from the east, were directed to operate in accordance with the sighting report of $U\,187$. In order to deploy the maximum number of boats against this important convoy, at 1058 $U\,456$ and $U\,614$, then still operating against HX 224, received orders to engage SC 118. In the same signal U-boat Command also ordered $U\,265$ to operate against SC 118, although monitored Allied radio traffic had indicated its possible loss to air attack on the previous day during the pursuit of HX 224. Thereafter the boat had failed twice to report its position on request. Lastly, at 1112 the five boats of Group Haudegen nearest to the convoy, $U\,438$, $U\,624$, $U\,704$, $U\,613$ and $U\,752$, together with $U\,266$, $U\,413$ and $U\,594$, which were still in the general area while returning to France, were also directed to intercept and attack the convoy. $U\,266$, previously belonging to Group Jaguar, had damaged its forward hydroplane on 2 February in a stopgap refuelling rendezvous with $U\,466$. A previous order early on 4 February to return to France after handing over surplus fuel to $U\,706$ was now cancelled by this new order. Thus, within an hour, twenty U-boats were sent to hunt for SC 118 although some of them were still more than 300 miles away from it. Except $U\,187$, $U\,266$, $U\,267$ and $U\,614$, all of these boats had completed at least one previous patrol in North Atlantic or Arctic waters with reasonable results against Allied shipping. The prospect of success for the U-boats seemed good and Grand Admiral Dönitz radioed to them: 'Convoy is probably destined for Murmansk. Attack! Operate ruthlessly, to relieve the Eastern Front.'[11]

Operators on the rescue ship *Toward* were quick to get a DF bearing on the second transmission of $U\,187$ at 1006, locating it right ahead of the port convoy column. Cdr Proudfoot immediately sent out *Beverley* (Lt-Cdr R. A. Price), then closing the convoy from its station ahead for refuelling, to search for the U-boat to a distance of 20 miles. At 1059

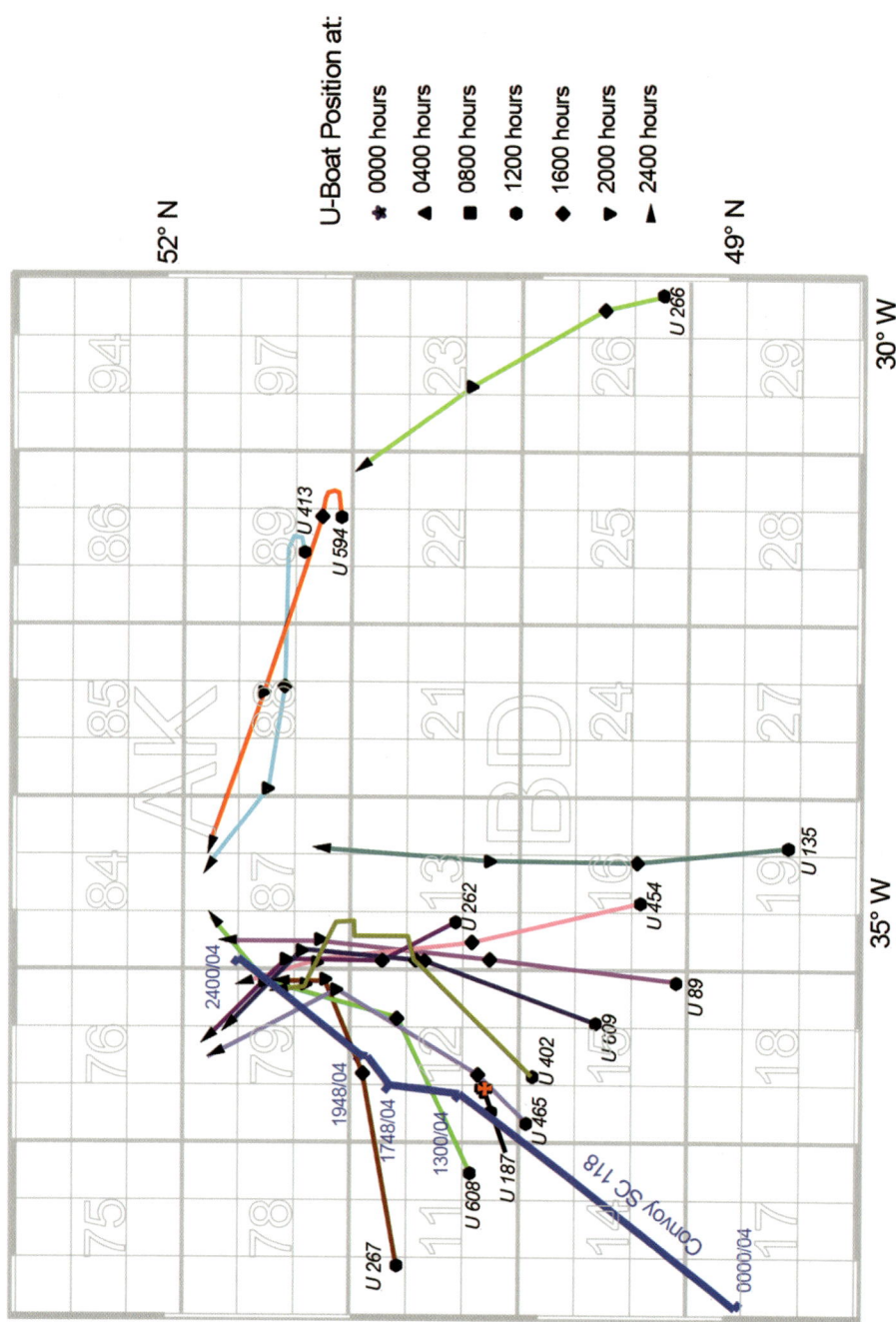

Fig. 8: Courses of U-boats near SC 118 on 4 February 1943.

Beverley's lookouts sighted *U 187* fifteen miles ahead of the convoy. In response to the destroyer's report Proudfoot sent *Vimy* (Lt-Cdr R. B. Stannard) to assist. *Beverley* meanwhile kept the U-boat on the starboard bow, thus forcing it to alter to the eastward clear of the convoy. When the destroyer then closed at high speed, *U 187* dived at a range of 4,000 yards at 1142. *Beverley* was sweeping the area of its dive at 15 knots in a line abreast with the upcoming *Vimy* when the latter gained an Asdic contact ahead at 1206. *Vimy* attacked the contact at 1241 with five depth charges set to 100 feet, followed by an unsuccessful Hedgehog attack at 1300. After two more depth-charge attacks set between 150 and 385 feet at 1315 and 1333 the badly damaged *U 187* broke surface five minutes later. The two destroyers immediately opened fire with their main armament and machine guns, scoring several hits. At 1343 the U-boat finally sank, stern first. Nine of its crew, including its commander, were killed in the fight or drowned, whilst forty-five others were taken prisoners of war.[12] The first round in the battle clearly went to the escorts who had knocked out the first contact-keeper in a textbook action.

In the afternoon of 4 February, the *Ingham*, under way to join the escort of SC 118, reported its sonar set as defective. The Commander Task Group 24.6 of the Iceland Escort Unit therefore directed the destroyer *Babbitt*, then on return to Iceland, to replace *Ingham* in the escort of SC 118 with the latter to return to Iceland after the arrival of *Babbitt*. However, after a request by the British C-in-C Western Approaches, Admiral Max Horton, *Ingham* was kept with the escort of SC 118 in view of the number of U-boats then in contact with the convoy. On the other hand, at 1000 the short-legged W-class destroyer HMS *Witch* (Lt-Cdr S. R. J. Woods) of the escort had to be detached to a port in Britain owing to its fuel situation.

At the same time as *U 187* sent its first sighting report, its left-wing neighbour *U 465* (Kptlt Heinz Wolf) also gained contact with SC 118 on its starboard bow. This sighting report at 1058 was not received by U-boat Command. With the starboard diesel out of service, *U 465* began shadowing the convoy then steering on course 37°. Soon afterwards Wolf observed the *Beverley* pursuing *U 187* on an easterly course. To avoid detection by the destroyer, *U 465* dived at 1100. Staying close

to the scene of *U 187*'s sinking, Wolf wrongly considered the depth charges dropped by *Beverley* and *Vimy* as being directed against his boat and remained submerged until 1455.[13] Meanwhile *U 402* (Kptlt Siegfried Freiherr von Forstner) made contact with SC 118 at 1110 and followed the convoy on the starboard side. Atmospheric conditions delayed his sighting report to U-boat Command until 1207. This signal, like the next one at 1339, was duly picked up by the HF/DF operators on *Toward*, indicating *U 402*'s position at 1339 bearing 154° from the convoy. Temporarily interrupted by a diesel breakdown, *U 402* was nevertheless able to shadow the convoy at long distance until 1441 when

The Flower-class corvette HMS *Anemone* in 1943, displaying a more compact bridge layout with the prominent round antenna of the Type 271 radar incorporated. Living conditions aboard the small escort vessels were often appalling, especially when subject to adverse weather in the North Atlantic. They were often delegated to rescue the crews of ships sunk in convoy battles; many merchant navy sailors owed their lives to the selfless performance of the crews on these ships.

it was driven off by one of the starboard escorts (*Beverley* or *Anemone*) zig-zagging routinely towards the east. At 1425 *U 262* (ObltzS Heinz Franke) and *U 609* (Kptlt Klaus Rudloff), joining the hunt from the

Kptlt Rolf Struckmeier as commander of *U 608*. The Commanding Officer U-boats commented: 'During the long patrol it was operated correctly against four convoys, regrettably without substantial success. The boat encountered a tough and resourceful defence.' Note the Iron Cross First Class award on his left-side uniform pocket in a unusual fabric version.

south, had come close to *U 402*, but were driven off towards the east by the same escort as *U 402*. Thereafter, all three boats failed to regain contact with the convoy. By assuming that the convoy had turned to a north-westerly course to move away from them, the U-boats apparently missed the convoy by passing behind its rear.[14] Actually, the convoy changed its general course at 1545 from 37° to 7° and again at 1948 to 52° in an emergency turn to starboard. Franke in *U 262* was the first to realise the mistake several hours later and searched again to the north.

At 1447 *U 608* (Kptlt Struckmeier), approaching from the western part of Group Pfeil, also made contact with the convoy and informed U-boat Command by short signal. Over the next five hours *U 608*, running on the convoy's port bow, remained in visual contact with the ships of the convoy, although movements of the portside escort ships repeatedly forced the boat to take evasive courses. During this time Struckmeier sent several contact reports to U-boat Command. Following an HF/DF fix bearing 0° from *Toward* at 1820, *Vimy* was sent to investigate and sighted *U 608* on the surface at 1913. Although the bridge watch on *U 608* had observed the approaching escort one minute earlier, Struckmeier was unable to escape the fast destroyer on the surface and crash-dived at 1929. Despite poor Asdic conditions *Vimy* quickly picked up the boat on its Asdic set and dropped two depth-charge patterns. After Cdr Proudfoot turned down a request for a second escort to assist in the hunt because four other warships were also absent from the convoy chasing HF/DF contacts, Lt-Cdr Stannard wisely considered that close convoy screen was more effective than hunting dubious contacts and *Vimy* set course to re-join. However, *Vimy*'s deterrent action successfully neutralised *U 608* for the rest of the night because, after surfacing again at 2205, contact with the convoy had been lost in the darkness.[15] By then, most of the eight escorts had again taken up their regular night-time positions around the convoy, as given in Fig. 9 overleaf.

The next to get a sight of the convoy was *U 267* (Kptlt Otto Tinschert), another Pfeil boat catching up with the convoy from the western end of the search line. Some 30 miles away from the convoy at the time when it was first sighted, Tinschert showed good navigational skill to intercept the convoy at 1520 following a four-hour high-speed chase.

Staying on the port bow of the convoy, he steamed ahead to attain a favourable position for attack at nightfall. At 1803 the lead escorts came in sight again. Now on the starboard bow of the convoy screen, *U 267* manoeuvred ahead of the convoy, following various courses to evade detection during the twilight period. A convoy sighting report timed at 2028 informed U-boat Command that contact with SC 118 had been re-established. At 2130 Tinschert finally started his high-speed approach towards the main body of the convoy. But only five minutes later *Beverley*, then stationed on the port beam of the convoy, picked up the U-boat on its radar at a range of 5,000 yards and ran down the contact bearing at 18 knots. Tinschert's lookouts recognised the approaching destroyer at a distance of 2,000 metres. At that time *Beverley* had still not gained visual contact and slowed down to locate the surfaced U-boat by using its Asdic set in the listening mode. Simultaneously, *U 267* was preparing for a stern torpedo shot on the destroyer when the destroyer lookouts eventually sighted the U-boat's wake at a distance of 500 yards. Only moments later *Beverley* illuminated the U-boat with its 10-in. searchlight and star shell and opened fire with its light AA guns. Tinschert immediately ordered the boat to crash-dive. Although *Beverley* failed to ram the diving boat, a pattern of five depth charges was dropped shortly afterwards by eye. After having gained Asdic contact, another ten-charge pattern was dropped at 2211. However, *U 267* had gone deep by that time and no damage was inflicted by the attack. At this point, the corvette *Anemone*, Lt-Cdr P. G. A. King, joined *Beverley*, and the two ships carried out a box search, dropping single depth charges at each turn. Held down by the presence of the two escorts, *U 267* could hear the convoy on its listening gear passing along its starboard side and then disappearing apparently sailing on an easterly course.

Tinschert eventually surfaced at 0048, but a search for the convoy to the east subsequently proved unsuccessful.[16]

● Night action
● Daylight action
◆ Nominal escort position taken up at nightfall

Note: All positions relative to convoy course. Contacts at more than ten miles are plotted without regard to the actual range

The series of disappointing encounters with the escorts of SC 118 was not yet over for the U-boats, which desperately tried to penetrate the screen of escorts to fire their torpedoes at the merchant ships in the convoy. The next to run into the protective curtain built up by the escorts was *U 454* under Kptlt Burkhard Hackländer. Previously stationed at the southern end of Group Pfeil, *U 454* was the last boat of this group to catch up with the convoy. At 1815 Hackländer met up with *U 262* well behind the convoy. Searching on a more northerly course, *U 454* did not fare any better than the other boats. At 2041 an

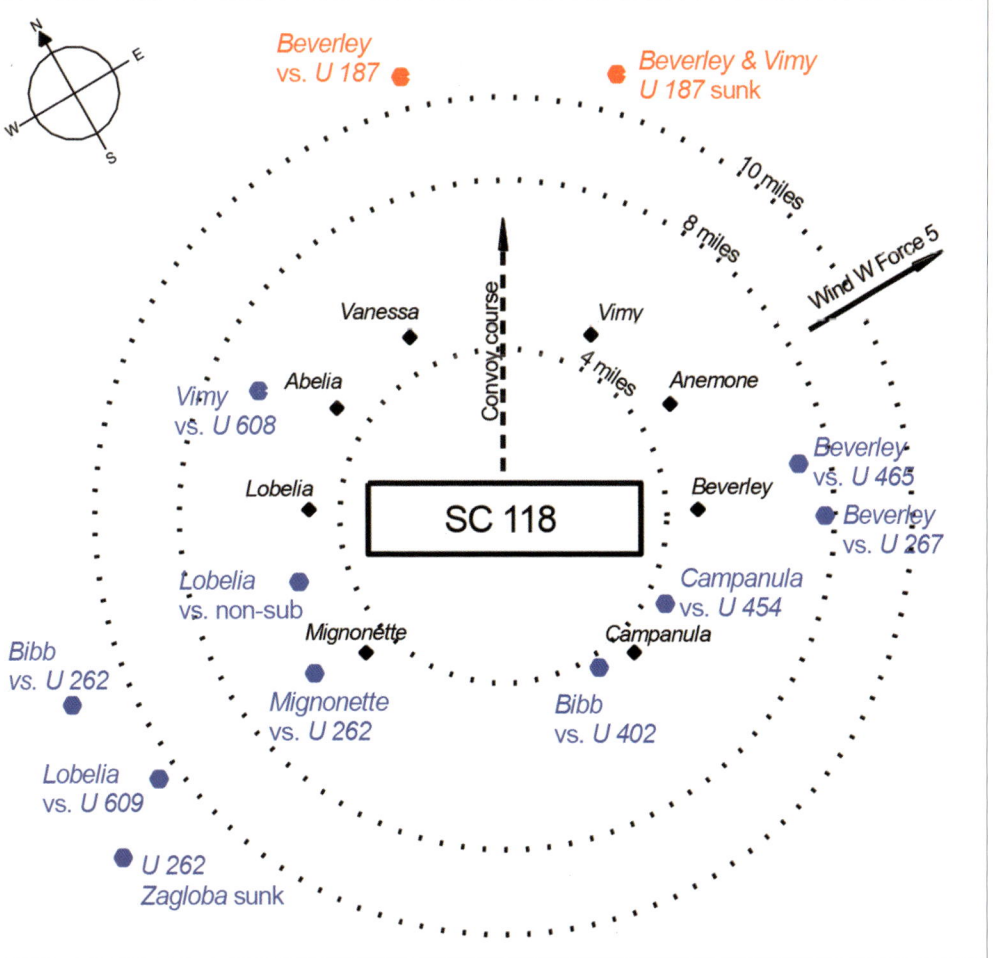

Fig. 9: Action around SC 118 between 1100/4 Feb. and 1100/5 Feb. 1943.

U 454 entering the lock at St-Nazaire on the afternoon of 8 March 1943 at the end of its hapless seventh patrol. The boat looks heavily battered by the severe weather in the North Atlantic. The cover plates at the magnetic compass housing and the port deck railing in front of the conning tower are both missing. In the background at right is the prominent building of the harbour lock pumping station. The houses to the west of the harbour entrance lock are also showing bomb damage from previous air attacks on the base, indicating the new situation in the air war to the returning U-boat crews.

---

escort vessel, identified as a destroyer in the darkness, was observed to turn towards the boat. Evasive manoeuvres on the surface failed to shake it off and at 2048 Hackländer dived to 100 metres. Fourteen minutes later ten depth charges were counted exploding harmlessly some distance away. Although not picked up by Asdic, the boat later listened to the explosions of depth charges dropped by other convoy escorts in the area. In fact, *U 454* had run into the corvette *Campanula*, Lt-Cdr B. A. Rogers, which was then returning to the convoy after being detached at 1715 to investigate a HF/DF contact bearing 143° from the convoy obtained nine minutes earlier by the *Toward*. After dropping a ten-charge pattern at a doubtful contact which was lost shortly afterwards, the corvette left the scene to re-join the convoy in accordance with Cdr Proudfoot's order from 2019 that all absentee escorts should return to their escort stations. *U 454* surfaced at 2204 but was still not out of trouble. Going north to follow the assumed course of the convoy, it ran into *Beverley* and *Anemone* still searching for *U 267*. Once again not picked up by the enemy ships, their presence nevertheless forced *U 454* to dive again at 2218. Frustrated by the apparent omnipresence of escort ships in the area, Hackländer now turned due south in order to get free from the convoy escorts. At 0107 *U 454* finally surfaced again. Without contact with the convoy, the boat then moved straight north, searching in accordance with various radio reports picked up from other boats that came into contact with convoy escorts or stragglers.[17]

Forstner in *U 402* had searched in vain for the convoy in a westerly direction until about 2100 when he heard the depth charges dropped on *U 454* in the distance. When he turned north to close the suspected position of the convoy, bad luck struck again. At 2132 a destroyer steaming up from port astern was observed. Due to the bad visibility during this night, the warship was only spotted when the distance was down to less than 500 m. Crash-diving at once, *U 402* heard a single depth-charge detonation one minute later. Thereafter only distant propeller noise and detonations were heard from the depth-charging of *U 267* and later *U 262*. But like *U 454*, Forstner considered it wise to stay submerged until the escorts had cleared the area to avoid being surprised in the darkness. Actually, the 'destroyer' was the US Coast Guard cutter *Bibb*, Cdr Roy L. Raney, on its way to re-join the convoy after having been directed at 1302 to investigate a HF/DF bearing astern. At 2120, about three miles astern of the convoy, the ship's radar obtained a contact. On closing the scene there was nothing to see but at 2131 a sonar contact believed to be a U-boat was picked up. Unable to hold the contact, and suspecting the use of a submarine bubble target by the U-boat, the cutter dropped only a single 600-lb charge set to 100 feet as a 'harassing charge'. At 2148 the *Bibb* watched the star shell and

HMS *Beverley*, taken from the air on 18 July 1942 while undergoing sea trials. During a previous refit at Belfast a new bridge structure with Type 271 radar, Hedgehog ahead-throwing mortar and additional close-range anti-aircraft machine-guns was installed. Commissioned in 1920 as USS *Branch*, the flush-deck destroyer was one of 50 ex-American destroyers transferred to Britain and Canada in autumn 1940 under the 'Destroyers for Bases' deal. Many of these vessels served as convoy escorts in the North Atlantic with notable results. *Beverley* took part in the destruction of *U 187*, but was itself sunk two months later by *U 188*.

gunfire from *Beverley* directed against *U 267*. Deciding not to interfere in this action, Cdr Raney continued towards the convoy and took over his assigned position in the screen at 0130. When *U 402* finally resurfaced at 0050, its renewed search for the convoy was fruitless. Like most of the other boats during that night *U 402* went north in the belief that the convoy had continued on its assumed previous course of

0°. Thus, all these boats missed the main body of the convoy, which in fact stayed to the east of them after the evasive turn at 1948 and which had returned to its general course of 37° at 2300 for the remainder of the night.[18]

The absence of further contact reports after dark left U-boat Command impatient. At 2122 it asked *U 267* to report forthwith the exact position of the convoy and advised all other boats on the importance of frequent contact reports. Star shells over the convoy were to be reported at once. Being well aware of the low fuel status of some boats directed to operate against the convoy, U-boat Command assured them in a further signal at 2240 that replenishment from a U-boat tanker was envisaged on the return trip.[19]

When the search of *Beverley* and *Anemone* for the submerged *U 267* proved unsuccessful, both ships informed the SOE at 2326 about their intention to re-join the convoy. But within minutes *Beverley* picked up a fresh radar contact and ran it down. At 500 yards the U-boat's wake was sighted and the destroyer increased speed to 22 knots in an attempt to ram. At a range of 160 yards *U 465* turned sharply to starboard inside HMS *Beverley*'s turning radius and began to dive. By this cold-blooded action Kptlt Wolf, whose lookouts had apparently seen the destroyer very late, saved his boat from destruction. Obtaining Asdic contact at 2333, *Beverley* dropped a ten-charge pattern, but failed to cause any damage. Contact was not regained thereafter and Lt-Cdr Price in *Beverley* set course to re-join in company with *Anemone*, reaching the convoy at 0139. *U 465* stayed submerged until 0050 and thereafter searched northwards without success for the rest of the night.[20]

The deck officers of *U 262* in front of the fully fitted-out boat on 16 January 1943 on the quay next to the U-boat pen at La Pallice. *From left*: 1st Watch Officer LtzS Hans Hellmann, the commander ObltzS Heinz Franke and 2nd Watch Officer LtzS Horst Dieter Hübsch.

In the meantime, the Free-French corvette *Lobelia*, then in convoy screen position 'P' on the port beam of the convoy, had obtained a radar echo on its port side at 1,800 yards. The echo disappeared at 1,000 yards and Asdic contact was gained immediately thereafter, indicating that the target had submerged. At 2302 five depth charges believed to have been accurate were dropped, followed by three more at 2307. Poor drill in the ship's company and the temporary breakdown of the radar set prevented further attacks and contact was finally lost. Because none of the boats then in the vicinity of the convoy reported this attack, *Lobelia*'s target must have been of a non-sub nature, all too common in the North Atlantic.[21]

By 2130 ObltzS Franke in *U 262* had finally realised that the convoy must have changed its course to the north-east and duly changed his own course in that direction. At 2208 *Beverley* and *Anemone*, using hand lights to identify their positions relative to each other, were observed in the distance and avoiding courses had to be steered. Nevertheless, at 2330 the corvette *Mignonette*, Lt H.H. Brown, then in screen position 'R' astern of the convoy, picked up *U 262* on its radar at 1,600 yards. At 2346 the lookouts sighted the U-boat at a distance of 600 yards. *U 262* had already recognised the corvette three minutes earlier and tried to evade on the surface. When Franke belatedly ordered the boat to dive after being fired on by the corvette, the escort's bow missed the submerging U-boat by a bare 50 yards. A ten-charge pattern dropped while passing along the submerging boat was apparently set too deep as *U 262* reported only slight damage, including the breakdown of its group listening gear. Unable to gain Asdic contact, *Mignonette* returned to its screen position in accordance with the SOE's order at 0015 that all escorts not in contact should take up their appointed stations. *U 262* stayed submerged until 0138 and then went after convoy in a north-easterly direction. In the meantime, *U 608* assumed that the star shells fired in the encounter had originated from the convoy itself and reported likewise by a short signal to U-boat Command at 0006.[22]

Unnoticed by the fighters, a serious misfortune had befallen the convoy on the evening of 4 February, which under adverse circumstances could have had grave consequences for the merchant ships in

The captain of *U 609*, Kptlt Klaus Rudloff, at the base after his return from a patrol. In the convoy battle around SC 118 he showed himself as a tough and skilful contact-keeper for the other U-boats over a period of more than two days. Rudloff was killed with his entire crew when *U 609* was sunk on the evening of 6 February 1943.

SC 118. As already mentioned, at 1948, shortly after twilight, the convoy commodore aboard the *African Prince* in position No. 81 had ordered an emergency turn of 45 degrees to starboard in an effort to shake off some of the pursuing submarines. Unfortunately, the radio room aboard the commodore's ship was out of action and the signal for the alteration of course was made by whistle only. The three port-wing columns and some of the ships at the rear of the convoy did not hear the signal and continued on the previous course of 7°. It took until 0015 for the escort commander and the escorts to appreciate the split in the convoy after all escorts had been ordered to take up appointed stations if not in contact. In the meantime, the convoy had reverted to its original course of 37°. As a result, at about 0300 the main convoy was steering 37° with the three port-wing columns standing about 15 miles to port still steering 7° True. Several other merchant ships which had appreciated the situation at varying times since the split stood in between the two portions. Cdr Proudfoot instructed the corvettes *Lobelia* and *Abelia* to retrieve these ships and escort them back to their proper station.[23]

Despite the confusion caused by the unintentional split of the convoy, the aggressive and skilful handling of the escorts during the first part of the night proved to have been highly successful in frustrating all attempts of the U-boats to press home a successful attack. Moreover, the radical change of course and the offensive sweeps by the escorts along the numerous HF/DF and radar bearings greatly confused both the U-boats at sea and U-boat Command about the position and course of the convoy. As a result, at the end of the day on 4 February, five of the seven U-boats of Group Pfeil then operating in the immediate vicinity of SC 118 had been forced to stay submerged astern of the convoy while the other two were out of contact.

Day Two – 5 February 1943

The only U-boat not yet having experienced a rough handling by the members of B2 Mid Ocean Escort Group was *U 609* under the experienced Kptlt Klaus Rudloff.[24] This was soon to change. This boat, which had been in company with *U 262* and *U 402* at 1425 the previous day on the starboard side of the convoy, apparently also passed behind the convoy while searching in a northerly direction until

ObltzS Klaus Rudloff of *U 609* directing manoeuvres inside the lock at St-Nazaire while leaving on 4 October 1942. The two MG 15 machine guns fitted to the conning tower fairing were to increase the anti-air armament.

Lieutenant de Vaisseau Pierre de Morsier, born in 1908 in Geneva, was called up into the French Navy as a reserve officer in September 1939. Following the French capitulation he joined the Free French forces in July 1940. After commissioning the corvette FFS *Lobelia* on 16 July 1941 he served as its captain until May 1943. Eventually, in 1948, he was awarded a Distinguished Service Cross for his part in defending SC 118.

after darkness. A request from *U 609* timed at 1648 for beacon signals to be sent by boats then in contact and a report timed at 2212 about star shells were the only messages received from *U 609* until midnight.

Assuming the star shells were an indication for the position of the convoy, U-boat Command ordered *U 609* at 2245 to commence shadowing duty. This was not unexpected, as Rudloff had already shown a talent for contact-keeping on a previous patrol in December 1942, when he successfully shadowed convoy ON 153 for more than three days in dreadful weather conditions. In a further message to U-boat Command at 0100 on 5 February Rudloff confirmed he was not in contact with the convoy but mentioned having seen three destroyers at 2300. Propeller noises from two more destroyers were heard at 0030 from a position he believed to be well to the west of the convoy.

The destroyers reported by *U 609* were probably *Beverley*, *Anemone* and *Mignonette* on their way to re-join the convoy.

However, two hours later *U 609* joined the battle and added to the list of unsuccessful attempts to sink one of the merchant vessels of the convoy. While searching for the missing port wing columns, at 0301 the corvette *Lobelia* sighted three ships, including the American troop transport *Henry R. Mallory*, carrying 383 passengers, 34 armed guards and 77 crew. Steering a course of 7°, these ships were still unaware of the alteration in convoy course at 1948 on the day before. Owing to the importance of the troop transport the corvette decided to remain with the *Henry R. Mallory*, taking station on its port bow. The wisdom of this decision was proved almost instantly because at 0305 a radar contact was picked up 5,000 yards astern of the troopship. This must have been *U 609* approaching the two ships for an attack. Closing at full speed around the stern of the transport, the contact disappeared at 1,100 yards, but the corvette soon gained Asdic contact at 600 yards. Due to lack of experience on the part of the A/S and recorder operators, four depth charges dropped at 0320 were released too early to cause any damage. Poor handling also prevented firing a full ten-charge pattern from the throwers. Due to the fact that the troop transport was left unescorted, the corvette abandoned the hunt and re-joined the *Henry R. Mallory*. It is interesting to note that the captain of the *Lobelia*, Lt de Vaisseau Pierre de Morsier, later complained bitterly in his report that none of the signals he sent to the *Mallory* during the whole night were answered. Eventually, both ships re-joined the main body of the convoy at 1515 in the afternoon. Unaware of the true nature of his target, Rudloff duly informed U-boat Command about his abortive attack and the subsequent counter-attack in a signal sent at 0435.[25]

The few and even conflicting reports about the convoy heavily strained the nerves of U-boat Command. At 0447 all boats of Group Pfeil were reminded to report more clearly. While *U 608* and *U 609* were specifically asked to confirm if they had contact with the convoy, the whole group was ordered to continue the search over an arc from 15° to 80° True, assuming a convoy speed of 6 to 8 knots.[26] Reacting to U-boat Command's request, *U 609* eventually reported in a further signal at 0607 that it had seen only two ships and one destroyer, but heard a strong noise band taken as an indicator that the convoy was nearby. Although *U 609* had clearly been out of touch with SC 118, many other boats then looking for the convoy nevertheless took *U 609*'s first report at 0435 as a clue for their further search. The confusion about the actual position of the convoy was further fostered by a short signal from *U 262* at 0636 claiming to be in contact with the

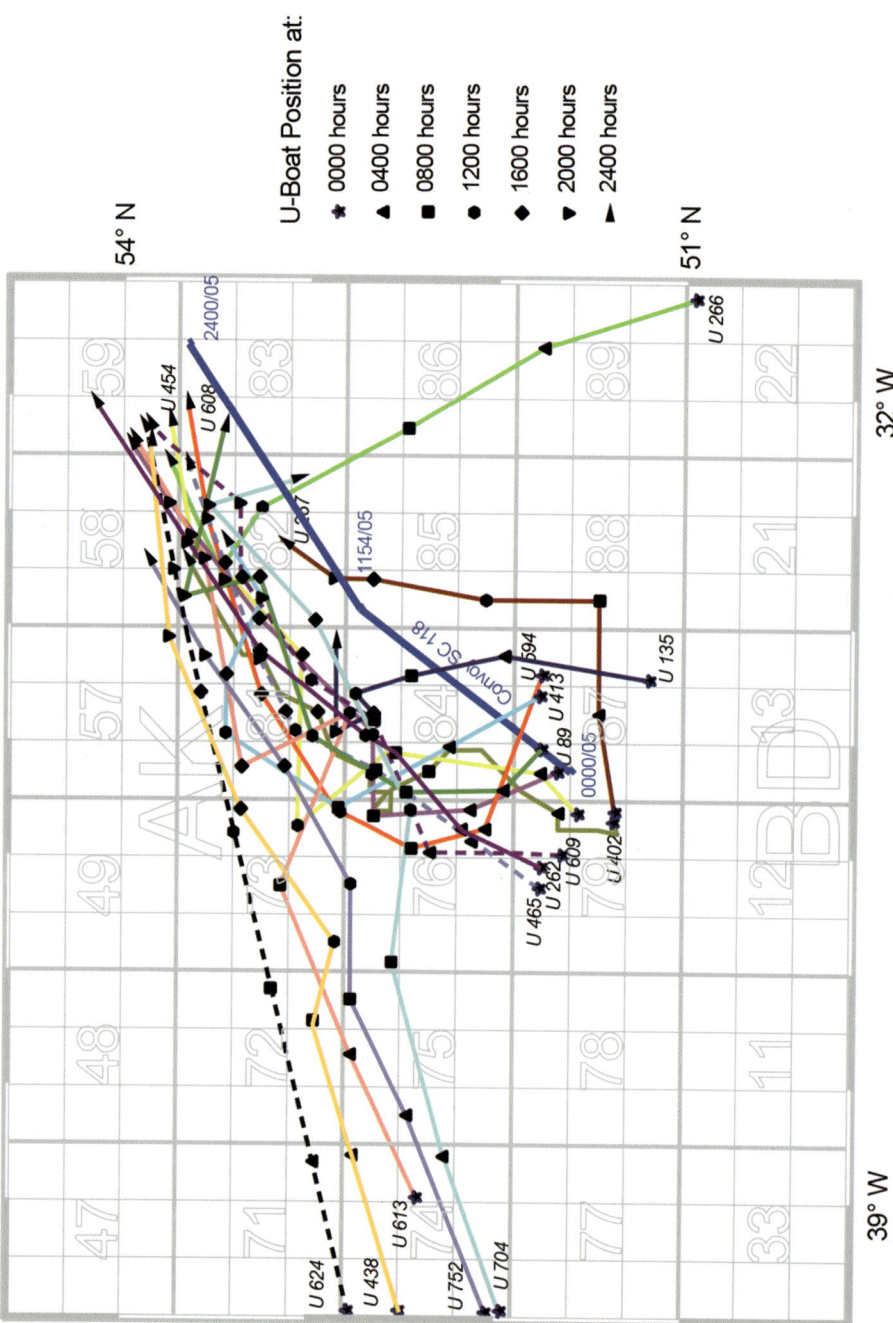

Fig. 10: Courses of U-boats near SC 118 on 5 February 1943.

convoy. The signal was picked up by *Toward*'s HF/DF operators, on a bearing of 261° from the convoy. In fact, *U 262* had run into another stray column of ships that had been diverted from the main convoy the previous evening. Chasing the convoy on a north-easterly course, the boat sighted four large shadows to port at 0544. Eleven minutes later *U 262* fired a spread of three torpedoes on the last ship in the row, identified as a 12,000-ton tanker. All three torpedoes were observed to hit the target, which was seen to sink slowly by the stern. A single shot at 0606 against the second-to-last ship and a stern shot at 0609 on the second ship in the column missed their targets owing to evasive manoeuvres or incomplete fire solutions. Although Allied reports do not mention the encounter, it is almost certain that the Polish steamer *Zagloba* was sunk in the first attack, thus becoming the first Allied victim in the running convoy battle. Assigned to convoy position No. 45 at the rear end of No. 4 port-wing column, the *Zagloba* had become separated from the convoy following the alteration of course at 1948 on the day before. *U 262* likely wrongly identified the ship as a tanker because it carried its funnel aft, and greatly over-estimated its size in the darkness. *Zagloba* was unable to send off a distress signal, so no Allied rescue effort took place. *Zagloba*'s entire crew of 36 men, including the master Captain Zbigniew Deyczakowski and 7 DEMS (Defensively Equipped Merchant Ship) gunners, perished with the ship. Interestingly, at 0806 *Toward*, sailing in the main body of the convoy, asked Cdr Proudfoot in *Vanessa* if he knew the position of convoy No. 45: *Zagloba*. Perhaps someone aboard the *Toward* had had a bad feeling about what had happened to the ship.[27]

While reloading its tubes on the surface next to the ships, *U 262* sent off another contact report at 0701. Half an hour later the ships moved out of sight in the prevailing weather with rough seas and low-lying haze. Trying to regain contact, the lookouts observed at 0800 a shadow believed to be one of the previously sighted ships. Attacking at once, ObltzS Franke identified the target as a British one-funnel destroyer only moments before he fired two torpedoes at 0812 at a distance of 1,500 metres. Missing with both his torpedoes when the target suddenly turned to starboard, Franke was forced to dive shortly afterwards when the warship came dangerously close to the boat.

U 262's target was almost certainly the *Bibb,* which had been ordered at 0634 to search outwards on 80° along *Toward*'s HF/DF bearing of *U 609*'s signal at 0607. *Bibb* was also to round up stragglers in that area at daylight. When *Toward* later also picked up the two signals from *U 262* coming from the same area to port astern of the convoy, their bearings were also passed on to the *Bibb*. However, without having noticed either the presence of the U-boat or its torpedoes, the *Bibb* had a lucky escape and both vessels went on their way. Due to the need to reload torpedoes and repair his defective listening gear, Franke remained submerged until 1155 before again going after the convoy.[28]

After all that excitement, the situation around SC 118 at daybreak on 5 February looked promising for the convoy escort. Despite the seemingly favourable situation for the U-boats on a dark night with moderate sea, no losses had been inflicted except the unnoticed sinking of the *Zagloba*. Moreover, most of the ships that had been separated from the convoy following the mishandled change of course on the previous evening had re-joined in the meantime. HF/DF bearings obtained by *Toward* indicated several U-boats still astern of the convoy, but none of them appeared to be in direct contact. With several escorts thrown out on various HF/DF bearings to put down these U-boats, the convoy seemed in no immediate danger. The only setback was that the ships had now reached the centre of the North Atlantic air gap where no air cover was possible due to the distance to the bases on Newfoundland and Iceland.

On the other hand, U-boat Command still had no clear idea about the position of the convoy. The last confirmed sighting by *U 267* was as far back as 2028 on the previous evening. All other sightings only gave U-boat Command an impression of stragglers and distant escorts meant to irritate and take the U-boats' attention away from the actual targets. The first fresh information about the enemy came at 0925 when *U 609* reported seeing one steamer, accompanied by a corvette, on course 45°. Once again, these ships were in all probability the *Lobelia* escorting the *Henry R. Mallory* back to the convoy. Half an hour later Kptlt Wolf in *U 465* also reported seeing one destroyer in the same area. His signal, indicating his position on a bearing of 190° from the convoy, was picked up by *Toward*. No doubt Kptlt Rudloff in *U 609*

The American troop transport *Henry R. Mallory*, which was sunk with heavy loss of life on 7 February 1943 by *U 402*. The master and officers had neglected their duty so that the ship was found repeatedly straggling behind the convoy; panic broke out among the crew and the embarked troops following the torpedoing.

took the course of the two ships sighted as a hint for the position of the convoy, for at 1036 he informed U-boat Command by short signal that he had found the convoy again in AK 8194. At 1111 Rudloff informed all other boats that he would send beacon signals. This signal, bearing 158°, caused Cdr Proudfoot to throw out *Beverley* in its direction. But instead of *U 609*, it was *U 465* which was sighted by *Beverley* at 1234 at five miles on its starboard quarter, placing the U-boat about 15 miles on the starboard quarter due south of the convoy. Shortly thereafter Proudfoot ordered *Vimy*, then returning from investigating an HF/DF bearing earlier in the day, to join the hunt. Diving at 1245, *U 465* was quickly picked up by the Asdic in *Beverley* and at 1305 a Hedgehog salvo was fired on the target. However, the twenty-four mortar charges exploded prematurely when hitting the water, causing no damage. Whilst attempting to regain contact, *Beverley* sighted a second U-boat at 1350 six miles away in a position 22 miles on the starboard quarter of the convoy. This was *U 267* under Kptlt Tinschert, who had

Renamed in 1939, the American steamer *West Portal* was previously called *Emergency Aid*. *West Portal* was sunk by U 413 on 6 February 1943 while straggling from SC 118. The survivors were lost in the severe North Atlantic winter weather.

searched due west until daybreak before turning north to intercept in accordance with *U 262*'s sighting report. At 1248 lookouts on *U 267* saw smoke clouds from the ships of SC 118 in the north. Tinschert then ordered *U 267* to steer an evasive course to the south-east when he heard the nearby explosions from *Beverley*'s attack against *U 465*. At 1300 the radio room on *U 267* received the BdU repeat message about the sighting report from *U 609* timed 1145, which confirmed the previous observations at 1248. Therefore, Tinschert turned north again to close the convoy and ran into *Beverley* for the second time since the previous night. Unable to escape the faster destroyer on the surface, *U 267* dived to a safe depth of 150 m and ran silent. Over the next two hours *Beverley*, joined shortly thereafter by *Vimy*, carried out a total of one Hedgehog and five depth-charge attacks, dropping thirty-five charges before the hunt was finally abandoned at 1745 when they re-joined the escort screen.

Unknown to the British destroyers yet a third boat was close by. During the morning *U 135* (LtzS der Res Heinz Schütt) had come up from the south to intercept SC 118 on its presumed north-east course, when two destroyers came in sight at 0908. Forced to dive, Schütt could hear the sound of the convoy to the north in his listening gear. The destroyers were probably *Vimy* and *Bibb* which had unintentionally come close to each other but failed to detect the U-boat. Within two minutes after resurfacing at 1137, Schütt had to dive anew when this time *Beverley* appeared out of a rain cloud. Again *U 135* escaped undetected. While submerged the crew of *U 135* heard the depth charges dropped on *U 465* and *U 267* some distance away. After the enemy ships had cleared the area, *U 135* finally surfaced at 1730. *U 465*, unaware of the presence of the other boats, again considered all attacks during this afternoon as being directed on itself and therefore remained underwater until 1835. *U 267* did not surface until 2106. Although all three boats suffered no damage in the attacks, the convoy by then was already some 45 miles further to the north-east and all chance of reaching a favourable position for a night-time attack had gone. Thus, the action of *Beverley* and *Vimy* effectively neutralised three U-boats for the following night. In the meantime, Kptlt von Forstner in *U 402* was troubled again by the breakdown of one of his main diesel engines at 1012. Running on its starboard engine for the next twenty-two hours, the boat could only limp after the convoy on its general course indicated by the shadowing signals sent by *U 609*.[29]

At noon on 5 February the five ex-Group Haudegen boats, *U 438*, *U 624*, *U 704*, *U 613* and *U 752*, now assigned to Group Pfeil, joined the wolf pack pursuing SC 118. Positioned up to 250 miles north-west of the convoy at the time of the initial sighting, these boats had travelled at high speed on north-easterly courses during the last twenty-four hours in the hope of intercepting the convoy in time to gain a favourable attack position for the following night. The lack of contact and the confusing information about the convoy's course during the previous night, however, delayed their approach. Therefore, none of the five boats got in contact with the convoy during 5 February. Moreover, when *U 704* (Kptlt Horst Wilhelm Kessler) observed an unidentified escort at 1937, probably belonging to the port-side convoy screen, and dived to escape detection, it developed serious damage on its port diesel exhaust valve. The badly leaking valve could not be repaired and the boat asked U-boat Command for permission to return to France, which was immediately granted. This reduced the number of U-boats still operating against SC 118 to eighteen.[30]

However, this did not save the American freighter *West Portal* from destruction. Originally assigned to position No. 94 at the rear end of a middle column of the convoy just ahead of the rescue ship *Toward*, the ship had lost touch with the convoy in the struggle during the previous night. Now sailing alone, the *West Portal* straggled on a course similar to the convoy's but somewhat north of it. Its theoretical top speed of 10 knots nevertheless should have offered a fair chance to regain contact with the convoy. Unfortunately, its path was to cross that of *U 413* (Kptlt Gustav Poel), which had chased the convoy in vain on a north-easterly course during the morning. It will be recalled that *U 413*, together with *U 266* and *U 594*, had been diverted to operate against SC 118 the day before after having already commenced their return to France owing to their low fuel status. Correctly appreciating his position to be well on the port flank of the convoy, Poel had given orders to turn on 120° True to intercept the convoy when his lookouts at 1010 sighted a smoke cloud fourteen miles on *U 413*'s starboard quarter. Its origin was soon identified as a 5,000-ton steamer believed to have been separated from the convoy. After having reached a favourable forward position, Poel dived for a daylight submerged attack. At 1305 he fired four torpedoes at the ship at 2,400 metres, achieving one hit just forward of the bridge. With the ship showing only a slight list after the hit, he fired another torpedo as a *coup-de-grâce* at 1330. Through a malfunction this torpedo stopped after twenty seconds of its run and missed. After reloading, another torpedo was fired at 1421, this time hitting the ship in the stern. With the list of the ship increasing steadily, the crew now took to their lifeboats. Surfacing at 1433, Poel saw the ship going down stern-first at 1450 in position 53°27′N, 34°25′W. An attempt to gain information from a rescue boat about the ship's name and to take the master aboard as a prisoner of war failed in the rough sea.

The *West Portal* had sent a distress signal after the first hit, giving its position as 53°N, 33°W. The signal was promptly picked up by *U 704*, then to the south-west behind the convoy, and the corvette *Abelia*, watching the distress wave at 500 kc/s while screening the convoy. *Abelia*'s radio operator, however, initially misrecorded the latitude as 55°N. Though later corrected, the first report placed the torpedoed ship in an unlikely position about three miles ahead of the convoy. A bearing obtained by *Toward* correctly positioned the *West Portal* well over to port. Confronted with two different positions for the *West Portal* and with several escorts absent from the convoy, Cdr Proudfoot considered it inadvisable to send off a further escort to render help. But when *Toward* at 1342 picked up another sighting report of *U 609* coming from close by in the same direction as the likeliest bearing on the *West Portal*, *Abelia* (Temp. Lt Frank Ardern), was thrown out 15 miles at 350° to press down the probable contact keeper and search for survivors from the ship as well. The corvette was also to sweep ahead for 15 miles before re-joining, thus covering quite a large area in very good visibility.

Having turned again south-east towards the convoy, *U 413* saw the corvette at 1519 close to the scene of the sinking, correctly assuming it had been sent out to pick up survivors. However, fate was against Captain O. J. Griffin and his crew of 39 men and 12 naval armed guards as *Abelia*'s lookouts found nothing and the lifeboats of the *West Portal* were never seen again. Instead, *U 413* ran into *Abelia* undetected for a second time at 1850 and was slowed down in pursuing the convoy because of evasive manoeuvres. Thus, at midnight the boat was still some 40 miles astern of the convoy.[31]

The other two boats coming up from the south, *U 266* (Kptlt Ralf von Jessen) and *U 594* (Kptlt Friedrich Mumm), fared no better. Running behind the convoy while trying to catch up with it according to *U 609*'s contact-keeping signals, at midnight they also were still astern of the convoy although somewhat closer than *U 413*. Quite naturally, all three boats were plagued by concerns about their fuel situation. Down to between 15 and 31 tons remaining, it was obvious that they had to turn home during the forenoon of the next day. Thus, the night of 5 February was their last chance to get on to the ships of SC 118.

Thanks to the tenacity and vigour displayed by Kptlt Rudloff and his crew in *U 609*, contact with the convoy was maintained almost continuously during the second half of 5 February. Following Rudloff's second contact report timed at 1145 U-boat Command was finally convinced that he in fact had found the main convoy and therefore at 1222 directed all boats of Group Pfeil to operate according to the latest position reported for the convoy. No doubt both U-boat Command and the U-boats operating against the convoy were somewhat disappointed by the outcome of the first twenty-four hours of the battle. Consequently, U-boat Command felt obliged to send the following advice to the boats at sea at 1521: 'The first night still counts for nothing. Experience shows that the heavy blow often only develops later, when the enemy is tired out by continuous attacks, has no more depth charges and then is no longer equal to the large number of boats. Consequently, follow up and attack without respite.'[32]

Rudloff's success in keeping contact with SC 118 was somewhat marred by the fact that his positions signalled on 5 February during the hours of daylight probably suffered from a large reckoning error, putting *U 609* approximately 15 miles to the north-west of its actual

The corvette *Abelia* at Hvalfjord in Iceland in late 1942.

position. With the course of the convoy unchanged as 56° True from 1154 on 5 February until the evening of the next day, the line between his convoy positions radioed until 1710 and those for the time period starting at 2000 does not make sense. Though large navigation errors were not uncommon among the boats operating against SC 118 – the low-lying clouds and changing visibility clearly made navigation difficult – this reckoning error partly explains why several other boats claiming to have been at or near the reported convoy positions failed to make contact with SC 118.

This applies especially to *U 262*, *U 454* and *U 608* and the newcomer *U 89* (Kptlt Dietrich Lohmann), which in the absence of air cover were able to work themselves up on the port side of the convoy for most of the day to achieve a favourable forward position by nightfall. *U 608* would have met the convoy twice during the afternoon if the positions reported by *U 609* were correct. When *U 609* temporarily paused sending sighting reports in the late afternoon while unsuccessfully attempting a twilight submerged attack against the convoy, U-boat Command apparently again got a bit worried. Fearing the convoy to have turned south-east, at 1936 it directed *U 135*, *U 608*, *U 465*, *U 267*, *U 262*, *U 454* and *U 89*, then all believed to be close to SC 118, to search for the convoy at best speed in the direction of 110° True in case contact was not re-established.[33] Although this radio order was soon cancelled by U-boat Command in a signal timed at 2041 after *U 609* had reported the convoy again half an hour earlier, not all boats immediately changed course towards the newly reported convoy

U 135 (centre) on 12 March 1943 inside the no. 19 Keroman III U-boat pen after entering Lorient as a guest boat of the 2nd U-boat Flotilla to hand over unused torpedoes. The two Type IX C boats lying in the pen with *U 135* are probably *U 525* (*left*) and *U 511* (*right*).

position. Due to a failure of his radio room personnel to decode the text of the second signal properly, Struckmeier in *U 608* continued to search south-east away from the ships until 0220 next morning, thus eliminating all chance of regaining contact during the night hours.[34]

To avoid another failure of the boats to come to grips with the convoy during the night, U-boat Command radioed the following reminder message to all Pfeil boats at 2154:

> 1. Attempt to obtain contact by all possible means. Convoy is not to be lost again as weather is favourable. The defence is powerless in view of the weather. Location, both on the surface and under water, greatly hindered.

2. Be hard and ruthless when operating. Remember the Eastern Front.[35]

But despite U-boat Command's appeal to his men, at the end of the second day of the battle *U 609* was still the only boat to keep visual or listening contact with the convoy. None of the other boats caught even a glimpse of the ships in SC 118 until the end of the day. Fifteen boats were spread at various distances in an arc around the rear of the convoy. Unknown to it at the time, only *U 262* had gained a favourable position close to the convoy's port bow after having followed a straight course similar to that of the convoy during most of the day. But the dark moonless night prevented the convoy from being located by the U-boats.

Unperturbed by the problems of the U-boats in pursuit, the convoy and its escort experienced a relatively quiet period during 5 February. In the late afternoon only the British steamer *Harmala* and the troop transport *Henry R. Mallory* were straggling from the convoy. These two vessels were soon able to re-join the main body. At 1813 *Beverley*, on re-joining the convoy, sighted the Greek steamer *Polyktor* 14 miles behind the convoy, steaming in circles with its steering gear out of order. Lt-Cdr Price advised the master not to use his radio, but to stop after dusk to repair and then to proceed on the straggler route.

The following night also passed without incident for SC 118. Although at times U-boat radio traffic was very intense, no contacts developed and no attacks were made. At nightfall, *Vimy* and *Beverley* were still returning from the afternoon hunt, and *Bibb* had been thrown out at 1715 on a HF/DF contact bearing 320° (probably *U 624*). *Beverley* was back on station at 2140 and *Vimy* at midnight. The latter was then ordered to take station 5 miles off the starboard beam of SC 118 in order to intercept any U-boats attempting to shadow the convoy.[36]

The absence of all the fast escorts except his own ship *Vanessa* and the known presence of several U-boats near the convoy made the escort commander reluctant to throw out any more escorts in the direction of the night-time HF/DF contacts. Instead Cdr Proudfout considered it advisable to keep whatever escorts he had in the close screen.

The regular night-time positions for the escorts around the convoy are shown in the diagram below.

Some relief came when the Coast Guard cutter *Ingham*, Cdr Albert M. Martinson, a sister ship of the *Bibb*, arrived at 2155 to join the escort after having been dispatched from Reykjavik two days before. However, with its sonar dome damaged, the *Ingham* reported its A/S-detection set inefficient and was therefore directed to take a screen station three miles astern of the convoy. This position offered the least chance of encountering a submerged U-boat attack.[37]

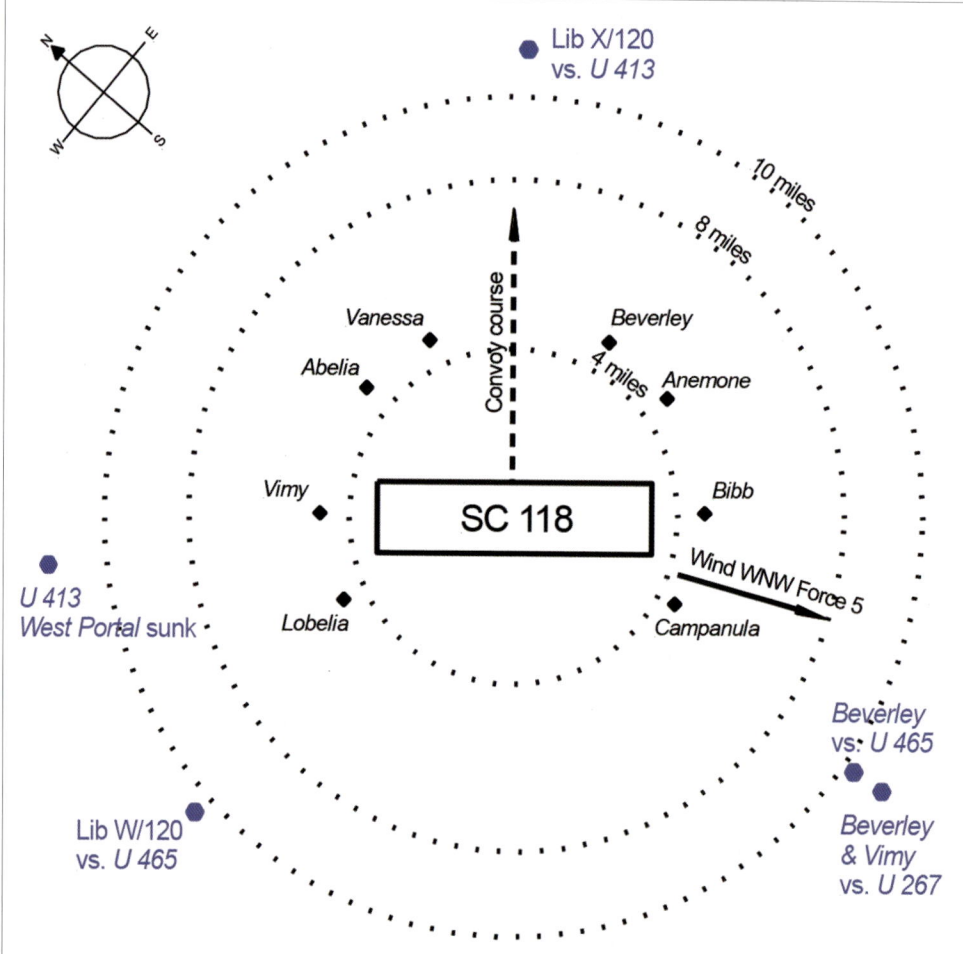

Fig. 11: Action around SC 118 between 1100/5 Feb. and 1100/6 Feb. 1943.

Day Three – 6 February 1943

Much to U-boat Command's annoyance the U-boats once again temporarily lost all contact with SC 118 in the early morning hours of 6 February. At first *U 609* was able to maintain listening contact until 0300, but later only *U 89* and *U 454* heard the convoy momentarily in the distance. Thus, for a second time, the U-boats missed their chance for successful attacks during the hours of darkness. Quite understandably U-boat Command complained at 0840 that: 'More boats should have gathered round when Rudloff made his reports. Proceed at high speed when searching. Make casts in various directions, listen to hydrophones, exploit every possibility to the utmost.'[38] But the only sign of the enemy observed by the boats during the morning came when *U 454* sighted a single unidentified merchant ship sailing east at 0730 well south of the convoy track. Believing this was a provisioning ship for the convoy escorts, Kptlt Hackländer nevertheless failed to press home a successful attack since he reported the enemy to have used radar. After his return to base U-boat Command judged this apparent lack of aggression as unacceptable. The reported ship was very probably the Greek steamer *Polyktor*, which had fallen behind on the previous evening following a rudder breakdown, as described above, and was now sailing east along the straggler route.[39]

With the convoy sailing unmolested along a general course of 56° from midnight, the group of escorts screening SC 118 was further strengthened at 1024 when the four-stack destroyer *Babbitt*, Lt-Cdr Samuel F. Quarles, arrived. The ship had been sent to the convoy by the Commander of Task Group 24.6 at 1415 on 4 February while it was returning to Iceland from escort duty. Cdr Proudfoot ordered Quarles to take station on the port bow of the convoy at maximum visibility distance. With this new arrival, the total number of escorts

- ● Night action
- ● Daylight action
- ◆ Nominal escort position taken up at nightfall

Note: All positions relative to convoy course. Contacts at more than ten miles are plotted without regard to the actual range

to protect SC 118 had risen to four destroyers, two Coast Guard cutters and five corvettes.[40] The nominal strength of the escort, however, was partly reduced by the lack of training and mutual understanding to act as a combined group. At the same time the convoy commodore reported the presence of 59 ships in convoy. While the *West Portal* was known to have been sunk on the previous day, the convoy commodore still considered the already sunk *Zagloba* and the *Polyktor* as stragglers.

The tactical situation, along with the balance of power, changed radically on the morning of 6 February when SC 118 came within range of very long range (VLR) aircraft based at Reykjavik in Iceland and Aldergrove in Northern Ireland. Flying at extreme range over a distance of some 800 miles from base, the mere presence of these aircraft over and around the convoy had an inhibiting effect on U-boat operations. RAF Coastal Command had designated four VLR Liberator aircraft of 120 Squadron to provide air cover during the day. At 0323 Liberator X/120, piloted by Sqn Ldr D.J. Isted, started from Aldergrove, but difficulties in locating SC 118 in the vast sea delayed its arrival over the convoy until 1154. Therefore, Fl Sgt J.H. Frewen in Liberator W/120, who left Reykjavik at 0538, was the first to arrive over the convoy at 0900. He was immediately told to put down a U-boat picked up at 0836 by *Toward*'s HF/DF set on a bearing of 271°. For the next nine and a half hours, aircraft stayed with the convoy almost continuously.[41] Cdr Proudfoot employed these in much the same way that he used his fast escorts by directing available aircraft to run down HF/DF bearings of U-boat radio transmissions, otherwise called 'mamba' patrols. This tactic seriously interfered with U-boat Command's intention to get the boats into a position ahead of the convoy for a daylight submerged attack or a surface attack after twilight. Instead of convoy sighting and sinking reports, the U-boats started to send numerous reports about aircraft sightings and attacks, which eventually prompted a frustrated U-boat Command to signal at 1500 that: 'Further reports about aircraft are superfluous.'[42] Slowed down by repeated crash dives, several U-boats fell behind the convoy while others experienced even worse.

The U-boats got the first indication of the presence of aircraft over the convoy at 0920 when *U 267* saw W/120 exchanging recognition signals

The Greek steamer *Polyktor* leaving Montevideo on 20 December 1935. This vessel was sunk by *U 266* on 6 February 1943 while straggling from SC 118 following a steering-gear failure. Two of its crew were later taken aboard *U 266* and survived the sinking.

with a convoy escort. However, consistent with the generally poor wartime performance of U-boat lookouts in aircraft identification, the Liberator aircraft were usually mistaken as Sunderland flying boats. At 1043 Liberator X/120, still on its way to meet the convoy, gained the first enemy contact during this day when it sighted a surfaced U-boat about 20 miles ahead of the convoy. But the lookouts on the bridge of *U 413*, which had searched for the convoy without success during the night, were alert and sighted the approaching aircraft in time to take the boat down before it could reach the spot.[43]

U 465 was less lucky when Liberator W/120 sighted the boat at 1056 about 31 miles on the port quarter of the convoy. Having failed so far to make contact with the convoy, Kptlt Wolf was trying to get ahead of it during daylight to reach a favourable position to fire his torpedoes. Attacking at once, the aircraft dropped six depth charges after the U-boat crash-dived during its approach. The bombs exploded close to the boat and caused considerable internal damage. Moreover, after resurfacing at 1230, there was a bright oil trail resulting from cracks in

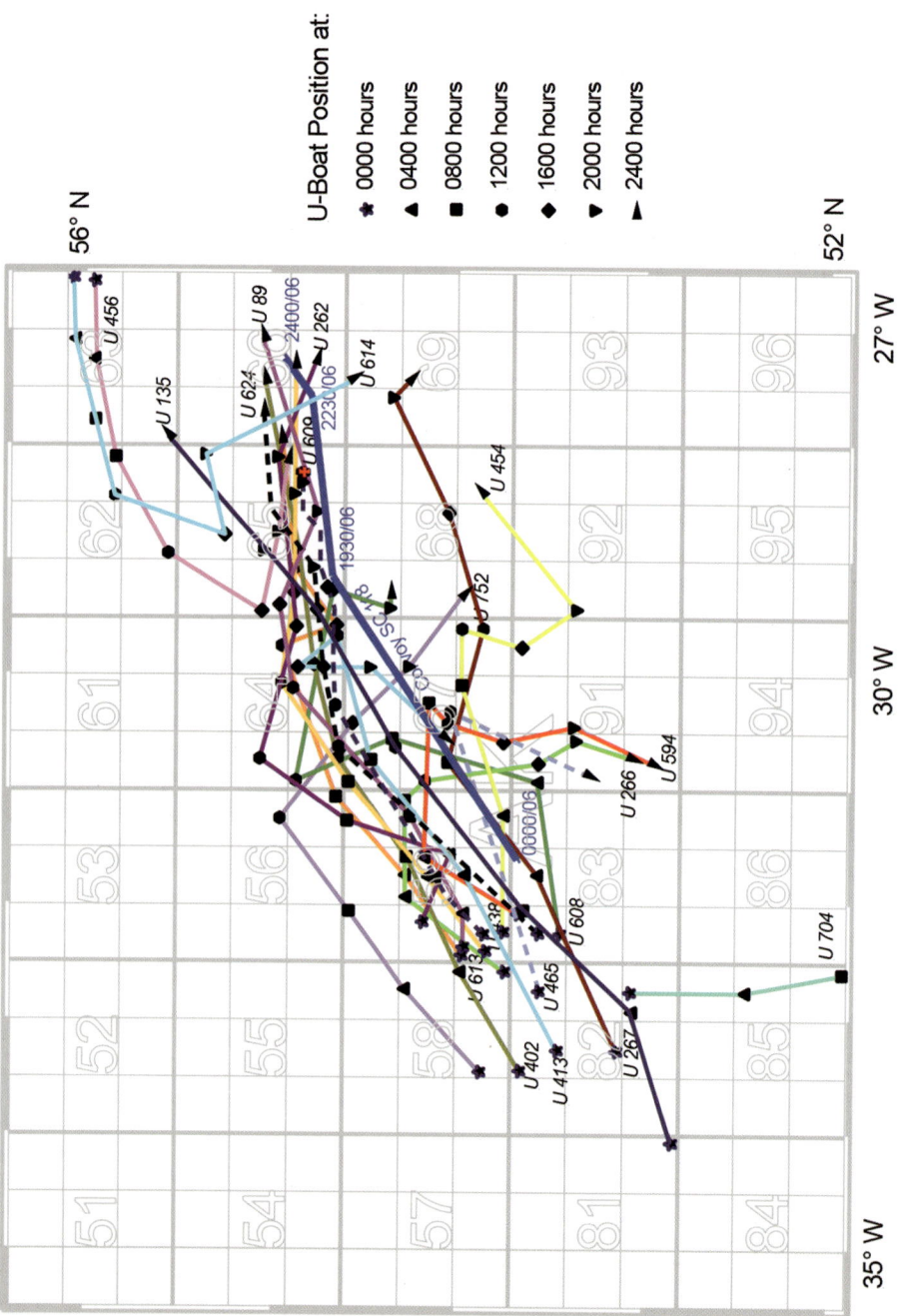

Fig. 12: Courses of U-boats near SC 118 on 6 February 1943.

No 4 starboard fuel ballast tank. Within a minute after resurfacing the lookouts reported another aircraft sighting and the boat crash-dived again. Finally, back on the surface at 1402 the boat was considered unfit for further convoy operations and Wolf set course to the south to make repairs. Meanwhile Liberator W/120 had sighted another U-boat at 1108 some miles to the south of the spot where *U 465* had been attacked. Dropping its remaining two depth charges on the diving boat, Fl Sgt Frewen considered the attack fairly accurate. In fact, *U 454*, which was targeted this time, suffered a long list of damage including its battery, attack periscope and an internal fuel tank. The second air attack was observed by the *Bibb* from a distance of five miles. On closing the attack scene, *Bibb* made a doubtful sound contact believed to be the U-boat. Following an unsuccessful Hedgehog attack at 1146 contact was not regained although a joint search was made with *Ingham* until 1601. *Bibb* certainly attacked a non-sub contact because Kptlt Hackländer in *U 454* did not even mention a nearby surface ship in his war diary and in addition no other boat reported being pursued at that time. Surfacing at 1348, *U 454* also turned south to begin repair work while Hackländer informed U-boat Command about his situation. It took until 1945 before the boat's combat readiness was restored although its attack periscope remained unusable. By then there was no possibility of regaining contact with the convoy during the next night and *U 454* could only follow its general course reported by the contact-keeper boat in the hope of finding another chance at daylight.[44]

The next boat to feel the new threat from the air was *U 624* (Kptlt Ulrich Graf von Soden-Fraunhofen) which was located visually by Liberator X/120 at 1404 when 18 miles on the port beam of the convoy. Following the convoy track on its port flank since midnight, this boat had also failed to make contact with the convoy so far. Shortly before 1130 *U 624* had exchanged information with *U 402* with the latter still nearby when the attack took place. Sqn Ldr Isted had just left SC 118 at 1358 to return to base when the U-boat was sighted five miles away. Dropping six depth charges from 40 feet as the boat was going down, Isted reported a direct hit with No. 3 charge, followed by air bubbles and some oil. Both *U 402* and *U 613*, which stayed nearby unseen, were also forced to dive at this time and recorded the depth-charge explosions in their diaries. Despite the rather optimistic claim of the aircrew, *U 624* later signalled U-boat Command that it had suffered only slight damage from the attack. Liberator X/120 eventually landed at 2123 at Ballykelly in Northern Ireland after a total flight time of 18 hours.[45]

At 1500 Liberator W/120, which had already expended its depth-charge load in the two previous attacks, sighted yet another U-boat 20 miles astern of the convoy. Showing a high degree of aggressive spirit, Fl Sgt Frewen nevertheless turned in to attack the diving boat

U 624 transferring from the harbour lock into one of the U-boat pens at St-Nazaire on 4 December 1942. There the boat was to be emptied before a yard overhaul started on 9 December 1942 in the dry-dock pen no. 5 further to the right. After being refloated on 20 December, and completion of final items of work at the quay, the basin motor trials were carried out on 30 December. Following successful sea trials the boat was finally declared ready for operations on 3 January 1943 and the crew started to stock the boat for front-line service with torpedoes, fuel oil and provisions. On 7 January 1943 *U 624* left on its second and final front-line patrol.

with machine-gun fire. Because the boat was almost completely submerged when the aircraft arrived over the spot, no hits were scored, but *U 608* had been successfully driven underwater. Assuming, like other commanders, that the convoy was following a general course of about 45° True, Kptlt Struckmeier had searched in vain for the enemy during the first half of the day. Only when the contact was re-established at 1046 by the indefatigable Rudloff in *U 609*, did the boat turn east to catch up with SC 118. Driven down repeatedly by aircraft and escorts thereafter, *U 608* suffered from Struckmeier's tendency to interpret many of the bomb and depth-charge explosions heard during the day as being directed against his own boat. He stayed submerged from 1835 until just after midnight, giving up any opportunity to intercept the convoy during the night.⁴⁶

Kptlt Ulrich Graf von Soden-Fraunhofen on the aft platform of his boat *U 624* inside the large sea lock at St-Nazaire on the return from his highly successful first patrol on 4 December 1942. This officer, whom Dönitz rated thereafter as tenacious, prudent and determined with good tactical skills, was lost with all his crew on the very next operational patrol on 7 February 1943 in the fight against the air escort of SC 118.

Liberator W/120 eventually left at 1704 after having stayed eight hours with the convoy and landed safely at 2136 at Reykjavik. In the meantime, two more relief aircraft had left Aldergrove and Reykjavik at 1142 and 1156. Still outbound from Reykjavik and trying to locate the convoy, at 1516 Liberator R/120, piloted by Fl Off D. C. Flemming-Williams, observed *U 614* (Kptlt Wolfgang Sträter) cruising on the surface 47 miles on the port beam of the convoy. Together with *U 456* (Kptlt Max-Martin Teichert) this boat had covered over 300 miles in the two previous days to intercept SC 118 from its position reached during former operations against convoy HX 224. A defective snap on the conning tower hatch delayed the boat's crash dive and the aircraft was able to drop four depth charges while the boat was still on the surface but overshot to port by about 300 feet. Before the aircraft could return for another attack, *U 614* finally went under undamaged. Fl Off Flemming-Williams's claim to have scored a direct hit or near miss with No. 1 charge, followed by some wreckage and considerable underwater disturbance, turned out to be over optimistic. After staying over the attack scene for a while, R/120 continued towards the convoy that was eventually met at 1823.

The second Liberator O/120, piloted by Fl Off R. G. 'Robin' Goodfellow, also sighted a U-boat at 1720 while homing towards the convoy. Located about 18 miles out at 160° on the convoy's starboard quarter, *U 267* was nevertheless quick enough to submerge that Goodfellow decided to withhold his charges. Informed about the sighting, at 1737 Cdr Proudfoot instructed Lt-Cdr Stannard in *Vimy* to head out 20 miles at 156° to hold down this U-boat whose position was considered uncomfortably close to the convoy. Later Liberator R/120 was sent to assist *Vimy* in the search. This proved to be a good move because Kptlt Tinschert had come back to the surface after just 25 minutes. Having sighted the smoke of the convoy at 1635 after following the convoy position signalled by the contact keeper *U 609*, he was determined to reach a forward position for a submerged attack at last light. However, his attempt was spoilt when R/120 forced the boat to crash-dive again at 1835. This time staying underwater until 1907, *U 267* had to dive for the sixth time this day only one minute later when the aircraft was found to be still circling over the area. With the aircraft having indicated the position of the U-boat by a flare, *Vimy* started a search at 1923 and quickly gained Asdic contact. A few minutes later *Vimy* dropped a single pattern of six depth charges. Contact was not regained and, as darkness was falling and the U-boat now some 25 miles astern of the convoy, *Vimy* set course to re-join. Lt-Cdr Stannard was later criticised for not having pressed home a more determined attack at this point.

Coastal Command GRIII Liberators M (FK228) and O (FL933) of No. 120 Squadron RAF, lined up with other aircraft at their base at Aldergrove, County Antrim. The two aircraft are equipped with the metric wavelength ASV Mark II anti-submarine radar with the related antennas clearly visible. Liberator O, piloted by Fl Off R. G. Goodfellow, was among the first aircraft to provide air escort to convoy SC 118 during the crucial daylight hours on 6 February 1943. (*IWM CH 18035*)

Unknown to the Allies, *Vimy*'s attack had in fact been extremely successful, severely damaging *U 267*. Still hearing the faint noise of the convoy to the north, Tinschert had started bringing the boat to periscope depth, when the listening gear operator suddenly heard the approaching destroyer. Despite his order to go down to a depth of 150 m, the boat was still at 20 m when the depth charges exploded on the starboard beam and astern. Losing trim, the boat went down by the bow, pointing down at an extreme angle of 45–50 degrees. Only the instant reactions of the cold-blooded control-room crew saved

The V&W-class destroyer HMS *Vimy* was the first vessel of its class to be converted into a Very Long Range Ocean Convoy Escort. During a refit at HM Dockyard Portsmouth in early 1941 *Vimy*'s forward boilers and forward funnel were removed to increase fuel oil storage.

the boat from destruction, finally stopping the downward plunge at 237 m. Surprised to hear the destroyer leaving eastwards, Tinschert then turned south to make emergency repairs. He did not surface until 0935 the next morning, when a thorough inspection revealed the full extent of the damage suffered by the attack. With his boat no longer fit for combat, Tinschert sought permission from U-boat Command to return to base, which was duly granted.[47]

The last U-boat to be forced down by the presence of aircraft this day was the long-time contact keeper *U 609*. Just two minutes after that, at 1932, Liberator R/120 departed from the convoy to return to base, landing at Reykjavik at 0129 early next morning. In his narrative of SC 118 Cdr Proudfoot expressed high praise for the support gained

from the aircraft covering the convoy during daylight on 6 February. The great effect of the air cover is shown by the statistic that U-boats near the convoy were forced to dive at least 35 times to escape being sighted or attacked from aircraft. A total of eleven U-boat sightings during the day resulted in four depth-charge attacks and one more with machine guns. With $U\,465$ forced to return to France and $U\,454$ temporarily out of action from these attacks, the benefit gained from the aircraft was much greater. Their ability to make the boats lose contact by forcing them to dive and stay submerged for varying periods of time turned out to be invaluable.

U-boat Command's concerns about the course of the battle were further heightened by the fact that apart from $U\,465$ and the yet unknown damage to $U\,267$, no fewer than five other boats had to break off operations against the convoy during the day. After two days of operations the fuel situation of $U\,266$, $U\,413$ and $U\,594$ was now critical. Previously ordered to continue the hunt until only 8–10 tons of fuel remained, their commanding officers finally had to break off operations. Since they were unable to reach their French bases directly with their remaining fuel, U-boat Command directed an emergency refuelling rendezvous to be made with $U\,465$ at a position some 150 miles to the south for it to divide its fuel equally among the other three boats. In addition, $U\,704$, suffering from leaky exhaust valves, and $U\,752$ (Kptlt Karl-Ernst Schroeter), with its starboard diesel permanently out of order, requested permission to return to France because the defects made further operations impossible. Thus, on the evening of 6 February, U-boat Command was left with only twelve boats to continue operations against SC 118.

However, the southward movement of the three boats low on fuel turned out to be disastrous for the Greek steamer *Polyktor* which had fallen behind the convoy on the previous evening. With his steering gear repaired but with the convoy then well ahead, the master followed the straggler route instructions. Travelling well to the south of the convoy track things seemed to go well until the ship was sighted first by *U 594* at 1455. At 1611, *U 266* also observed the mast tops of the *Polyktor*, then steering on a general course of about 80° without zig-zagging. Both boats immediately went after the ship to attack. By 1735 Kptlt von Jessen in *U 266* had gained a favourable forward position and dived for a daylight underwater attack. He fired a single torpedo from the stern tube at 1817; this exploded amidships after a run time of 25 seconds. The *Polyktor* stopped immediately but remained afloat on an even keel. At 1830 Jessen fired another torpedo as a *coup-de-grâce*, this time hitting under the bridge. This increased the slight port list but otherwise had no further effect. Therefore, two minutes later he fired a third torpedo, which exploded in the forward section of the ship. The resulting damage caused the ship to capsize and sink quickly by the bow. Shortly thereafter *U 266* surfaced and approached the survivors in a lifeboat and two floats nearby. According to standing war orders issued to front-line U-boats, the master, Captain Nikos Kontisas, and the chief engineer officer were taken aboard as prisoners of war. Too slow to take part in the action, Kptlt Mumm in *U 594* could only watch the sinking of the ship from nearby. Within an hour both boats were continuing on their way to the rendezvous.

The *Polyktor* had been unable to send a distress signal before it went down, and the remaining survivors were now struggling for life in their open boats with a long night ahead. Sadly, none of these men were ever seen again, making the two men aboard *U 266* the only survivors of the crew of 34 aboard the *Polyktor*.[48] The ship and its crew had become the third Allied victim in the running battle around convoy SC 118. Despite the tragic loss of three ships so far (*Zagloba*, *West Portal* and *Polyktor*) with most of their crews, the fact that all three were straggling

U 752 making fast to the eastern quay in the new entrance harbour lock at St-Nazaire on 15 February 1943 at the end its seventh patrol. No torpedoes were fired during the 37 days at sea and a diesel breakdown eventually forced Kptlt Karl-Ernst Schroeter to return to base prematurely. The houses in the background were heavily damaged during the American air raids on the city in November 1942 and January 1943.

from the convoy when sunk indicates the hitherto great success of the B2 Escort Group in holding the U-boats of Group Pfeil at distance from the main body. Meanwhile the escort group had been further augmented by the destroyer *Schenck* (Lt-Cdr William S. Estabrook), which had left Reykjavik at 2025 on 4 February and joined the escort at 1240, taking station on the starboard bow of the convoy.[49]

But U-boat Command was far from giving up and indeed the prospects for the coming night looked promising again. Like on the day before, the indefatigable Rudloff in *U 609* had maintained almost continuous contact with SC 118 since his first sighting report at 1046. Initially shadowing the convoy from a position on its port quarter, he later shifted to the port beam. Once again, his shadowing signals were duly picked up by the HF/DF operators aboard the *Toward*. The expertise of Rudloff in maintaining contact with the convoy is shown best by the fact that neither the *Ingham* nor the *Bibb*, ordered at 1054 and 1445 respectively to search in the direction of individual bearings, nor several aircraft thrown out on mamba patrols, even got a glimpse of *U 609*. Unlike the day before, the convoy positions radioed by *U 609* during the afternoon were calculated correctly and despite the air cover all other boats still operating against SC 118 set course to intercept before dark.

The first boat to observe the tell-tale smoke clouds of the 59 ships still in convoy was *U 456* at 1651, then positioned slightly astern of *U 609* at the port quarter of the SC 118. Although twice forced to dive to escape searching aircraft during the next three hours, Kptlt Teichert each time quickly regained visual contact. At 1801, two other U-boats were observed close by. This must have been *U 609* and *U 262*, the latter having gained visual contact with the convoy at 1705. Eager to use his first chance for an attack after having successfully intercepted the convoy following a hunt in the two days before from a position more than 300 miles ahead of it, Teichert tried to slip through the escorts astern of the convoy at high speed. In the early darkness, one of the port rear escorts sighted at 1930 was successfully out-manoeuvred. But the next one sighted at 2015 was more alert. Three minutes after *U 456* had sighted its enemy, the corvette *Lobelia*, then stationed in screen position 'Q' for Queen, gained a radar contact bearing 345° on its port side, 4,200 yards away and moving rapidly to the right. Soon realising that he had been observed and unable to escape into the darkness, Teichert crash-dived at 2026. *Lobelia* quickly gained Asdic contact and attacked. Owing to the lack of experience of the crew, the first two depth-charge patterns dropped at 2031 and 2036 numbered only five and six charges respectively instead of a full ten-charge pattern. Set to a maximum depth of 140 feet, they exploded harmlessly above *U 456*, which had gone straight down to 160 metres. Asdic contact was lost thereafter.

However, at 2046 *Lobelia* gained another radar contact, bearing 32°, distance 4,600 yards, also moving to the right. Turning towards the new contact, the corvette fired six star shells two minutes later to illuminate its forward arc, but saw nothing. At 2056 the radar contact disappeared at a distance of 3,000 yards, but a few minutes after that Asdic contact was established at 1,400 yards. Finally, at 2104 a full ten-charge pattern, set to explode between 50 and 140 feet, was dropped. The pattern was slightly scattered to allow for the slow speed of approach. Asdic contact was regained after the attack, but became progressively less sharp during the following minutes until it was eventually lost completely. At 2112, *Lobelia* carried out an unsuccessful Hedgehog attack, but Lt de Morsier later believed the contact to have been a submarine bubble target ejected from the U-boat.

Following *Lobelia*'s first report, Cdr Proudfoot dispatched the corvette *Mignonette* to join the hunt. It arrived on the scene at 2115 and both ships carried out a thorough search for the U-boat, but no fresh contact was gained. However, much oil spreading in patches on the surface over a large area was observed after the attack. Stern lookouts aboard *Lobelia* also reported the smell of warm oil. Unfortunately, a bath towel towed for a while failed to collect any sample.

Kptlt Max-Martin Teichert photographed while captain of *U 456*. Before his first patrol in the North Atlantic in January/February 1943, when the boat operated against SC 118, *U 456* had been employed in northern waters, where Teichert torpedoed the cruiser HMS *Edinburgh*, which had to be scuttled thereafter by its own crew. Teichert and his crew were killed on 12 May 1943 attempting to dive their severely damaged boat in the face of an approaching destroyer. On 19 December 1943 he was the 108th member of the U-boat arm decorated with the Knight's Cross of the Iron Cross.

Originally built as HMS *Lobelia*, this Flower-class corvette was transferred to the Free French Navy in 1941, but retained its name. *Lobelia* escorted many North Atlantic convoys from September 1941 until 1944. Late on 6 February 1943, the long-time convoy shadower *U 609* succumbed to a depth-charge attack from *Lobelia*.

Nevertheless, de Morsier believed the U-boat attacked was at least damaged. With *Mignonette* having already left at 2320 to catch the convoy, *Lobelia* also set course to re-join at 0020.[50]

While *Lobelia*'s first two depth-charge attacks were undoubtedly directed against *U 456*, Teichert stayed submerged until 2220, overhearing the subsequent depth-charge attack and *Mignonette*'s arrival. Therefore, *Lobelia*'s second radar contact and third depth-charge attack at 2104 must have been directed against another U-boat. Nevertheless, *U 456* was forced to dive a second time between 2255 and 0004 when it ran again unobserved into the two corvettes still searching the area for the second contact and lost all chance to intercept the convoy during the night.

But more important, none of the other U-boats then operating against SC 118 that returned from patrol to base, can be identified as the target of *Lobelia*'s third attack. Of the two boats that did not return, Kptlt von Soden-Fraunhofen in *U 624* reported in his last signal sent after daybreak on the next day that he had passed a search group dropping depth charges at 2055 the previous day, escaping a pursuit on the surface by zig-zagging away in naval grid square AK 6559. The given time and location indicate that *U 624* must have been present close to the scene of *Lobelia*'s action as no other escorts of SC 118 dropped depth charges at that time. But Soden-Fraunhofen explicitly mentioned that he had evaded the enemy on the surface. Neither did he mention being depth-charged or receiving any damage. It is reasonable to conclude that yet another boat must have been involved. The only alternative is *U 609*, which also failed to return from its patrol.

Rudloff reported for the last time at about 2040 that he had lost contact with the convoy at 1930 after being forced under by an aircraft (actually Liberator R/120). Although *U 609*'s signal carried the sender's time group as 2030, the radio logs of *U 89* and *U 402* recorded the actual time of sending as 2040 and 2044 respectively. The time lag is easily explained by the necessary time to encipher the signal before it was actually sent off by the radio operator. From the previous sighting reports monitored by the *Toward* it is known that *U 609* shadowed the convoy at last on its port beam. Thus, it is likely that the boat had drifted astern to a position to port during the time submerged following the air alarm and that it stayed submerged for the shortest possible period to be able to regain contact quickly. It is accordingly very probable that *U 609* was the boat picked up by *Lobelia*'s radar at 2046, just minutes after having sent its last signal to U-boat Command. Knowing that the official post-war attribution of its loss to another of *Lobelia*'s attacks in the morning of the following day has turned out to be wrong, and that all other anti-submarine attacks carried out over the next days are also known to have been directed against other boats, it is evident that the scattered patches of oil seen after *Lobelia*'s last attack at 2104 in fact marked the destruction of *U 609*. Kptlt Klaus Rudloff and his 45-man crew were all killed in the sinking. Thus, a second member of Group Pfeil, led by a most energetic and skilful commander, had fallen victim to an escort of the B2 Escort Group protecting convoy SC 118.

In the meantime, other boats had made contact with the convoy during the evening of 6 February. At 1700 *U 438* (Kptlt Rudolf Franzius) sighted smoke clouds over the horizon about 14 miles away. Situated

ObltzS Heinz Franke is welcomed to La Pallice following his arrival with *U 262* on 15 February 1943. On the ladder behind him 2nd Watch Officer Hübsch. After three more patrols this energetic and aggressive U-boat commander was decorated on 30 November 1943 with the Knight's Cross of the Iron Cross.

also on the port quarter of the convoy, Franzius immediately tried to gain a forward position for the night. But within minutes of his first sighting report at 1730 he was forced down by one of the Liberator aircraft closing his position. When he resurfaced almost an hour later, the convoy was gone. Using *U 456*'s sighting report at 1848 as a beacon, *U 438* tried again to reach a forward position along the convoy's port flank. However, the change in the convoy's course from 56° to 83° ordered by the commodore at 1930 caused the boat to miss to the north. The only signs of the enemy were distant lights and star shells fired by *Lobelia* during the action against *U 456*. Anticipating a more easterly course of the convoy, Franzius eventually searched to the south-east. At 2110 the shadow of an unidentified escort on the port flank of SC 118, probably the *Abelia*, came in sight but soon disappeared again in the darkness. But while overtaking the corvette on the inner side, *U 438* was picked up by *Abelia*'s radar at 2 miles at 2125. Due to the U-boat running at a higher speed, the corvette was unable to close the unidentified contact. A quarter of an hour later the bridge watch on *U 438* saw the corvette following in its wake. After recognition signals were left unanswered, *Abelia* eventually opened fire on the contact, now believed to be a U-boat, forcing *U 438* to crash-dive at 2156. After dropping a full pattern of depth charges on an underwater contact picked up from the diving position, the corvette soon lost it again and Lt Ardern finally left the area at 2223 to re-join the screen. Although Franzius went deep to 150 metres, *U 438* sustained damage, which caused a loud noise in the starboard propeller shaft glands. Repeated bearings gained on escorts in the following hours kept the boat submerged until 0101.[51]

The only boat to penetrate the convoy screen before midnight was *U 262*. Reluctant to dive despite repeated aircraft sightings, ObltzS Franke closed the convoy from starboard astern after dark. Skilfully manoeuvring the boat unobserved through the rear escorts *Schenck* and *Campanula*, he suddenly brought numerous merchant ship silhouettes in sight at 2049. Finding himself right aft of several convoy columns, Franke decided to pass between two columns to reach a forward firing position. After several abortive attempts due to the short distance between the columns *U 262* was eventually able to move directly between two columns of ships, still sailing unaware of the U-boat's presence right amongst them. With the way forward blocked by a steamer travelling apparently out of line 300 metres ahead and unable to fire torpedoes at the ships running on parallel courses 400 metres away, Franke soon found himself in a very unpleasant position. Although his lookouts expected the boat to be spotted by the ships every moment, everything remained silent. At last, Franke decided to attack. At 2155 two torpedoes were fired on a tanker running on the boat's port beam as the rear ship of its column. Both torpedoes were heard to hit the target but apparently failed to explode. The tanker then turned to port and fired three white rockets while exchanging light signals. Five minutes later two more torpedoes were fired, this time at a large tanker running as the rear ship of its column on the starboard beam of *U 262*. Again *U 262* recorded hearing two detonations after 67 seconds, but the only reaction of the ship was that it changed its course thirty or forty degrees to starboard. Finally, at 2205 Franke fired his last torpedo from the stern tube at another tanker running in front of the tanker attacked first. Seventy-five seconds later a detonation was heard. Lights illuminating the ship's side were seen when the U-boat passed the ship, which was believed to settle on an even keel. However, from the available reports it is evident that no ship was hit at this time. Surprisingly, none of the ships in convoy reported any incident that could relate to the attacks recorded in *U 262*'s war diary. Therefore, this attack remains something of a mystery.

Although the war diary entries of *U 262* on this attack offer some conflicting details, a reconstruction of the events suggests that the boat must have entered the convoy from the rear between columns 11 and 13. The first attack was then probably directed against the American steam tanker *Robert E. Hopkins* in position No. 115, while the second attack must have been aimed at the Norwegian tanker *Daghild*, then sailing as the last vessel of column 13 in position 135. The rear ship in column 12, the British motorship *Deido*, was apparently out of position or had slipped into position No. 134, vacated by the

Fig. 13: Action around SC 118 between 1100/6 Feb. and 1100/7 Feb. 1943.

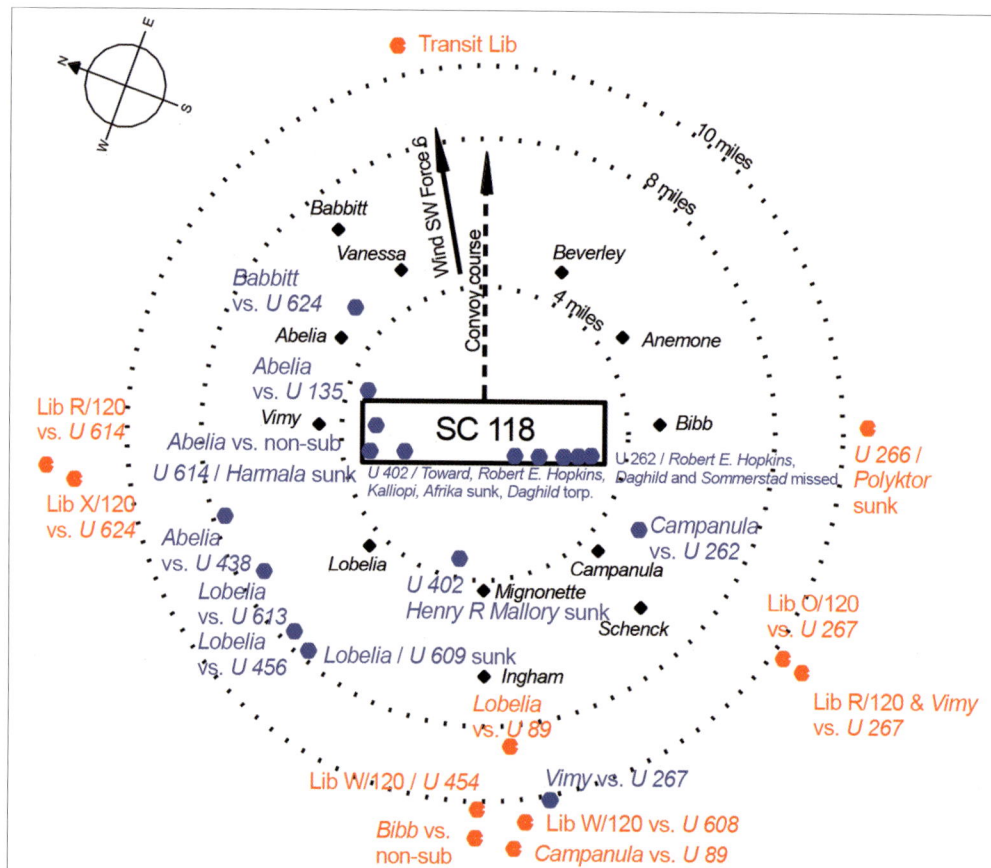

Polyktor after it became a straggler on 5 February. The last torpedo fired at 2205 may have been fired either at the British steamer *Radport* in position No. 114 or the Norwegian tanker *Sommerstad* in position No. 113. One explanation for the absence of reports on the Allied side could be the fact that both the *Robert E. Hopkins* and the *Daghild* were torpedoed within hours the same night. With no more torpedoes left under deck, Franke in *U 262* then acted as contact keeper, still sailing boldly inside the convoy columns. His reports and beacon signals sent over the next hours enabled several other boats in the vicinity of the convoy to gain contact with SC 118. But still none of the U-boats of Group Pfeil had yet been able to launch a successful attack against any of the ships inside the convoy screen.[52]

Day Four – 7 February 1943

Weather conditions during the night were typical for the North Atlantic at this time of the year with winds of force 6 to 7 blowing from the south-west, a moderate sea and visibility of 1 to 2 miles, sometimes reduced even more by rain showers and low-lying mist. SC 118, sailing at 7.5 knots on course 53° since 2230, still numbered 59 ships. The escorts had performed well during the first part of the night but, unlike the nights before, the U-boats remained in firm contact despite the fact that some of them had been forced underwater by the depth-charge attacks on the port quarter. Of those U-boats still pursuing the convoy, *U 624* had worked itself ahead of the convoy on the port side since the previous evening, but failed to locate the convoy in the darkness before midnight owing to the side-step in the convoy's course executed after dusk. Operating on *U 262*'s last convoy sighting report from 2245, *U 624* eventually requested beacon signals from the boat in contact at 2321. These were duly sent by *U 262*, but *U 624*'s radio signal had also been picked up by the *Toward*, putting the U-boat on a bearing

- ● Night action
- ● Daylight action
- ◆ Nominal escort position taken up at nightfall

Note: All positions relative to convoy course. Contacts at more than ten miles are plotted without regard to the actual range

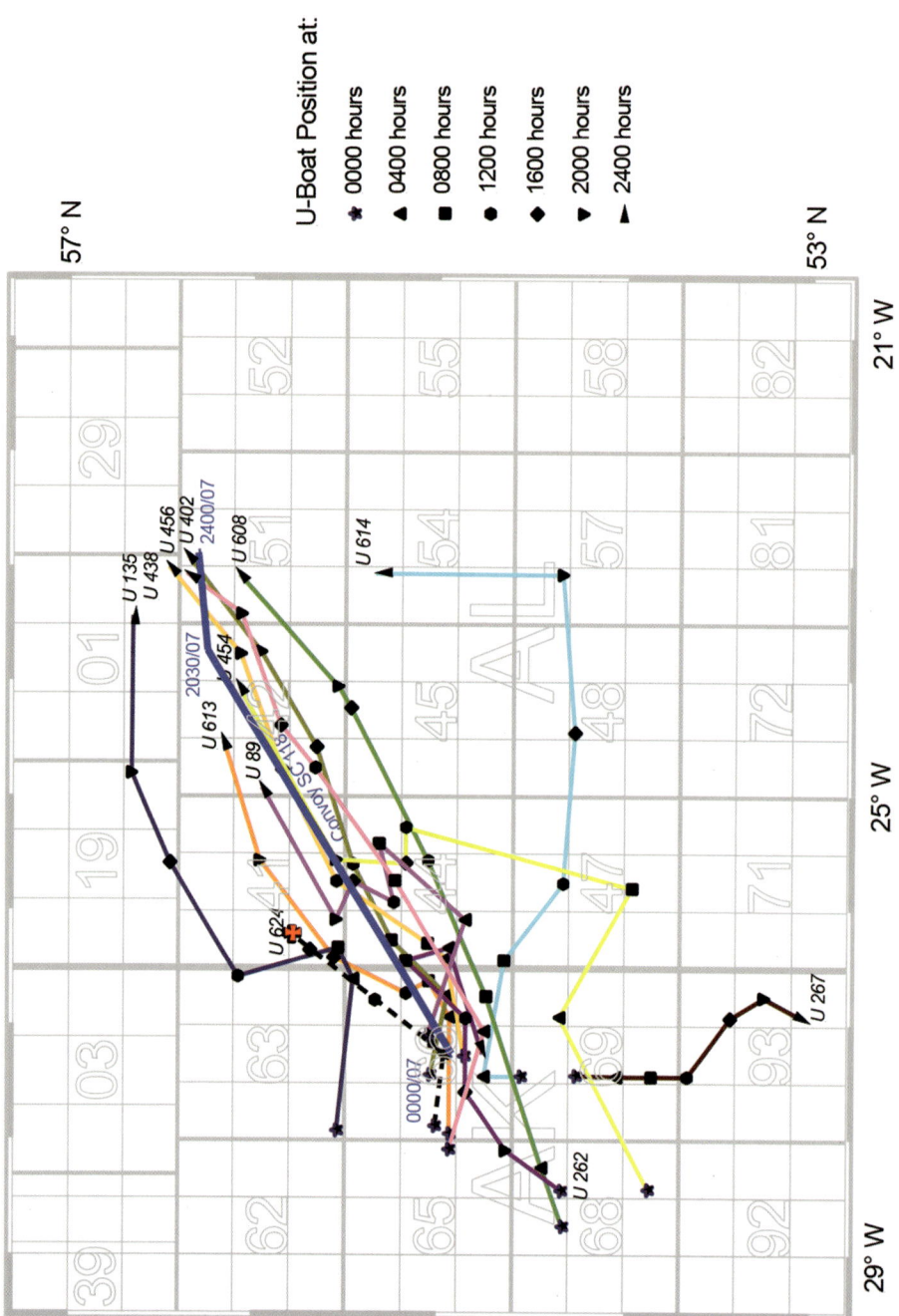

Fig. 14: Courses of U-boats near SC 118 on 7 February 1943.

almost due east and ahead of the convoy. Just six minutes later the escort commander ordered Cdr Martinson in *Ingham*, then stationed on the starboard bow of the convoy screen, to stand out in this direction in an attempt to force down this boat whose position was considered dangerous for the convoy. While *Ingham* failed to make contact with the boat, U 624 homed successfully onto the beacon signals and may have found the convoy soon after midnight, preparing immediately for attack. But again, radar proved to be a decisive advantage for the escorts in defending the convoy when the old SC-type set installed on the destroyer *Babbitt* picked up the surfaced U-boat in the darkness at 0045. Trying to close the convoy from the port bow, U 624 had already managed to slip through the escort screen at the centre of the gap between the destroyer, then stationed about 10,000 yards ahead of the outer port column, and the corvette *Abelia* running some 6,000 yards behind. With the U-boat almost astern of the *Babbitt* at the time of initial contact, Lt-Cdr Quarles turned the destroyer around and closed at 20 knots. Obviously U 624 soon realised that it been detected and, unable to escape on the surface, crash-dived at 0056 with the destroyer 2,000 yards away. Sound contact was established just three minutes later, but Kptlt Graf von Soden-Fraunhofen steered the U-boat into a sharp underwater turn to get inside the destroyer's turning circle and was almost successful in this. *Babbitt* could only fire its three port thrower charges at 0102 to make at least a harassing attack. The depth charges were set shallow, between 50 and 100 feet, and U 624 escaped undamaged. Before another attack could be executed, danger from a collision with the ships of the convoy heading directly towards the destroyer forced *Babbitt* to abandon the hunt. At 0133 Cdr Proudfoot in *Vanessa* warned all escorts that a U-boat was passing under the convoy. Below, the frustrated crew of U 624 could hear the propeller noises from the ships passing over, which then disappeared slowly in a north-easterly direction. Held down until about 0700 by the numerous escort ships then running back and forth behind the convoy, the boat eventually informed U-boat Command about its experience in a radio signal timed 0830.[53]

Meanwhile U 262 had dropped out of the convoy to a somewhat safer position a few miles astern of it on the starboard quarter. But low-lying

Before *U 402* entered La Pallice on 23 February 1943, the figure of 113,000 grt for the total tonnage claimed until then was painted on the port side of the conning tower.

mist and the presence of one of the rear escorts caused the boat to lose visual contact at 0221. While attempting to regain contact, at 0249 the bridge watch observed a shadow, later identified as a destroyer, heading directly towards the boat. Left with no alternative to escape, the boat crash-dived a minute later. The 'destroyer' was actually the corvette *Campanula* stationed in screen position 'G' on the starboard quarter, which had gained radar contact with the surfaced boat at 1,200 yards at 0245. After dropping a single depth charge pattern less than two minutes after the U-boat disappeared from the surface, *Campanula* lost contact. On receipt of *Campanula*'s radio report about the sighting, at 0300 the SOE detached the *Schenck*, then stationed in position 'Q' on the port quarter of the screen, to assist in the hunt. Unable to regain Asdic contact, the corvette soon abandoned searching for the U-boat to re-join. When arriving on the scene at 0358, *Schenck* nearly rammed the corvette when mistaking the radar echo from the escort as that of a U-boat. Although not known at the time, *Campanula*'s attack proved to be accurate because *U 262* suffered a crack in its air intake and exhaust pipe. Already without torpedoes, Kptlt Franke quickly decided to return to his French base and informed U-boat Command accordingly after daybreak.

Apart from *U 262*, *U 89* was also close by after having homed on *U 262*'s beacon signals. Taking star shells fired by *Campanula* as being directed against his own boat, Kptlt Dietrich Lohmann crash-dived at 0250 and heard the depth charge dropped on *U 262* close by. With escorts and numerous depth charges heard thereafter *U 89* remained submerged until 0532. However, by then it was too late to reach the convoy before daylight. So, Lt-Cdr Rogers in *Campanula* effectively pressed down two U-boats by his action.[54]

In its post-action analysis of the U-boat attacks against SC 118 the Anti-Submarine Warfare Division of the British Admiralty later stated that early on 7 February, after the escorts' latest successes in keeping the U-boats at distance, the situation was now one to inspire at the least some sober confidence in the outcome of the battle.[55] After a classic start with the first convoy shadower immediately sunk and nearly all attempts to attack the convoy successfully repelled over the next two days, the chance of escaping from the U-boats still pursuing the convoy looked good. The presence of a total of ten escorts stationed around the convoy (see Fig. 15, p. 174) with two more vessels in offensive action in the immediate vicinity behind and the prospect of continuous air cover starting at first light meant that the U-boats around the convoy were virtually outnumbered by the Allied forces. Moreover, the ability provided by the HF/DF set installed on the *Toward* to locate and engage all U-boats using radio in the vicinity of the convoy had been invaluable. But unexpected destruction struck at the merchant ships of SC 118 right at the height of these hopes when the U-boats suddenly gained the initiative in the early morning hours of 7 February.

Sixty-two hours after *U 402* had made its first visual contact with SC 118, the boat was back in contact with the convoy at 0055, having travelled nearly 600 nautical miles in the meantime. Determined to take every chance to attack after the long hunt, its tenacious and highly experienced commander finally succeeded in getting into a favourable firing position after manoeuvring the boat successfully through the rear screen. This had been partly weakened through the absence of the *Lobelia* and the *Bibb* at that time from their regular escort positions 'Q' and 'R' on the starboard quarter. The *Lobelia* was still trying to rejoin since 0020 after its successful action against *U 609*, while the *Bibb* was also behind the convoy after being sent out on 180° True at 2115 on the previous evening to force down any U-boats trailing behind the convoy. Although *Schenck* had been ordered at 0007 by Cdr Proudfoot to shift its screen position from 'H' to 'Q', which was duly taken up at 0040, this order created another gap on the starboard quarter. After *Bibb* had turned around at 0200, she was ordered at 0224 to take up the screen position 'H' formerly occupied by *Schenck*, while *Lobelia* received similar orders at 0248 to move into position 'R' to fill up the rear screen for the rest of the night. But all these tactical measures by Cdr Proudfoot came too late to avoid the coming disaster that befell SC 118. Finally approaching the convoy from between the starboard beam and the starboard quarter, *U 402* at 0247 first fired a single torpedo at a freighter estimated at 6,000 tons. Greatly underestimating the distance for the shot, Forstner was lucky that the torpedo nevertheless hit the target amidships after 135 seconds, causing the ship to sink rapidly. Two minutes later a double torpedo shot aimed at a large tanker running next to the torpedoed ship failed to find its mark, but another torpedo fired at 0252 on the same target finally hit the ship. Doubting that the second ship would sink, at 0302 he fired a fifth torpedo on the tanker as a *coup-de-grâce*, this time hitting aft in the engine room. This last torpedo hit achieved the desired results and the tanker was seen to go down within 20 minutes.

The victims of this attack were the rescue ship *Toward*, then approximately in convoy position No. 126 on its way back to its regular position of No. 95, and the American steam tanker *Robert E. Hopkins* in position No. 115. Struck forward of the bridge, the small rescue vessel was doomed from the beginning. Of the 69 men aboard *Toward*, including five naval and eleven military gunners, two signalmen, one surgeon and one sick bay attendant plus two injured sailors carried as passengers, only 26 men were picked up by the corvette *Mignonette*. The master, Captain Gordon K. Hudson, who was last seen running

HMS *Mignonette* was another Flower-class corvette of Ocean Escort Group B3 defending SC 118. Here the vessel is shown in its 1943 outfit with Type 271 radar and the typical North Atlantic paint scheme. Under its long-time captain Lieutenant H. H. Brown, RNR, *Mignonette* took part in the sinking of U 135 and U 1199 later in the war.

The modern British steamer *Harmala*, sunk by *U 614* from SC 118 on 7 February 1943. A number of survivors in the water were later abandoned by the corvette *Lobelia* in favour of following up a U-boat radar contact.

to the wireless room to get off a distress call, went down with the *Toward*. The *Robert E. Hopkins* was first hit beneath the dry cargo hold, buckling the forward decks. The engines were shut down after the ship became unmanageable. The second hit in the engine room caused the boilers to explode resulting in widespread devastation. The ship eventually went down by the stern. Cdr Proudfoot, stationed ahead of the convoy on *Vanessa*, reacted swiftly to the new situation at 0257 by directing Lt Brown in *Mignonette*, then stationed next to the torpedoed ships, to assist and render help to survivors. Twenty-four crew members of the tanker, including the master Captain Rene Blanc and 18 naval armed guards, were rescued by the corvette, 15 others were killed by the explosions or went down with the ship. At 0313 the *Lobelia*, about to re-join the convoy after sinking *U 609*, was ordered to screen *Mignonette* during the rescue mission.[56]

The loss of the *Toward*, the designated rescue ship, was a severe blow. Now the escorts had to take over this job, thus stripping the convoy screen in its fight against the U-boats. Another disaster for the senior officer was the loss of the HF/DF set installed on the *Toward*. Now the *Bibb* with its inexperienced operators was the only ship left carrying HF/DF. At 0328 Proudfoot signalled the Coast Guard cutter that the convoy was now relying entirely on it in this respect. In this critical situation, after the U-boats had struck their first serious blow against the convoy and its escorts, it became a serious tactical disadvantage that Cdr Proudfoot in *Vanessa* choose to stay at the head of the convoy to organise the defence. As a result, he failed to realise at this time that the new tactical situation and his recent orders had drawn away all three escorts then stationed at the rear end of the convoy screen from their nominal positions. This left the back of the convoy, including escort positions 'Q', 'R', 'S' and 'G', wide open to attack. The slow-speed corvette *Lobelia*, which he had directed partly to fill the gap, never reached its assigned new position 'R'. Only the faster Coast Guard cutter *Bibb* reached its assigned screen position 'H' at 0345. But no blame can be put on Proudfoot that his general order at 0410 to all escorts not in contact with the enemy to take up their appointed stations was intentionally disobeyed by several commanding officers on humanitarian reasons to rescue survivors. At that time the U-boats had already struck twice more with the next attack taking place on the opposite side of the convoy.

Led to the convoy by taking a listening bearing on the propeller noise generated by the armada of ships, *U 614* made visual contact with the ships of the port-wing column at 0015, but at first a destroyer, probably *Vimy*, soon forced the boat away. Two hours later an unidentified U-boat, now known to have been *U 613*, passed abeam 300 metres away into the darkness. Finally, *U 614* got into position to fire a triple torpedo fan at a large steamer at 0311. Three detonations were heard, assumed to be two hits on the steamer, estimated at 8,000 grt, and the third torpedo possibly achieving a chance hit on another ship further behind not seen before in the darkness. In fact, only one torpedo hit the British steamer *Harmala* on the port side by No. 2 hold just forward of the bridge, causing only a dull explosion without a flash and no water thrown up. The *Harmala* had left its designated convoy position after the earlier hits on its starboard side and proceeded towards the port flank of the convoy to place as much room as possible between it and the attack position. With 8,500 tons of iron ore in the holds, the ship now sank within just three minutes. Due to the rapid sinking no distress signal was sent and only one boat containing twelve men was lowered in time. Several other crew members simply jumped into the water when the ship went down and were heard shouting afterwards.[57]

Meanwhile the crew of *U 402* had started to reload their empty torpedo tubes while the boat went after the other ships of the convoy. After comparing the size of several ships in sight, Forstner selected a large tanker of the *Victor Ross* type as the next target. At 0338 *U 402* fired a single torpedo, but right afterwards an approaching destroyer forced the boat to crash-dive. During the dive the torpedo explosion was heard after a run time of 90 seconds, equalling a distance of 1,400 metres. Unobserved by the escort, *U 402* resurfaced sixteen minutes later and found the tanker lying stopped nearby. As before, Forstner wanted to make sure that the ship was going down and fired a *coup-de-grâce* at 0412. Much to his embarrassment the torpedo missed the ship. Unwilling to sacrifice another torpedo for the tanker, he gladly accepted the fact that the ship's bow had already settled below the surface as an indication of its imminent sinking and turned east. But things did not quite happen this way. It was the Norwegian tanker *Daghild*, carrying 13,000 tons of diesel in its tanks that was torpedoed in the attack. In addition to its normal load the ship carried the tank landing

Kptlt Helmut Köppe caught during a cigarette break on the bridge of his boat *U 613*. As a pre-war officer, he was one of the older captains operating against SC 118. He was killed on the his next-but-one patrol when his boat was sunk on 23 July 1943 with all hands in the mid-Atlantic south of the Azores.

craft *LCT 2335* and several crated aircraft as deck cargo. After the ship was hit, all 39 crewmen went into two lifeboats but stayed nearby throughout the rest of the night during which no further attack took place. Seeing the ship remaining afloat, the master, Captain Olaf K. Egidius, wanted to re-board the vessel at daylight to check if it could be saved.[58]

At 0336 the *Lobelia*, on its way to join *Mignonette*, saw lights on the water. Closing the scene, the wreckage and crewmen of the *Harmala* were discovered floating in the water. After the escort commander had granted permission, the corvette tried to pick up the men with life-buoys and heaving lines, but managed to get only one man aboard before the ship's life-boat was seen. After having taken its twelve occupants on board, the corvette was just closing a raft showing red lights when a radar contact, bearing 143° True, was picked up at 0412 at a range of some 6,000 yards. After dropping a Carley float for the remaining men in the water to take refuge on until its return, the *Lobelia* turned towards the contact. Seeing the corvette leaving obviously dashed all hopes of the men left behind; no one was found when the corvette returned to the scene two hours later. Therefore, out of *Harmala*'s crew of 53 men, only 13 were rescued while the rest, including the master Captain H. C. Walker, went down with the ship or perished in the cold water.[59]

Lobelia's radar contact was *U 613* (Kptlt Helmut Köppe), which had sighted the convoy just twelve minutes before being picked up on the radar. Before Köppe was able to make up his mind on the best way to attack, star shells were observed at 0420 in line with the boat and soon exploding right in front of it. At 0430 a searchlight appeared, but the heavy rain obscured its origin. Ten minutes later flashes from gun fire were observed astern, soon followed by the silhouette of an escort. Moments later machine-gun fire started to come in the direction of the boat and *U 613* pulled the plug and crash-dived, going straight to 150 metres. Shortly after the radar echo had disappeared from the screen, the corvette's Asdic picked up the U-boat. At 0446 *Lobelia* dropped a full ten-charge pattern set between 50 and 140 feet, but the charges exploded harmlessly above the U-boat. About thirty seconds after the explosion of the last charge a rumbling noise, followed by a

The British motor ship *Afrika* was sunk by *U 402* on 7 February 1943. The *Afrika*'s unusual silhouette without a prominent funnel differs greatly from that of the transport *Henry R. Mallory*. Yet the two losses were mixed up for a long time.

loud explosion ending with the same rumbling noise was heard on the corvette. A large bubble about three feet high with a dark hollow centre was also seen by several officers and ratings. The echo then became vague and gradually faded. Based on the observation the attack was later graded 'B – U-boat believed sunk'. Post-war, the attack was wrongly credited with the destruction of *U 609*. Comparison with the war diary of *U 613* clearly reveals that this boat was the target, but the event gives a fine example of the difficulties in the correct assessment of anti-submarine attacks. *U 613* remained submerged for the time being because propeller noise from ships criss-crossing on the surface was heard constantly over the next hours. Following the attack *Lobelia* continued to search for survivors of the *Harmala*, but only floating corpses sustained by their life jackets and two dead ratings on a raft from the American Liberty ship *Jeremiah van Rensselaer* were found. This last ship had been sunk five days earlier by *U 456* while in convoy HX 224. Later in the day the location of the sinking of the *Toward* was also searched by the corvette, but only fresh wreckage was found.⁶⁰

While *Lobelia* harassed *U 613* through the night on the port quarter of the convoy, *U 135* (LtzS der Res Heinz Schütt) unexpectedly found SC 118. Although he heard the distant detonations resulting from the various depth-charge attacks all night, Schütt apparently gained no clear idea about the position of the convoy, until at 0440 the whole armada suddenly came into sight astern of the boat in the light of exploding star shells. With the lead ship of the port wing column just 600 metres away and heading directly for the boat, Schütt turned to port to open the distance in order to attack the merchant ships on the port beam of the convoy. But even before *U 135* saw the convoy it had already been picked up by the radar aboard the corvette *Abelia*. *Abelia* got a contact at a distance of 3,500 yards and the corvette went to maximum speed to investigate. The U-boat was eventually sighted dead ahead at 400 yards. With the U-boat manoeuvring sharply to port and then to starboard, it got inside the turning circle of the escort before it crash-dived. This smart reaction saved the boat from being rammed. A pattern of eight depth charges dropped by *Abelia* on an Asdic contact gained shortly afterwards exploded well above *U 135*, which had already reached a depth of 80 metres. Contact with the U-boat was lost thereafter and *Vimy*, which had been told by the escort commander to assist in the hunt, arrived too late to take part. Assuming the U-boat to have escaped underneath the convoy, Lt Ardern of the *Abelia* warned all escorts at 0502 that a U-boat was passing under the ships of the convoy and eventually returned to his assigned screen position.⁶¹

At 0541 it was again the *Abelia* which noticed the next incident in the course of the convoy battle, however, without realising the full extent of the disaster about to follow. Listening to the radio wavelength at 500 kc/s, *Abelia* picked up a distress signal identified as coming from the British freighter *Afrika*. The escort commander ordered a 'Raspberry' operation shortly afterwards to illuminate the starboard flank of the convoy. 'Raspberry' was the code-name for a night-time escort manoeuvre, when some or all of the escorting warships turned

90 degrees outward from the convoy body and swept their own patrol sectors with radar and sonar, and could additionally fire illuminating star shells over the whole arc, if ordered to do so. The operation, however, gave no results this time. This was hardly surprising because the ship most recently torpedoed was somewhat behind the main convoy body. Delayed by the action around the torpedoing of the *Daghild*, *U 402* had temporarily lost contact with SC 118. Trying to catch up after leaving the torpedoed tanker, Forstner was able to watch *Lobelia*'s action against *U 613* on his port side. At 0527 he selected a large ship, apparently straggling some distance behind the convoy for his next attack. The target was identified as a flush-deck freighter estimated at 8,000 tons with an unusually long superstructure and a tall funnel. A single torpedo fired at 0536 hit the target amidships after 90 seconds. As Forstner watched the results in the darkness, at first the ship apparently listed to starboard. Later white rockets were fired while the crew was seen to abandon the ship, now beginning to sink on

Kptlt Freiherr von Forstner, together with the commander of the 3rd U-boat Flotilla, Korvettenkapitän Richard Zapp, taking the salute from the honour company and the crew of *U 402* at La Pallice on the afternoon of 23 February 1943.

Two portraits of the freshly decorated Knight's Cross holder Kptlt Siegfried Freiherr von Forstner on 23 February 1943 at La Pallice. According to Dönitz in the war diary of *U 402*, 'The commanding officer took every opportunity to attack with great determination.' Forstner was killed in action with his entire crew two patrols later.

an even keel. *U 402* left the scene at 0549 when the vessel had already settled down to the railings.[62]

Contrary to a signal from the *Abelia*, the ship hit at this time was the troop transport *Henry R. Mallory*, carrying 494 persons besides a cargo of clothing, food, trucks, cigarettes and 610 bags of mail. The silhouette of the target and the circumstances of attack described in the war diary of *U 402* leave no doubt that it was the *Mallory* and not the *Afrika* that was hit in this attack. The torpedo hit, striking the vessel on the starboard side by No. 3 hold, was the beginning of one of the most tragic events during the battle around SC 118. Most of the 383 passengers aboard were caught asleep or in their quarters below decks when the torpedo exploded. Many of the troops violated a basic rule by failing to wear sufficient clothing while sleeping. Some men came on deck simply wearing shirts and trousers, and had no shoes. Once in an open boat or swimming in the icy North Atlantic water, these men were to suffer much more from exposure than others with complete equipment. No alarm was sounded after the hit and without orders or control from the bridge, panic rather than discipline prevailed on the ship. Although wind and sea conditions for launching the numerous boats and rafts to rescue most of the survivors were good, inadequate training and lack of boat drills before the attack resulted in only three out of nine lifeboats and four rafts successfully getting away before that ship went down. Although available reports are somewhat contradictory on this point it is likely that it took no longer than 30 minutes after the attack until the ship was gone. Apart from the misleading distress signal picked up by the *Abelia*, apparently none of the convoy escorts or the other merchant ships in convoy realised that the troopship had been torpedoed. Therefore, many of the hundreds of men drifting in the sea were dead long before help finally arrived on the scene about four hours later.[63]

Unaware of the extent of destruction caused by its last attack, *U 402* continued on its way to sink one ship after the other, totally unmolested by any of the escorts. Following closely behind the convoy at the rear, Forstner drew maximum advantage from the failure of several escorts to obey the order given by Cdr Proudfoot at 0410 to take up their appointed stations if not in contact. At that time only the two corvettes *Mignonette* and *Lobelia* had been explicitly granted permission to pick up survivors from the torpedoed ships. Proudfoot later considered it an understandable but regrettable mistake that other escorts took it upon themselves to keep picking up survivors in the water around them rather than return to their stations as ordered. In his narrative he noted that he did not appreciate until after 0600 that other ships were also picking up survivors.

Just twenty-three minutes after the attack on the *Mallory*, *U 402* fired another single torpedo on a *Jersey City*-type freighter estimated at 6,000 tons. Fifty-three seconds later the torpedo exploded right in front of the aft mast, starting a fire. As the ship settled down by the stern, the crew were seen to abandon ship immediately. The torpedo

The fully loaded Greek steamship *Kalliopi*, sunk by *U 402* on 7 February 1943. This photo was taken on 23 May 1937 during coaling at Montevideo.

had struck the Greek freighter *Kalliopi*, nominally assigned convoy No. 44 and carrying 6,500 tons of lumber and steel. At the time of the hit four other vessels in the convoy were in sight from *U 402*. In his letter of proceedings Cdr Proudfoot correctly assumed that the *Kalliopi* was torpedoed at this time. Despite the seeming presence of four other vessels, none of them made any effort to rescue the Greek crew. With three men lost in the torpedo explosion, the master, Captain Nikos Pontikos, and 19 men left the ship in the lifeboat and 13 others on a life raft. These men were lucky that they were eventually discovered and picked up from the rising sea by the *Bibb* at 1550 the same day.[64]

With six ships already torpedoed in the last three hours, the ordeal of SC 118 was far from over. After the many days of fruitless hunting Forstner was determined to use every chance to attack. As though it was a training exercise in the Baltic, he picked up another target for his torpedoes. As he reloaded his tubes within sight of the convoy, the convoy battle must have reminded him of the 'Happy Time' in

Kptlt Heinz Wolf with the obligatory flowers on 18 February 1943 after returning to the U-boat base at St-Nazaire from his second patrol with U 465. Like many other U-boat commanders Wolf achieved no sinkings. He was killed together with his crew on 2 May 1943 while attempting to cross the Bay of Biscay outbound on his fourth patrol.

September/October 1940 when he had served for one patrol on *U 99* under the famous Otto Kretschmer as supernumerary commander under instruction. At that time, he took part in the battle around convoy SC 7, when Kretschmer likewise torpedoed ship after ship. Now Forstner selected another large ship for his next torpedo. Firing at 0635 on a *Mathura*-type freighter of 8,900 tons estimated, he hit the target after 48 seconds (a run of 740 metres) with a high white explosion plume. The ship was seen to settle by the stern with a starboard list, firing a signal rocket. This was seen by *Vanessa* which ordered a fresh Raspberry operation astern of the convoy. After 25 minutes the freighter finally sank with its bow rising steeply out of the water before going down. Although Allied times do not match, the comparison of German and Allied reports leaves no doubt that the British motor ship *Afrika*, sailing as No. 105, the rear ship of the tenth column, was sunk in this attack. The *Afrika* carried 11,457 tons of government and general cargo including 5,000 tons of steel. When it was hit in No. 5 hold, the neighbouring No. 4 hold also flooded, causing the ship to sink stern first after a short time with the bow rising vertically. The surviving crew abandoned the vessel in three lifeboats and one raft. After some time, an escort vessel appeared but stopped close to the No. 1 boat on seeing light signals from this boat. Much to the horror of the survivors in the boat it eventually went away without attempting to pick them up. In all probability the escort was the *Schenck* which reported sighting several lights bobbing in the water at 0750. For a long time, it was wrongly thought that *Schenck* had sighted survivors from the *Henry R. Mallory*. The escort commander refused *Schenck* permission to remain in the vicinity until daylight in order to pick up the survivors, stating that *Lobelia* was remaining in the area to pick them up. Therefore, *Schenck* set course to resume escort station 'H' with the convoy which it did at 0945. By this time 25 survivors of the *Afrika* had already been taken aboard the *Campanula*; 12 more from the No. 2 boat were later picked up by the *Mignonette*. The remaining men including the master, Captain Emanuel Broholm Jensen, 18 crewmen and 4 gunners were lost.[65]

Still full of fighting spirit, Forstner attempted to torpedo another steamer from the convoy at 0750, but the torpedo became a surface runner and missed the unidentified target. With only one torpedo left in the stern compartment, *U 402* finally dived at 0754 to reload the stern tube. Ranking highest among the U-boats was *U 402*, claiming no fewer than six vessels sunk. In less than four hours the U-boats had indeed caused deadly havoc amongst the ships of SC 118, actually sinking six in total, with enormous loss of life among the terrified crews, and leaving behind one badly damaged tanker.

The only two boats of Group Pfeil not in contact with the convoy during this fateful night were *U 454* and *U 608*. Having fallen behind the convoy the previous afternoon owing to repairs necessary after the air attack by Liberator X/120, Kptlt Hackländer on *U 454* was unable to catch up during the night and saw nothing. The commander of *U 608* continued to attribute all kind of detonations heard underwater as being directed against his boat although it was never really picked up. In fact, the explosions recorded in the boat's war diary resulted from depth charges dropped on *U 614*, *U 267*, *U 456* and *U 609*, often miles away from its position. Nevertheless, when Kptlt Struckmeier chose to stay submerged almost continuously from 1500 on 6 February until 0006 on 7 February, he forfeited any possibility of making an attack.[66] U-boat Command tried to exploit the situation and advised the Pfeil boats at 0755: 'Despite air, by daylight today "Pfeil" group is to make repeated attempts to get ahead to attack. A dispersed formation is the most favourable for underwater as well as for surface attack. Contact must be ensured by constant reporting and intelligent cooperation.'[67]

While trying to catch up with the convoy, *U 89* observed three escorts in the mist at dawn. Evasive manoeuvres on the surface proved unsuccessful: two of them were seen to turn towards the boat. Tell-tale black smoke clouds emerging from their funnels indicated that extra boilers were alight for higher speed. *Campanula* and *Mignonette* had just completed the rescue of survivors from the *Afrika* when *Campanula* sighted *U 89*'s conning tower 4,000 yards away at 0935. The two corvettes were then about 27 miles astern of the convoy. The U-boat dived three minutes later, but was soon picked up on the Asdic. Several depth charge patterns and an unsuccessful Hedgehog attack failed to cause any damage because of the prevailing poor Asdic conditions. *U 454* also happened to run into the two escorts and was forced to dive, though not actually observed by the corvettes. Eventually the two escorts continued to re-join the convoy.

Well behind the convoy, the full tragedy caused by the sinking of the *Henry R. Mallory* became obvious when the *Bibb* sighted one of its lifeboats at 1000. Soon realising that there were hundreds of survivors and dead bodies floating in the sea, Cdr Raney and his crew started heroic efforts to pull the men out of the water. Later joined by the *Ingham* and screened by the *Campanula* and *Mignonette*, the two Coast Guard cutters rescued 227 men, of whom five died subsequently despite all care given to them. The death toll of the *Henry R. Mallory* therefore probably numbered 272 men including its master, Captain Horace R. Weaver. Most of them died of exposure from long immersion in the cold water.[68] The total number of persons aboard the *Henry R. Mallory* is uncertain and variously given as 494 or 499. There are unconfirmed reports that *Mignonette* and *Campanula* also picked up four survivors each. Therefore, loss figures should be treated with caution. Nevertheless, the sinking of this troop transport was one of the worst disasters during the many battles in the Atlantic convoy lanes.

Kptlt Rolf Struckmeier of *U 608* and his 1st Officer, LtzS Karl-Ernst Kaiser, proudly display sinking pennants for a 12,000-ton tanker from SC 118 on 7 February 1943 and a destroyer on 19 March 1943 from HX 229, following the arrival of the boat at Bordeaux on 29 March. In fact, both attacks were unsuccessful. At SC 118, the torpedo missed the damaged Greek steamer *Adamas*, while at HX 229 Struckmeier mistook supposed sinking noises and a presumed explosion as certain indications for the destruction of the destroyer attacked (actually HMS *Highlander*).

Severely damaged by an earlier air attack, *U 465* transferred 20 cubic metres of fuel to *U 413* while both were returning to France. Owing to adverse weather conditions, which allowed no work on deck, the transfer was made by fire hoses visibly fixed directly between the conning towers while the boats travelled at low speed on electric motors.

Taking an all-round look through his periscope before surfacing at 1306, Kptlt Lohmann in *U 89* was surprised to find a large modern tanker lying stopped barely 2,000 metres away. After surfacing, the boat closed the ship to make an inspection and saw a large hole on the starboard bow believed to have resulted from a torpedo hit. The tanker was the damaged *Daghild* now floating on an even keel. Unobserved from the U-boat the master had already sent his first mate aboard to inspect the damage to decide if the ship could be re-boarded. To his horror the man saw the approaching U-boat and left the tanker as fast as he could. At 1326 *U 89* fired a first torpedo as a *coup-de-grâce*; this hit forward but failed to sink the ship. Therefore, at 1339 Lohmann fired a second torpedo, which resulted in a large explosion, sending the tanker listing heavily to starboard, so that the complete deck load went overboard and much oil spilled into the sea. While watching the tanker slowly settling deeper, *U 89* suddenly came under gunfire out of a rain cloud, forcing the boat to dive at 1353. This time it was the corvette *Lobelia*, which had sighted the U-boat as it closed the tanker which it sighted in the distance. After a search for the U-boat proved unsuccessful, the corvette picked up the complete crew of the *Daghild*. Following a discussion with its master it was agreed that the tanker was damaged beyond salvage. This was signalled to Cdr Proudfoot, who ordered the hulk to be sunk by gunfire. As the *Daghild* was now heeling over, *Lobelia* fired several rounds into its deck before leaving the slowly sinking ship at 1600 to re-join the convoy, then already 75 miles away. Still in the area, $U\,454$ had watched the action from a distance. Intending to finish off the tanker later, in the twilight, the boat submerged in the meantime. Returning two hours later, $U\,454$ found the *Daghild* had already gone, leaving a widespread oil slick and much wreckage including several landing craft floating on the surface. $U\,89$ had also overheard the sinking of the tanker while submerged. Shortly after 1700 both boats turned east in response to the sighting reports of $U\,456$, which had been in contact with the convoy since 1442.[69]

At 1205 the convoy commodore reported all 52 remaining ships present in convoy. With no fewer than five escorts (*Bibb*, *Ingham*, *Campanula*, *Mignonette* and *Lobelia*) known to be still far astern of the convoy, at 1338 Proudfoot ordered all of them to re-join at maximum speed. Fortunately, none of the U-boats were in contact with SC 118 during the forenoon and the convoy sailed unmolested throughout the day on a course of 53°. After U-boat Command had received the first reports about the successful attacks from the boats, Dönitz praised Forstner for his results. At the same time, he was somewhat disappointed that only three boats had reached a position to fire torpedoes. In a signal timed at 1154 he therefore directed all boats: 'Keep at it and keep contact. All boats must get to grips now. The depth charges will also run out. Be tenacious. The convoy is enormously important.'[70]

With the convoy well within range of Allied anti-submarine aircraft from Iceland and Northern Ireland, Coastal Command was able to provide continuous air cover during the day. But things did not go as smoothly as on the day before. Although five Catalina flying-boats of USN Squadron VP-84 had been dispatched between 0256 and 0603 from the Fleet Air Base at Reykjavik to give close escort during the first part of the day, the first aircraft failed to meet the convoy, while the other four either returned owing to radio trouble or were recalled because of the worsening weather. Likewise, Liberator C of 120 Squadron (Fl Off R. T. F. Turner), starting from Aldergrove at 0730, failed to find the convoy and returned to Ballykelly empty-handed at 2220. The second Liberator sent to provide close cover fared somewhat better. Liberator S/120 (Fl Off J. K. Moffat) started from Ballykelly at 1023 and successfully met the convoy at 1737 in position 55°56′N, 24°38′W. Seeing no U-boats at all, this aircraft stayed with the convoy until 1950 when its Prudent Limit of Endurance was reached and it had to return, landing safely at its home base at 0015 the next day. Bad weather grounded the Liberator detachment of 120 Squadron at Reykjavik on this day. A further six B-17 Flying Fortress aircraft of 206 and 220 Squadrons, RAF, starting during the day from their bases on Benbecula and at Ballykelly, were to fly ahead of or on parallel sweeps along the convoy course to prevent the U-boats from getting in front of the convoy before the next night. The start was made by Fortresses G/206 (Fl Off R. L. Cowey) and B/206 (Fl Lt L. M. Nelson), which took off at 0644 and 0658 from Benbecula to patrol from 0807 to 1339 up and down between 17°W and 26°W along the convoy course planned for the afternoon. Both aircraft returned safely, at 1615 and 1641. They were followed up at 0934 from Benbecula by Fortress L/206 (Fl Off W. Roxburgh) with the same orders, returning to base at 2002.[71]

During the afternoon three B-17s of 220 Squadron, which set out in rapid succession between 1225 and 1230 from their home base at Ballykelly, took over the search for the U-boats ahead and behind the convoy. The first two aircraft, N/220 (Fl Lt J. Wright) and R/220 (Sqn Ldr W. E. Edser), patrolled unsuccessfully between 1411 and 1944 along their search lines and returned to Ballykelly at 2315 and 2240 respectively. Only Fortress J/220 (Plt Off G. P. Roberson), met a U-boat during its search starting at 1412, but this encounter proved to be lethal for *U 624*. This boat had travelled behind SC 118 since dawn, following the convoy on its general course. At 1707 Roberson's crew sighted the surfaced U-boat about 15 miles astern of the convoy. With the target then some 9 miles off, Roberson climbed into cloud

Boeing Flying Fortress IIA (B-17E) long-range bombers were employed from 7 February 1943 to escort SC 118. Fortress J (FL 459) of No. 220 Squadron RAF, flown by Plt Off. G. P. Roberson, RAFVR, operated from Ballykelly and sank U 624 with depth charges. During the war FL 459 also took part in the destruction of U 469, U 707 and U 575. (IWM CH 11131)

and approached, finally breaking into the open three-quarters of a mile from the U-boat. Seven depth charges were dropped at 1712 from 50 feet on the surprised boat, which had started to dive after being slow to spot the aircraft but still had its conning tower half out of the water at the time of release. The charges straddled the boat, U 624 was mortally hit and went straight to the bottom, leaving only debris and an increasing oil slick on the sea. The belated order to dive had caught the boat in the most dangerous moments of a crash dive, presenting an almost stationary and defenceless target for the bomb aimer. Kptlt Ulrich Graf von Soden-Fraunhofen and his crew of 44 men were all killed in the sinking. Fortress J/220 landed safely at Ballykelly at 2308.

The deployment of aircraft to assist in the defence of convoys had paid another dividend for the Allies, causing the loss of the third U-boat during the battle around convoy SC 118. Though the result could not be determined, U 613 saw the air attack from some distance away. Others like U 135, U 402 and U 608 were also nearby and either saw the aircraft or heard the depth-charge detonations, soon followed by several other loud noises indicating the breaking-up of *U 624* on its way down.[72]

Reduced by the loss of two boats but reinforced by the return of *U 262* during the previous 24 hours, only nine boats of Group Pfeil remained in operation against SC 118 on the evening of 7 February. However, *U 89*, *U 454* and *U 613*, the last troubled by filter problems in the fuel lines, were up to 70 miles astern of the convoy at dusk and

Fig. 15: Action around SC 118 between 1100/7 Feb. and 1200/9 Feb. 1943.

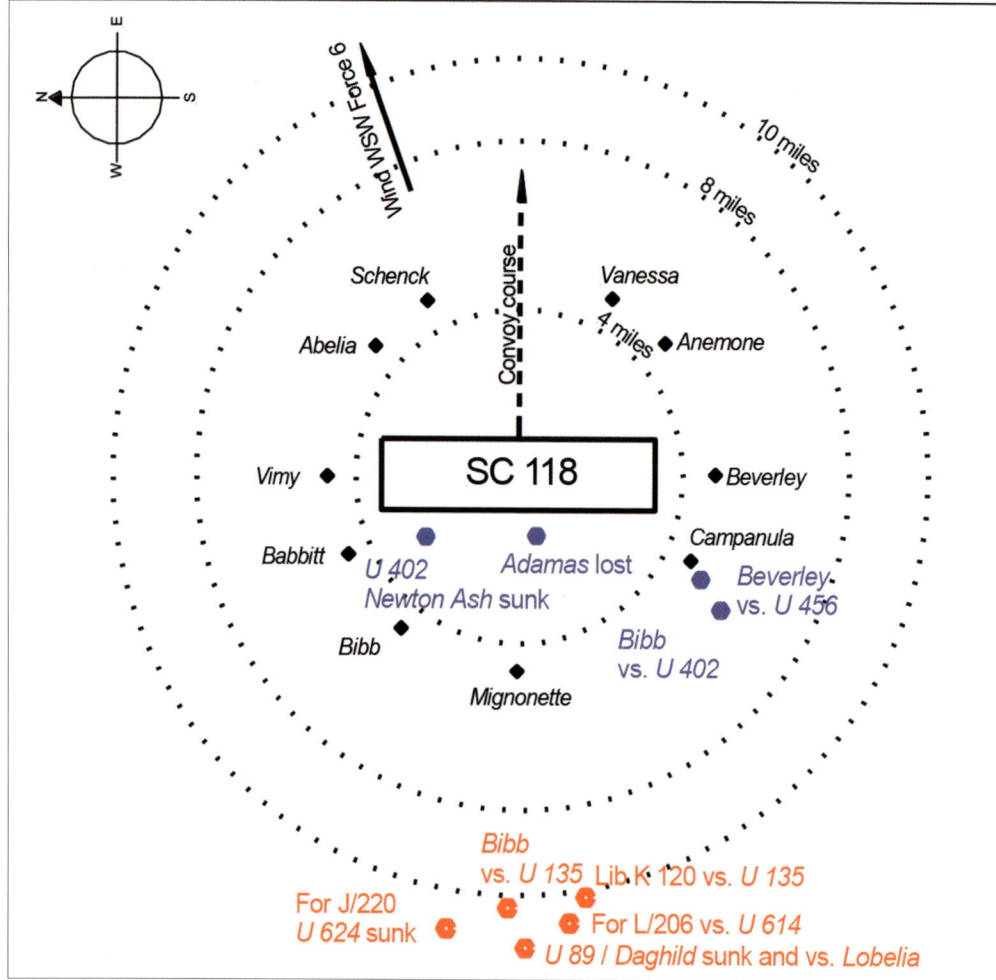

played no part during the coming night. On the Allied side, the ships in SC 118 sailed on after a relatively quiet day. The regular night-time positions of the escorts then with the convoy are shown opposite.

When *U 456* finally reported it had regained contact with the convoy at 1444, U-boat Command immediately directed all Pfeil boats at 1512 'Attack on Teichert's report. Endeavour to be on the spot at dusk. Then fire as soon as possible to clear the way for the other boats.'[73] With *U 456* sending contact reports every hour, other boats set course to get into a favourable position for a night attack. By 1900 *U 456* had moved along the port side to a waiting position ahead of SC 118. After the convoy appeared on the horizon two hours later and the surfaced boat had already passed through the forward screen, a destroyer turning towards *U 456* spoiled the attempt by forcing the boat to dive at 2120. Minutes later the crew heard the whole convoy pass over the boat, unaware of the presence of the 'wolf' below. But Kptlt Teichert was not one to give up easily. Surfacing right after the last escort of the screen went over, he now tried to approach the convoy from astern. Boldly trying to manoeuvre his boat through the clearly seen escorts astern of SC 118, *U 456* was nevertheless picked up by the radar aboard the *Beverley*. The destroyer was about to occupy screen station 'G' on the starboard quarter of the convoy, when the U-boat was detected at 2,400 yards. *Beverley* closed the target and fired star shells at 2240, whereupon *U 456* crash-dived and went down to 160 metres. Instant Asdic contact was gained and *Beverley* carried out an unsuccessful Hedgehog attack at 2251. With only six depth charges left and contact lost, *Beverley* dropped a single scare charge at 2304. Thereafter the destroyer and *Anemone*, which had been directed to assist, searched the area for another 25 minutes until both ships set course to re-join.[74]

U 438 accidentally ran into the hunt for *U 456*. Although failing to spot its enemy, a destroyer closing unintentionally

- Night action
- Daylight action
- Nominal escort position taken up at nightfall

Note: All positions relative to convoy course. Contacts at more than ten miles are plotted without regard to the actual range

to just 200 metres eventually forced the boat to crash-dive at 2355. During the dive the outer caps of two of the forward torpedo tubes failed to close. Water pressure while diving to 150 metres destroyed the torpedoes loaded in the tubes. Half an hour later the unintentional flooding of a torpedo tank, probably caused by a leaky drainage valve, resulted in a loss of trim which eventually forced the boat back to the surface at 0110. Luckily, *U 438* remained undetected and Kptlt Franzius set off to the south-west at high speed. After inspections during the next hour had established the full the extent of the damage, he decided to break off operations against the convoy and told U-boat Command about his decision to return to France.[75]

Shortly after *U 456* had been forced down, the last U-boat contact before midnight turned up, again behind the convoy. At 2255 the *Babbitt* obtained a radar contact resembling a U-boat astern of the convoy at 3,700 yards. Although the destroyer fired a total of 22 rounds of star shell in the direction of the contact, nothing could be seen. After searching the area for 30 minutes, *Babbitt* abandoned the hunt. It is likely that the target was *U 135*, which had observed the illumination of *U 456* and had turned northwards to evade the search group believed to be ahead. *U 135* was unaware of the presence of the convoy in the immediate neighbourhood, so this evasive manoeuvre drew the boat away from SC 118 for the rest of the night.[76] Likewise, none of the other boats were able to make direct contact with the convoy until midnight although *U 402*, *U 608* and *U 614* were only a few miles astern of it at that time. At 2220 Dönitz reminded all Pfeil boats: 'If you have no contact continue search at dusk with big sweeps and at high speed. It will be more difficult tomorrow because of air. We assume convoy will proceed, after dusk has set in, to the east, direction North Channel.'[77]

Although the convoy escorts of the B2 Escort Group kept the U-boats at bay during the second part of the day, this fateful 7 February was nevertheless bound to end in another disaster. At 2335 the Greek steamer *Adamas*, convoy No. 65, but then out of station somewhere between position Nos. 63 and 73, reported seeing a U-boat between columns 7 and 8. The ship then in position No. 73, whose identity is in doubt, turned to port away from the supposed U-boat. *Adamas* was forced to do the same and veered across the bows of the American

Liberty ship *Samuel Huntington* in position No. 63. Although the *Samuel Huntington* went full astern, it still rammed the *Adamas* amidships. Extensive flooding of the engine room and several of the cargo holds resulted from the impact. The *Adamas* was carrying iron and timber under the deck and additional timber as deck cargo. The Greek crew feared the ship would go down quickly and some panicked. With the port lifeboat destroyed in the collision, the starboard lifeboat was lowered unsuccessfully without orders by the second mate. Other men also left without orders on three rafts, leaving only one raft for the rest of the crew still on board.[78]

Day Five – 8 February 1943

The fifth day of the battle around convoy SC 118 began like the day before. Just before midnight *U 402*, having used *Beverley* hunting *U 456* as a beacon to find the convoy, observed the stopped *Adamas* but passed by in order to make contact with the main body of ships. At 0030 the rear ships of SC 118 finally came in sight. Once again, his approach from astern was made easier by the absence of *Beverley*, *Babbitt*, *Bibb*, *Campanula* and *Mignonette* from the convoy screen. Losing no time Forstner selected a large ship identified as a 10,900-ton freighter of the *Cumberland* type and fired his last electric torpedo at 0042. The torpedo was seen to hit after 95 seconds and the ship settled down instantly. This time *U 402* had hit the British freighter *Newton Ash* sailing as convoy No. 54, which became its seventh victim in the running battle. The torpedo struck on the starboard side by No. 5 hold and the explosion detonated the stern ammunition magazine and caused the ship to sink within 20 minutes. Frightened by the very rough sea at the time with a Force 8 south-west gale blowing with hail and rain, some of the men aboard the *Newton Ash* panicked. The port lifeboat containing 32 men was heavily overloaded when lowered, while the starboard boat carried only a single man. In the following hour 14 men were washed out from the port lifeboat by the huge seas. The torpedoing of the *Newton Ash* was not known by the escort commander until 0103 when *Abelia* reported that the ship required assistance. This incident proved again the tactical disadvantages, when the SOE sailed at the head of the convoy during night hours and was likely to lose his overview in rapidly changing tactical or visibility situations. Four minutes later Cdr Proudfoot ordered the *Ingham* to assist the damaged ship. At 0139 the Coast Guard cutter saw lights on the water, soon identified as two boats. Temporarily diverted thereafter by picking up a sound contact and a fruitless search, Cdr Martinson returned with his ship to the scene about an hour later. During an attempt to pick up the men from the crowded port lifeboat first, the boat capsized in a huge wave while coming alongside the cutter, drowning most of the men who had already been exposed to the cold water and could not help themselves. Others drifted away into the darkness and were not found again. Thus, just three men from this boat could be picked up. Later the sole man in the starboard lifeboat was also picked up, resulting in only four survivors from the *Newton Ash*. Forty-one men, including the master Captain James Purvis, were lost.[79]

After firing his last ready torpedo, Forstner was left with only two air driven torpedoes stored outside the pressure hull in pressure-proof upper-deck containers. Loading them into the tubes inside the hull was impossible in the prevailing weather and the proximity of the convoy escorts. Therefore *U 402* acted as contact keeper, shadowing the convoy on its port side on a roughly parallel course. At 0124 Forstner radioed his latest success to U-boat Command. However, this signal was picked up by the *Bibb*, then about to re-join the convoy after rescuing the survivors of the *Henry R. Mallory* the day before. Simultaneously *Bibb* gained a radar contact several thousand yards ahead. After closing to 1,700 yards without making sound or visual contact, Cdr Raney fired two star shells to illuminate, which exploded right above *U 402*. Luckily, *U 402* was able to escape unobserved into the darkness as the exploding star shells completely blinded *Bibb*'s bridge watch and their radar temporarily failed because of the gunfire concussion. In the following hours *U 402* was the only U-boat to keep contact with SC 118, trying to facilitate attacks by other boats.

None of the other seven U-boats still operating against the convoy reached a position to attack in the following hours. Instead, Kptlt Struckmeier in *U 608* ran into the ships that had assembled around the damaged *Adamas* in order to take off its crew after the master had

The British steamer *Newton Ash* off Avonmouth in the Bristol Channel before the war. On 8 February 1943 this ship was *U 402*'s final victim from SC 118.

signalled that the ship would go down soon. The lookouts on *U 608* sighted the stopped Greek steamer and the nearby *Babbitt* at 0125. The latter had sighted the *Adamas* shortly before while returning to station after unsuccessfully investigating a radar contact astern of the convoy. After an exchange of blinker signals with the freighter, Lt Cdr Quarles informed the escort commander about the situation and was told to pick up the crew with all dispatch. In the darkness Kptlt Struckmeier wrongly identified the *Adamas* as a tanker of the *Pennsylvania Sun* type. A torpedo fired at 0137 at the stopped freighter missed the ship. A second torpedo fired at 0150 was heard to explode after three minutes. Originally aimed at the *Babbitt*, it was believed to have hit the merchant ship behind after the destroyer had turned towards the U-boat, forcing it to crash-dive. However, *Babbitt* did not report a contact or record an explosion at this time when trying to pick up survivors floating on the rafts astern of the *Adamas*. Sinking noises noted by *U 608* might

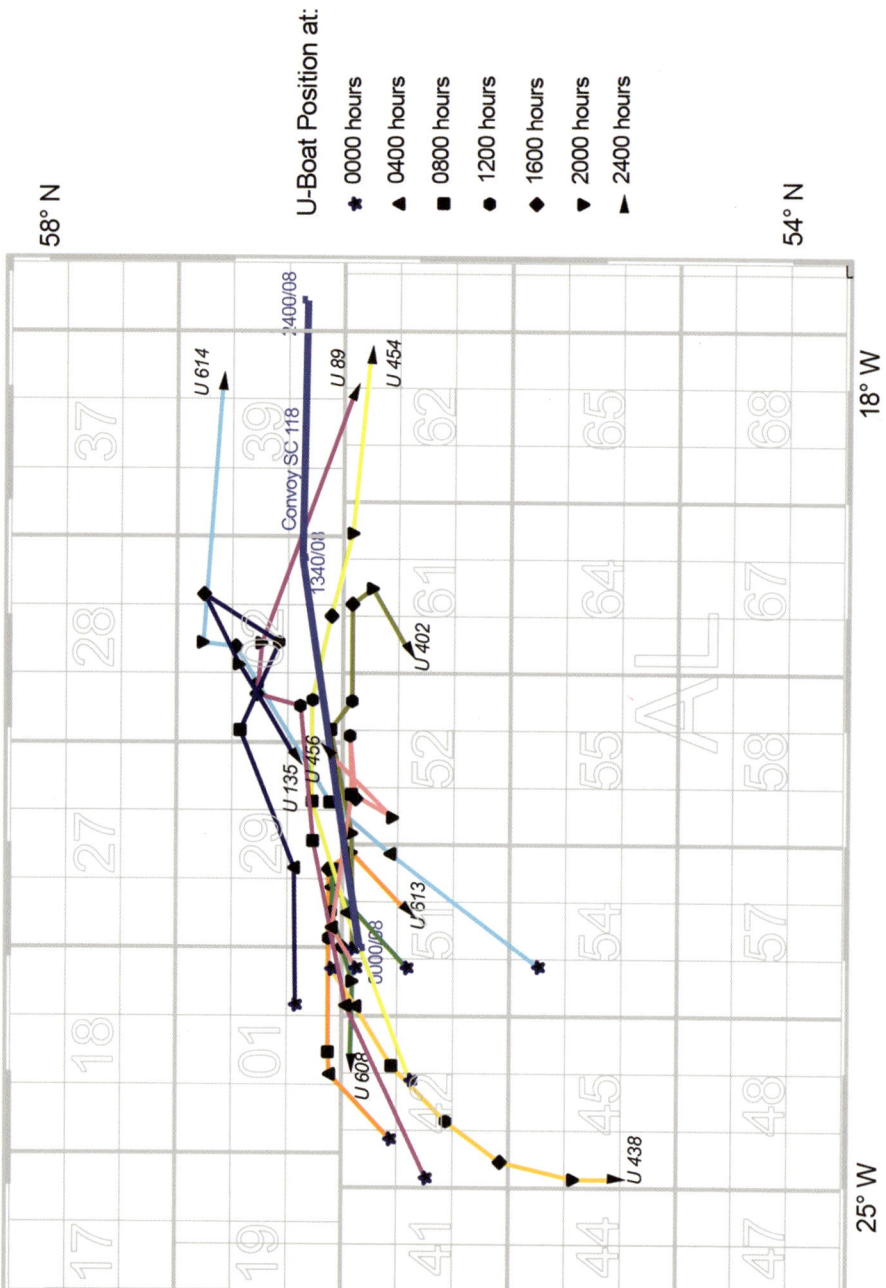

Fig. 16: Courses of U-boats near SC 118 on 8 February 1943.

have been caused by collapsing bulkheads aboard the *Adamas* in the prevailing heavy swell. After resurfacing at 0343 to investigate, *U 608* observed only a large oil slick and a strong smell of petrol but found no wreckage. In any case, the claim to have sunk a 12,000-ton tanker was just wishful thinking. The *Adamas* continued to float all night. Despite the adverse weather *Babbitt* and *Lobelia* were able to pick up 25 men, including the master Captain Fragkopoulos Sgourdaios, out of the 32-man crew of the *Adamas*. After completion of the rescue work, *Babbitt* was forced to cease escorting SC 118 at 0550 owing to shortage of fuel and proceeded independently to Reykjavik. Shortly afterwards the *Beverley* arrived on the scene. The destroyer had received instructions from the escort commander at 0510 to sink any derelicts astern of SC 118 if salvage by tug was considered impracticable. At daylight salvage of the damaged Greek vessel seemed impossible and with the master having left all his secret papers aboard, *Lobelia* eventually sank the *Adamas* by gunfire at 1140. Three hours later *Beverley*, which was also running short of fuel, left Escort Group B2 to proceed independently to Moville at the head of Lough Foyle in Northern Ireland.[80]

At 0440 *Bibb* obtained a sound contact close to the starboard quarter of the convoy and dropped a full pattern of depth charges in an urgent attack. No evidence for damage was observed thereafter and *Bibb* quickly resumed its station. However, none of the U-boats chasing the convoy recorded being attacked at that time. Therefore, the attack must have been directed against a non-sub contact. Operating on the sighting reports from *U 402*, *U 456* was the first on this day to come near to SC 118 but lost the race against the upcoming dawn. Unable to reach the merchant ships before daylight, at 0720 Kptlt Teichert instead tried to attack one of the destroyers screening astern. After he had closed the target to 3,500 metres, the improving visibility forced him to break off the approach. With only 18 cubic metres of fuel left, he too started his return to France. For Teichert and his crew this marked the end to a nerve-shredding eight-day period of nearly continuous pursuit of the convoys HX 224 and SC 118.[81]

At 0912 *U 89* sighted mast tops and smoke from the convoy after a twelve-hour high-speed chase during the night. (It will be remembered that on the evening before *U 89* was about 70 miles behind the convoy after sinking the wreck of the Norwegian tanker *Daghild*.) Only minutes later the lookouts on the nearby *U 402* also spotted the convoy in the distance. Forstner preferred to maintain a safe position well behind the convoy, while Lohmann set off to overtake the convoy to attack at dusk. But by now the odds were greatly against the attacking U-boats.

As in the days before, RAF Coastal Command aircraft were sent out to strengthen the convoy escort during the hours of daylight. Two Liberators of 120 Squadron and no fewer than six Flying Fortresses of 206 and 220 Squadrons were detailed as close cover over the convoy or conducted protective sweeps ahead and along its flanks. This completely tipped the tactical balance in favour of the Allied side. At 0742 Fortress H/220 (Fl Lt R. P. Drummond) appeared as the first aircraft over the convoy. From then on up to four aircraft at a time were in the vicinity of SC 118. H/220, together with Fortress R/220 (Fl Off R. D. Cunningham) and Fortress D/206 (Plt Off P. M. Hill), made up the first group of three aircraft detailed to sweep around the convoy. They started from their bases at Ballykelly and on Benbecula between 0513 and 0532. When D/206 came across the vessels assembled around the stationary *Adamas* at 1036, Lt-Cdr Price in *Beverley* asked the aircraft to search for other possible survivors from *Adamas*, but unfortunately none were found. At 1233 the last of the three aircraft set course for base. As a replacement, Fortress L/206 (Plt Off K. B. Bass) and the Liberators K/120 (Sgt B. W. Turnbull) and N/120 (W Off H. J. Wilson) departed from Benbecula, Reykjavik and Aldergrove between 0837 and 1012. All three aircraft duly found the convoy in the open Atlantic. On reaching its endurance limit, the last aircraft of this group left the convoy at 1838.

A final trio of aircraft detailed to cover the path of SC 118 on this day were the Fortresses B/206 (Plt Off R. S. Weir) and G/206 (Fl Off W. Roxburgh), starting from Benbecula at 1208 and 1425, which were joined by the Sunderland T of 228 Squadron. T/228 was piloted by Fl Off H. J. H. Debnam with the squadron commander, Wing Cdr N. F. Eagleston, aboard as supernumerary officer. However, bad weather forced the flying boat to return early and no U-boats were seen by the other two aircraft. Fortress G/206 as the last of this group finally set

A VLR Liberator of 53 Squadron RAF, before loading with eight 250-lb Mk VIII depth charges, like those used in the destruction of *U 624*. This weapon was introduced in April 1941. Its 170-lb (77-kg) charge of Amatol, later Torpex explosive, went off at a prescribed depth by the use of a hydrostatic pistol. From 1942 onwards its standard depth setting was 25 feet (7.6 m). To crack the pressure hull of a Type VII C U-boat, the distance between the point of explosion and the target had to be less than 10 metres. (*IWM CH 12373*)

course for base at 1929. Three minutes after midnight on 8 February, Liberator K/120 touched ground at Reykjavik as the last member of the air escort on this day.[82]

It was this intense support from the air on 8 February which finally forced the U-boats to lose contact with the convoy permanently at 0950 when the remaining contact keeper *U 402* was driven under by an approaching aircraft. This put an end to the threat to SC 118 from the U-boats, which had intermittently maintained contact with the convoy for almost exactly 96 hours since the first sighting by *U 187* in the forenoon of 4 February.

Despite this, the fighting was far from over on this fifth day of the battle. At 1152 Fortress R/220 sighted a U-boat 28 miles astern of the convoy but *U 89* submerged before Fl Off Cunningham could reach the spot. However, the next U-boat sighting was turned into an attack. On its way from Reykjavik to meet the convoy, at 1312 Liberator K/120 sighted a surfaced U-boat about 19 miles astern of the convoy. Using cloud cover in the approach, Sergeant Turnbull was able to surprise *U 135* and it was too late to dive. To the astonishment of ObltzS der Res Schütt no charges fell in the first attack and following a crash-dive only a single depth charge could be dropped owing to mechanical problems in the second run-in. Landing 15 feet to starboard of the diving swirl, the explosion caused moderate damage to the electrical system aboard *U 135*. This attack was also noted by *U 454* and *U 614*, which were close by and submerged on spotting the aircraft.

At 1504 the *Bibb* was sent out on a bearing of 273° to investigate the position of the air attack. The crew of *U 135* were still repairing the damage, when the *Bibb* picked up the submerged boat by chance on its sonar at 1537 and dropped three depth-charge patterns over the next thirteen minutes. These attacks resulted in an oil slick and two large air bubbles coming to the surface. Unable to regain contact thereafter, Cdr Raney in *Bibb* cancelled the search at 1745. Curiously, ObltzS Schütt remained completely unaware of the escort's presence. Instead, he considered the depth charges to come from an aircraft, believed to have used a possible oil trace from a ruptured fuel tank as an aiming mark. Again, the neighbouring *U 89*, *U 402*, *U 454* and *U 614* recorded the explosions and partly mistook them as being directed against themselves. Reluctant to surface after the recent attacks, *U 135* stayed submerged until 1945 and then set off to the south-west to investigate the damage.[83] This left only *U 89*, *U 402*, *U 454* and *U 614* operating against the convoy after *U 613* had reported its position at 1330 to be about 90 miles behind the convoy, thus indirectly requesting permission to break off operations. Within half an hour U-boat Command approved its return. However, none of the four boats continuing the operation was able to get ahead against the strong air cover. Repeatedly forced to dive by the patrolling aircraft, the boats quickly fell well behind the convoy. Although U-boat Command had reminded *U 402* twice in the early afternoon to maintain contact until dusk to facilitate attacks by other boats, at 1732 Forstner eventually broke off his effort to regain contact with SC 118. At 2113 U-boat Command advised: 'Boats which still have the chance of getting on to it are to search at high speed on zig-zagging courses during the hours of darkness. The others are to withdraw to south-westward. Boats which are still operating will be withdrawn to south-westward tomorrow at first light. Withdrawing boats are to report fuel status by short signal.'[84] *U 89* and *U 614* gave up the pursuit shortly afterwards after considering the tactical situation. At last Kptlt Hackländer in *U 454* finally abandoned the hunt at 0330 on 9 February.

End of the Fighting

Apart from a false Asdic contact obtained by the *Abelia* just before dawn on 9 February, the further passage of SC 118 was uneventful. At daylight most of the escorts were on their assigned stations. In addition, four B-17 Flying Fortresses of 206 and 220 Squadrons provided close cover or A/S sweeps around the convoy. Only *Vimy* and *Lobelia* were still far astern of the convoy. The Free French corvette had developed machinery problems the day before, following an action to sink a derelict ship with only its bow sticking out of the water. This wreck had been sighted earlier by the Fortresses H/220 and R/220. It was probably one of the torpedoed ships from convoy HX 224, possibly the British tanker *Cordelia*. After gunfire to sink the wreck had shown no effect, *Lobelia* dropped depth charges alongside it. The explosions sunk the ship but also caused serious damage to the thrust blocks of the corvette, eventually reducing the ship's speed to three knots during the afternoon. After receiving a signal from *Lobelia* about its mishap, Proudfoot sent *Vimy* to assist, which arrived at 0605 on 9 February and eventually took the corvette in tow. Later in the day Lt-Cdr Stannard aboard *Vimy* requested one of the aircraft at SC 118 to give air cover against possible U-boats. Flying in wide circles around the two ships, Fortress L/206 (Sqn Ldr R. C. Patrick) in fact sighted a U-boat at 1142 about 19 miles astern of them. *U 614* had just surfaced and was caught completely by surprise. The aircraft dropped six depth charges, which exploded some 20 metres away on the starboard beam before the boat was able to dive. With both periscopes, its magnetic compass and the diesel air compressor out of order, damage to one of the fuel cells and only 28 cubic metres of fuel left, ObltzS Sträter requested permission to return to France which was duly granted.[85] Unaffected by the action astern, the bearings in *Lobelia*'s thrust block apparently settled to a new position while the ship was being towed. Thus, after *Vimy* had slipped the tow at 1936 to search for survivors reported by the aircraft to be ahead of the ships, the corvette was able to proceed again without assistance and both escorts then sailed on individually to British ports. *Lobelia* eventually arrived at Greenock at 2104 on 11 February.

At 1330 on 9 February seven ships destined for Iceland, designated convoy SCL 118, were detached belatedly from the main convoy at 14° West when the Iceland Ocean Meeting Point (ICOMP) was reached. Escorted by the cutters *Ingham* and *Bibb* and the destroyer *Schenck*, these ships reached Reykjavik on 14 February. With the main body of SC 118 carrying on towards Britain, at 1640 on 9 February a number of fast ships bound for Liverpool were detached under the escort of *Mignonette*. Other ships bound for Loch Ewe departed at 1300 on 10 February. At 2330 on the 10th *Vanessa* with Cdr Proudfoot left the convoy to proceed independently to Liverpool, arriving at daylight the next morning. This left *Abelia*, *Anemone* and *Campanula* to escort the remaining combined Clyde, Belfast and Mersey portion of SC 118, all of which arrived in port by 12 February.

The BdU ended the operation against SC 118 on 9 February with the following radio message to the Pfeil Group: 'My gratitude for your tough and hard battle with the convoy. In particular to Forstner, Rudloff and Franke for success and shadowing. However, out of such a large group, more boats should have come to grips with the convoy. C-in-C.'[86] Nevertheless, it had a happy ending for Kptlt Siegfried Freiherr von Forstner, whose reported combined sinking figure during his six patrols in *U 402* now crossed the mark of 100,000 gross tons, which automatically led to his decoration with the coveted Knight's Cross on 9 February 1943. At 0828 on the same day the following radio signal was received: 'To Kptlt Frhr. von Forstner: Sincere congratulation to you and your brave men on the award of the

Two survivors of *U 187* (*left* Steuermann Heinrich Skrzipek, *centre* Maschinenobergefreiter Bernhard Römer) aboard HMS *Vimy* at Liverpool shortly before being taken ashore for processing and interrogation. The destroyer picked up nine ratings after the destruction of *U 187*. However, four later died of their wounds and were buried at sea. (*IWM A 15020*)

Knight's Cross. Your Flag Officer (U-boats) and C-in-C of the Navy.'[87] *U 402* made a triumphant return to La Pallice on 23 February, but the last of the Group Pfeil boats did not enter port until much later when *U 608* arrived at Bordeaux on 29 March.

Tactical Analysis of the Battle

Following the end of operations against SC 118 U-boat Command ordered all boats that took part in it: 'to prepare an exact route chart of the operation against the convoy with own route and enemy route based on shadowers' report on which operations were carried out. Draw charts on tracing paper. Charts 1897 large and 1872 large. Mark every time you dived, surfaced, aircraft attacks, etc.'[88] Although Allied naval intelligence was somewhat surprised about this request, U-boat

Kptlt Wolfgang Sträter, captain of *U 614*, at a reception given by the officers of 7th U-boat Flotilla on 26 February 1943. As one out of only three commanding officers from that flotilla operating against SC 118, he was able to carry out a successful attack against the convoy itself during his first patrol with *U 614*. Hence, he was heartily greeted at his new operational base in western France.

Command had finally seen the need to prepare a thorough evaluation of an individual convoy battle. The written report covering convoy SC 118, issued on 25 March 1943 to all front-line and training commands within the U-boat arm, thus became the first such analysis prepared during the war.[89]

Despite the numerical success in terms of ships sunk, U-boat Command was far from satisfied with the operations against the convoy. Although a total of twenty boats operated against the convoy over the five-day period, only eleven boats were able to make contact with the convoy or its close-range escorts. Of these, only three boats were able to launch successful attacks. More U-boats ought to have come to grips with the convoy out of such a large U-boat group in the view of U-boat Command. Based on torpedo-firing reports submitted by the U-boats, U-boat Command assumed that 15 ships of 120,277 grt were sunk from SC 118. In fact, only 11 ships totalling 59,765 grt were sunk by the U-boats. In exchange for the number of ships sunk during the convoy battle, the German Navy paid a high price with three U-boats lost to air or sea escorts. A further four had been damaged so seriously that they were forced to return to base. According to U-boat Command the reasons for the failure to achieve even better results were manifold.

U 614 on 26 February 1943 in the lock before the inner harbour at St-Nazaire on the happy return from its first patrol. Note the pennant for the sinking of the British steamer Harmala flying aft of the half-extended attack periscope

During the first night unusual darkness and the aggressiveness of the escorts stationed at long distance around the merchant ships prevented the boats from keeping contact with the convoy. Further confusion was caused by the unintentional split of the convoy, seen by U-boat Command as a well-planned ruse to deceive the pursuing U-boats. After contact had been firmly re-established before the second night, numerous boats were close by but missed the convoy because of a considerable navigational error in the convoy positions reported by the contact-keeper. On the third day the strong air cover provided during daylight together with the presence of distant escorts astern of the convoy track prevented a large number of boats from catching up with the convoy from behind. Only boats already in close contact with the convoy or coming from a position ahead of its track were eventually able to press home successful attacks inside the escort screen during

The officers of *U 135* on 10 March 1943 following their return to Lorient. *Left to right*, Engineer Officer Lt Ing der Res Dietrich Stölting, the supernumerary meteorologist Dr Werner Reichelt, 2nd Watch Officer LtzS Helmut Karstens, commanding officer LtzS der Res Heinz Schütt and 1st Watch Officer LtzS der Res Ludwig Cohen-Lade.

the following night, sometimes running even within or close to the convoy columns. Naturally, their commanders reported favourable opportunities for attack and fully exploited the situation at the climax of the battle. On the fourth day strong air cover again forced most of the boats still operating against the convoy to drop behind during daylight. Only the most energetic and aggressive commanders were able to keep contact at this time and attacked again during the night. The constant wear and tear on the U-boat crews during the pursuit of the convoy and the now continuous air cover finally led to the end of the fight on the fifth day.

In its summary U-boat Command attributed the unsatisfactory course of the action to the following points:

1) The sea escort was numerically very strong owing to the assumed importance of the convoy and cooperated smartly with

the air escort behind the convoy. This ensured that the boats continually dropped further astern and failed to reach a forward position.

2) The large navigational error on the part of the contact keeper on the second night, when many boats were close by, resulted in no success.

3) With more experience in dealing with the sea escorts at night a number of boats could have reached the convoy despite the strong defence. Proof of this is given by the opinions of the two most successful commanders against the convoy who both judged the chances for success on the convoy as most favourable.[90]

U-boat Command seemed to be unaware or unwilling to accept that existing U-boat designs and combat tactics were rapidly becoming obsolete due to Allied technical and tactical innovations, apart from the enormous advantage from the ability to read the German naval radio traffic including U-boat signals. Instead, Grand Admiral Dönitz as Commander-in-Chief of the Kriegsmarine as well as Flag Officer U-boats, still believed that pure will and aggressive attitude could overcome technological and tactical disadvantages to tip the Battle in the Atlantic towards the German side.

The British perspective on the battle around convoy SC 118 was somewhat different. In his narrative on SC 118, delivered at a conference at the HQ of the Commander-in-Chief Western Approaches at Derby House, Liverpool, on 13 February, Cdr Proudfoot pointed out several aspects and lessons from the operation. This included the extraordinary usefulness of aircraft in combating the U-boats, using direct voice communications. The only trouble experienced by the escorts was correctly to identify the aircraft they were speaking to when several were in the area. Likewise, he praised the work done by the *Toward* in making HF/DF contacts, which in his eyes had helped greatly to reduce losses. Knowing that his escort group was a mixture of vessels that had not been trained as a unit before, Proudfoot was nevertheless rather critical of the performance of some of the American escorts, mentioning incidents of bad station keeping or outright disobedience of his orders. This included the *Ingham* and *Schenck*. The latter had been ordered at 2328 on 6 February to take up screen position 'Q' at the port rear end of the convoy to replace *Lobelia*, then absent from the screen after engaging *U 456* and *U 609*. But instead, Proudfoot believed the destroyer to have stayed in screen position 'L' at the port bow, where it became a nuisance to both *Abelia* and *Vanessa* running in their assigned positions.[91] It seems that Proudfoot had misidentified *Schenck*'s sistership *Babbitt*, which was then engaging *U 624* on the port bow of the convoy. *Schenck* correctly stayed in its assigned position 'Q' from 0040 until 0310 on 7 February, when it shifted to convoy screen position 'G' to assist *Campanula* in accordance with the order from the SOE. Proudfoot also considered it an understandable but regrettable mistake that some escorts took it upon themselves to keep picking up survivors in the water around them, rather than return to their stations when ordered, thus weakening the convoy screen at critical moments.[92]

In his comment on the Proudfoot narrative, the destroyer flotilla commander (Captain [D] Liverpool), Captain F.J. Walker, critically questioned Proudfoot's decision to lead convoy SC 118 from a forward position in the screen during the night hours. In his opinion: 'The correct position of the SOE at night was astern of a slow convoy, so as to be in the best position to see his convoy and control his escorts.' From the astern position the SOE would have been far more likely to see what was happening, including ships torpedoed, and thus be well placed to pounce on U-boats that attacked. The next senior officer should be ahead and should be given authority to order emergency alterations of the convoy course for such contingencies as a U-boat right ahead. Walker expressed his belief that, had Proudfoot in *Vanessa* been astern on the night of 6/7 February, there would have been: '... little doubt that he would have known more of what was happening and could have controlled the ugly rush of escorts to pick up survivors, which left the stern of the convoy open to further attack'. Despite his criticism, Walker was well aware that the escort group had not been a well-drilled team, but considered it a 'collection of individual ships under a strange Senior Officer'. He nevertheless rated the results obtained, mostly by individual initiative, as very creditable, whereas in most such cases they were disastrous.[93]

The final analysis of the U-boat operations in the vicinity of convoy SC 118 by the Anti-Submarine Warfare Division of the British Admiralty summed up all previous comments and criticism.[94] It acknowledged the fact that the ships in the escort were individually efficient, proved by the number of encounters with the enemy and the amount of damage inflicted. At the time it was assessed that one U-boat was known sunk, one was probably sunk, two were severely damaged and one was slightly damaged. It even expressed the belief, that had the escort been equally well trained as a group, the encounter might well have been one of the highlights of the U-boat war. As it was, eight ships were torpedoed while in convoy, seven of them during a period of three hours. Even so, the price the U-boats had to pay in losses inflicted both by aircraft and surface ships was considered a heavy one.

The inability of the escort to fend off the attacks on the night of 6/7 February was seen as due to the fact that it was a scratch team. From its numerical size it should have been large enough to deal with the given situation. However, the ships had not worked together previously and were led by a new senior officer. In addition, a number of the ships had joined the escort while the convoy was already under way. Despite various criticisms the Admiralty concluded that the sort of things which went wrong during the operation could always be expected to go wrong when an escort was made up of a miscellaneous collection of warships with no previous experience of each other. But the Anti-Submarine Warfare Division fully supported the criticism expressed by Walker on the positioning of the senior officer within the screen. Positioned astern, he would have realised that escorts stationed on the threatened sectors were absenting themselves for long periods and thus would have been able to re-organise the screen so as to fill the gaps or order them back to the convoy.

In the following weeks all the points and criticisms raised in the discussion and analysis of the operation were quickly disseminated to the appropriate stations within Western Approaches Command. Just three months later the battle around convoy SC 130 showed that Allied shore commands and escort group commanders had learned their lessons well, when Mid-Ocean Escort Group B7, supported by the 1st Escort Group and VLR aircraft from RAF Coastal Command, successfully fought off a group of 29 U-boats, sinking three of them without losing a single merchant ship. The Allies had finally gained the initiative against the U-boats, which suffered terrible losses from then on, without any reasonable return, until the end of the war in Europe.

Notes to Chapter 2

1. Karl Dönitz, *Ten Years and Twenty Days, Memoirs 1935–1945*, Frontline Books, Barnsley, 2012, p. 322.
2. John M. Waters, *Bloody Winter*, United States Naval Institute, Annapolis, 1994; David Syrett, 'German U-Boat Attacks on Convoy SC 118: 4 February to 14 February 1943', *American Neptune*, 1984: 44 (1), 48–60.
3. Clay Blair, *Hitler's U-Boat War – The Hunted: 1942–1945*, Random House, New York, 1998, App. III; Jürgen Rohwer, *Axis Submarine Successes of World War Two*, United States Naval Institute, Annapolis, 1994.
4. In the following all times are given in Greenwich Mean Time (GMT).
5. TNA DEFE 3/709 ZTPGU-4287 TOO 2031/27 Jan. 43, decoded 1535/31 Jan. 43, DEFE 3/709 ZTPGU-4334 TOO 1536/28 Jan. 43, decoded 1223/1 Feb. 43.
6. NARA RG 38 Box 125, CNO Convoy and routing section, Convoy SC 112–SC 120.
7. BA/MA RM 87/25, KTB Befehlshaber der Unterseeboote, 1 Feb. 43; TNA DEFE 3/709 ZTPGU-4748 TOO 2131/1 Feb. 43.
8. TNA DEFE 3/709 ZTPGU-4757 TOO 1732/1 Feb. 43, decoded 0026/8 Feb. 43, DEFE 3/709 ZTPGU-4748 TOO 2131/1 Feb. 43, decoded 0016/8 Feb. 43.
9. Stephen Roskill, *The War at Sea*, London, 1956, Vol. II, 356; Waters, *Bloody Winter*, 141.
10. BA/MA RM 98/1105, KTB *U 632*, 3 Feb. 43 to 4 Feb. 43; TNA DEFE3/710 ZTPGU-5063 TOO 2314/3 Feb. 43.
11. NARA T1022, 2887, KTB *U 266*, BdU radio signal 1212/4/187.
12. TNA ADM 199/579, Narrative report HMS *Beverley* 12 February 1943; TNA ADM 186/808, Report on interrogation of survivors from *U 187*.
13. NARA T1022, 2839, KTB *U 465*, 4 Feb. 43.
14. NARA T1022, 2938, KTB *U 402*, 4 Feb. 43.
15. NARA T1022, 3373, KTB *U 608*, 4 Feb. 43.
16. NARA T1022, 2887, KTB *U 267*, 4 Feb. 43; TNA ADM 199/579 Narrative report HMS *Beverley* 12 Feb. 1943.
17. BA-MA RM 98/948, KTB *U 454*, 4 Feb. 43; TNA ADM 199/2017, Analysis of U-boat operations in the vicinity of convoy SC 118, 4–9 Feb. 1943.
18. NARA T1022, 2938, KTB *U 402*, 4 Feb. 43; www.fold3.com, War Diary USS *Bibb*, Feb. 1943.
19. BA-MA RM 98/910, Radio log *U 413*, TNA DEFE 3/710 ZTPGU-5164, TOO 2122/4 Feb. 43.

20. NARA T1022, 2839, KTB *U 465*, 4 Feb. 43; TNA ADM 199/579 Narrative report HMS *Beverley* 12 Feb. 1943.
21. TNA ADM 199/579 Narrative report FFS *Lobelia* 12 Feb. 1943.
22. NARA T1022, 2886, KTB *U 262*, 4 Feb. 43; TNA ADM 199/2017, Analysis of U-boat operations in the vicinity of convoy SC 118, 4–9 Feb. 1943.
23. TNA ADM 199/579, Narrative Act. Comdr. Proudfoot of SC 118, 3.
24. *U 609* was lost with all hands in the course of this patrol. Its movements have been reconstructed from radio signals and other sources.
25. TNA ADM 199/579 Narrative report FFS *Lobelia* 12 February 1943.
26. TNA DEFE 3/710 ZTPGU-5157 TOO 0447/5 Feb. 43.
27. NARA T1022, 2886, KTB *U 262*, 5 Feb. 43.
28. Ibid.; www.fold3.com, War Diary USS *Bibb*, February 1943.
29. NARA T1022, 2887, KTB *U 267*, 5 Feb. 43; NARA T1022, 2839, KTB *U 465*, 5 Feb. 43; NARA T1022, 2938, KTB *U 402*, 5 Feb. 43; BA-MA RM 98/957–60, KTB *U 135*, 5 Feb. 43; TNA ADM 199/579 Narrative report HMS *Beverley* 12 February 1943.
30. BA-MA RM 98/913, KTB *U 704*, 5 Feb. 43.
31. BA-MA RM 98/910, KTB *U 413*, 5 Feb. 43; TNA ADM 199/579, Narrative Act. Comdr. Proudfoot of SC 118, p. 4.
32. BA-MA RM 98/910, Radio log *U 413*, 5 Feb. 43; TNA DEFE 3/709 ZTPGU-4539 TOO 1621/5 Feb. 43.
33. TNA DEFE 3/709 ZTPGU-4571 TOO 2036/6 Feb. 43.
34. NARA T1022, 3373, KTB *U 608*, 5 Feb. 43.
35. TNA DEFE 3/709 ZTPGU-4666 TOO 2254/5 Feb. 43.
36. TNA ADM 199/579, Narrative Act. Comdr. Proudfoot of SC 118, pp. 71–9.
37. www.fold3.com, War Diary USS *Ingham*, February 1943.
38. TNA DEFE 3/709 ZTPGU-4631 TOO 0940/6 Feb. 43.
39. BA-MA RM 98/948, KTB *U 454*, 6 Feb. 1943.
40. www.fold3.com, War Diary USS *Babbitt*, 1–28 February 1943.
41. TNA AIR 27/911/35 No. 120 Squadron ORB, 6 Feb. 1943.
42. TNA DEFE 3/709 ZTPGU-4578 TOO 1600/6 Feb. 43.
43. BA-MA RM 98/910, KTB *U 413*, 6 Feb. 43; TNA ADM 199/2017, Analysis of U-boat operations in the vicinity of convoy SC 118, 4–9 Feb. 1943; TNA AIR 27/911/35 No. 120 Squadron ORB, 6 Feb. 43.
44. NARA T1022, 2839, KTB *U 465*, 6 Feb. 43; BA-MA RM 98/948, KTB *U 454*, 6 Feb. 43.
45. NARA T1022, 3385, reconstructed KTB *U 624*, 6 Feb. 43; TNA AIR 27/911/35 No. 120 Squadron ORB, 6 Feb. 43.
46. NARA T1022, 3373, KTB *U 608*, 6 Feb. 43.
47. NARA T1022, 2887, KTB *U 267*, 6 Feb. 43; NARA T1022, 3374, KTB *U 614*, 6 Feb. 43; TNA AIR 27/911/35 No. 120 Squadron ORB, 6 Feb. 43; TNA ADM 199/2017, Analysis of U-boat operations in the vicinity of convoy SC 118, 4–9 Feb. 1943.
48. NARA T1022, 2887, KTB *U 266*, 6 Feb. 43.
49. www.fold3.com, War Diary USS *Schenck*, 1 to 28 Feb. 1943.
50. BA-MA RM 98/950, KTB *U 456*, 6 Feb. 43; TNA ADM 199/579, Narrative report FFS *Lobelia* 12 Feb. 1943.

51. NARA T1022, 2887, KTB *U 266*, 6 Feb. 43; TNA ADM 199/2017, Analysis of U-boat operations in the vicinity of convoy SC 118, 4–9 Feb. 1943.
52. NARA T1022, 2886, KTB *U 262*, 6 Feb. 43.
53. NARA T1022, 3385, reconstructed KTB *U 624*, 7 Feb. 43; www.fold3.com, War Diary USS *Babbitt*, 1 to 28 Feb. 1943.
54. NARA T1022, 2886, KTB *U 262*, 7 Feb. 43; TNA ADM 199/2017, Analysis of U-boat operations in the vicinity of convoy SC 118, 4–9 Feb. 1943.
55. TNA ADM 199/2017, Analysis of U-boat operations in the vicinity of convoy SC 118, 4–9 Feb. 1943, 4.
56. NARA T1022, 2938, KTB *U 402*, 7 Feb. 43; TNA ADM 199/2144, Report Interview Chief Officer Rescue Ship *Toward*, 23 Feb. 1943; TNA ADM 199/579, Narrative Act. Comdr. Proudfoot of SC 118, 3; Capt. Arthur Moore, *A Careless Word ... A Needless Sinking*, American Merchant Marine Museum, King Point NY, 1990, 127.
57. NARA T1022, 3374, KTB *U 614*, 7 Feb. 43; TNA ADM 199/2144, Report Interview Chief Officer SS *Harmala*, 3 Mar. 1943.
58. NARA T1022, 2938, KTB *U 402*, 7 Feb. 43; http://www.warsailors.com/singleships/daghild.html.
59. TNA ADM 199/2144, Report Interview Chief Officer S.S. *Harmala*, 3 Mar. 1943.
60. NARA T1022, 3374, KTB *U 614*, 7 Feb. 43; TNA ADM 199/579, Narrative report FFS *Lobelia* 12 February 1943.
61. BA-MA RM 98/957-960, KTB *U 135*, 7 Feb. 43; TNA ADM 199/579, Narrative Act. Comdr. Proudfoot of SC 118.
62. NARA T1022, 2938, KTB *U 402*, 7 Feb. 43.
63. http://freepages.military.rootsweb.ancestry.com/~cacunithistories/hr_mallory.htm
64. NARA T1022, 2938, KTB *U 402*, 7 Feb. 43; TNA ADM 199/579, Narrative Act. Comdr. Proudfoot of SC 118.
65. NARA T1022, 2938, KTB *U 402*, 7 Feb. 43; TNA ADM 199/2144, Report Interview Chief Officer SS *Afrika*, 24 Feb. 43; www.fold3.com, War Diary USS *Schenck*, 1 to 28 Feb. 1943.
66. NARA T1022, 3373, KTB *U 608*, 7 Feb. 43.
67. TNA DEFE 3/709 ZTPGU-4696 TOO 0855/7 Feb. 43.
68. www.fold3.com, War Diary USS *Bibb*, February 1943; www.fold3.com, War Diary USS *Ingham*, February 1943.
69. BA-MA RM 98/307 KTB *U 89*, 7 Feb. 43; http://www.warsailors.com/singleships/daghild.html.
70. TNA DEFE 3/709 ZTPGU-4881, TOO 1216/7 Feb. 43.
71. TNA AIR 27/911/36 120 Squadron RAF ORB, 7 Feb. 43; TNA AIR 27/1223/352 206 Squadron RAF ORB, 7 Feb. 43; TNA AIR 27/1366/48 220 Squadron RAF ORB, 7 Feb. 43; TNA AIR 27/1415/28 228 Squadron RAF ORB, 7 Feb. 43; www.fold3.com, War Diary Compatron 84, 2/1-28/43.
72. TNA AIR 27/1366 220 Squadron ORB, 7 Feb. 1943.
73. TNA DEFE 3/709 ZTPGU-4935, TOO 1612/7 Feb. 43.
74. BA-MA RM 98/950, KTB *U 456*, 7 Feb. 43; TNA ADM 199/579, Narrative report HMS *Beverley*, 12 Feb. 1943.
75. NARA T1022, 2978, KTB *U 438*, 7 Feb. 43.

76. BA-MA RM 98/957-960, KTB *U 135*, 7 Feb. 43; TNA ADM 199/579 USS *Babbitt*, Report of Escort Operations with SC 118, 18 Feb. 1943.
77. TNA DEFE 3/709 ZTPGU-4886, TOO 2220/7 Feb. 43.
78. TNA ADM 199/579, Narrative Act. Comdr. Proudfoot of SC 118.
79. NARA T1022, 2938, KTB *U 402*, 8 Feb. 43; TNA ADM 199/2144, Report Interview Able Seaman SS *Newton Ash*, 15 Mar. 43.
80. NARA T1022, 3373, KTB *U 608*, 8 Feb. 43; TNA ADM 199/579 USS *Babbitt*, Report of Escort Operations with SC 118, 18 Feb. 1943; Ibid, Narrative report FFS *Lobelia* 12 Feb. 1943.
81. BA-MA RM 98/950, KTB *U 456*, 8 Feb. 43.
82. TNA AIR 27/911/36 120 Squadron RAF ORB, 8 Feb. 43; TNA AIR 27/1223/352 206 Squadron RAF ORB, 8 Feb. 43; TNA AIR 27/1366/48 220 Squadron RAF ORB, 8 Feb. 43.
83. BA-MA RM 98/957-960, KTB *U 135*, 8 Feb. 43; TNA AIR 27/911/35 No. 120 Squadron ORB, 8 Feb. 43.
84. TNA DEFE 3/710 ZTPGU-5107 TOO 2213/8 Feb. 43.
85. NARA T1022, 3374, KTB *U 614*, 9 Feb. 43; TNA AIR 27/1223/52 No. 206 Squadron ORB, 9 Feb. 43.
86. TNA DEFE 3/710 ZTPGU-5550, BdU signal TOO 0108/10 Feb. 43.
87. TNA DEFE 3/710 ZTPGU-5549, BdU signal TOO 0928/10 Feb. 43.
88. TNA DEFE 3/710 ZTPGU-5551, BdU signal TOO 1849/9 Feb. 43.
89. NARA T1022, 1725, OKM/2.Abt. Skl/BdU op, B.-Nr. Gkdos 1877, Geleitzugoperation Nr. 1, 25 Mar. 43.
90. NARA T1022, 1725, OKM/2. Abt. Skl/BdU op, B. Nr. Gkdos 1877, Geleitzugoperation Nr. 1, 25 Mar. 43, p. 6.
91. www.fold3.com, War Diary USS *Schenck*, 1 to 28 Feb. 1943.
92. TNA ADM 199/579, Narrative Act. Comdr. Proudfoot of SC 118.
93. Ibid., Captain (D), Liverpool, to C-in-C Western Approaches, 26 Feb. 43.
94. TNA ADM 199/2017, Analysis of U-boat operations in the vicinity of convoy SC 118, 4–9 Feb. 1943.

3.
The Final Convoy Battle
JW 66 & RA 66 – April/May 1945

U-boat War in the Arctic in 1945

IN 1944 THE U-BOAT CAMPAIGN against Allied shipping turned into a desperate struggle to stem the seemingly inevitable advances of the Allied land forces in the war in Europe. Encouraged by unrealistic hopes for a renewal of the Battle of the Atlantic, U-boat Command considered this phase of the campaign as a transition period until the arrival of the long-awaited new Type XXI and XXIII U-boats, to be followed by the high-speed Walter Types XVII and XXVI. Until then, existing U-boats patrolling in British and American coastal waters were employed in partisan-like operations against superior Allied naval and air forces, resulting in heavy losses.

The retro-fitting of schnorkel equipment was seen as a major step in improving the fighting power of the old Type VII and Type IX U-boats. A schnorkel allowed them to run their diesel engines and ventilate their boats

The Castle-class corvette HMS *Alnwick Castle* escorted several Arctic convoys in 1945 as part of the 7th Escort Group. Late on 29 April *U 968* missed the ship with a T-V acoustic homing torpedo.

while they travelled submerged at periscope depth. Simultaneously, the U-boats could recharge their batteries without surfacing. This made the U-boats generally very much less vulnerable to detection and attack. Although modern Allied centimetric-wavelength radar sets could detect an extended schnorkel head a metre above water level at four to eight miles distance, practical trials by RAF Coastal Command in September 1944 revealed that, in bad weather or at night, the chance of locating one visually for attack was only about 2 per cent. German efforts in the following months to camouflage schnorkel heads against radar further increased the difficulty of locating a schnorkelling U-boat from the air. Statistical analysis by the Operational Research Department of the British Admiralty in August 1944 showed that U-boats using schnorkel to recharge their batteries were nearly eight times safer from air attack than non-schnorkel boats. However, the top speed of the old U-boat types while schnorkelling hardly exceeded 6 knots. This greatly reduced the operational range of the common Type VII C U-boats, which made up roughly two-thirds

of the German front-line boats right until the end of the war. Hence, the schnorkel eventually forced the previously highly mobile U-boat campaign in the open Atlantic into a more confined role, with the future operational areas mostly confined to waters off the British coasts and other major Allied ports. This strategic change was propelled by the Allied landings on the French Normandy coasts in June 1944, when the interruption of the naval supply traffic across the Channel became the main focal point for the U-boat campaign. In August 1944, this new inshore campaign spread all around Britain and, using schnorkel-equipped long-range Type IX boats, to the distant east coasts of Canada and the United States. Results against Allied shipping were only moderate and never became more than a nuisance for the Allied war effort. However, the small number of U-boats in their allocated operational areas, which never exceeded more than seventeen boats at a time in the Atlantic and around Britain during the second half of 1944, continued to tie down a huge part of the Allied naval and air forces. In this role, the U-boat campaign during the final year of the war was far more effective.

Combat conditions for U-boats in the Arctic theatre greatly differed from those prevailing in other regions. Allied naval forces appeared only intermittently in these waters, mostly in connection with supply convoys running to and from Soviet ports along the coast of the Kola Peninsula. The lack of nearby air bases prevented regular patrols by British and American shore-based ASW aircraft, though there were some patrols by insufficiently trained Soviet air units. Soviet naval forces likewise lacked sufficient effective training and tactics to fight successfully against U-boats operating off their coast. Hence, U-boats operating in the Arctic theatre still enjoyed significant operational freedom during this phase of the war and were still able to spend considerable time on the surface during patrols. Non-schnorkel boats were employed against Allied Arctic convoys and Soviet coastal shipping as late as March 1945. Even the old pack tactic, which had been finally abandoned in the Atlantic by March 1944, was still used in the albeit unsuccessful attempts to intercept Allied shipping. In comparison, operational losses were extremely low with just seven U-boats lost to enemy action between mid-October 1944 and May

1945.¹ During this period the 32 U-boats employed in this theatre carried out 89 patrols, totalling 1,974 days at sea, which resulted in 10 merchant ships of 51,518 grt and 14 escorts sunk or damaged.²

During the first months of 1945, Fregattenkapitän Reinhard Suhren, Führer der Unterseeboote (FdU) Nordmeer, in charge of all U-boat operations in the Arctic, had moved a number of boats into waiting positions directly off the Kola Inlet, where they became a considerable nuisance for the Allies. The U-boats succeeded in sinking several merchant ships and escorts from convoys bringing supplies to the port of Murmansk during February and March 1945 in exchange for just one loss. For the next convoy operation in April 1945, code-named Operation 'Roundel', the Royal Navy, which controlled the system of convoys to the North Russian ports, decided to employ new tactics against the developing U-boat inshore campaign in this part of the seas to the north of Norway.

The first convoys to suffer from the new U-boat disposition right in front of Kola Inlet were the outbound JW 64 and the return convoy RA 64 in February 1945, which lost three escorts and one merchant ship in exchange for one U-boat sunk. In addition, the U-boats sank two more merchant ships off Kola Inlet from a Soviet feeder convoy bringing ships from White Sea ports to join RA 64. In his summary report on the combined convoy operation JW 64/RA 64, code-named Operation 'Hotbed', Rear Admiral R. R. McGrigor pointed out that:

> The problem of entering and leaving Kola without losses, or even of safety while at Kola is now in a very unsatisfactory state. The approach is confined to a 40-mile passage eastward along the shore before turning north, a fact of which the enemy is well aware… How to get an unformed convoy through those U-boats unscathed is a major problem to which the only answer would seem to be, so to hunt and harry the U-boats as to force them to withdraw further from the coast. This the Russians should do but don't. I consider it most important that each convoy should be so strong in long-endurance escort vessels that a continual offensive can be undertaken in the approaches during the whole period the convoy is at Kola, so as to drive the U-boats further away.³

In addition, the Senior Officer 7th Escort Group covering both convoys remarked in his report that:

> ... owing to the large prohibited area off Kola the convoy route is so stereotyped that it is easy for the U-boats to get into the tracks of the convoys and when Asdic conditions are bad there is practically nothing that the escorts can do to help. It therefore seems that it is high time that the Russians undertook some sweeping so that the route can be changed and some degree of surprise thereby achieved ... Escorts sweeping the approaches before the convoy sails undoubtedly achieve a certain amount but if Asdic conditions are poor, they really only give warning that a convoy is leaving without any commensurate gain to counterbalance the loss of surprise.
>
> Possibly as the days get longer more value will be obtained from Russian aircraft in keeping the U-boats down, though this may well be nullified by the use of more Schnorkel-fitted U-boats. There is, however, no doubt that it is no longer a suitable area in which to operate a carrier prior to the convoy sailing and the only other possibility would be to land some of their aircraft at Vaenga.[4]

The next outbound convoy, JW 65, experienced the same problems on entering Kola Inlet on 20 March 1945, losing the sloop HMS *Lapwing* and two merchant ships to U-boat Group Hagen waiting right outside the entrance channel. Adverse weather conditions with snowstorms had stopped all flying from the escort carriers attached to the screen at this critical juncture. However, the Soviet Navy had meanwhile carried out a British request to sweep a new channel through the German minefield north of Kola to enable convoys to approach or leave Murmansk by a more direct route. The return convoy RA 65, sailing on 23 March 1945, was the first to use this new route. The frigates of the escort went ahead of the convoy to harass the nine U-boats of Group Hagen lying in wait off Kola Inlet, while four destroyers put up a pyrotechnic display on the old route to draw the U-boats in that direction. This ruse, and the strong anti-submarine measures, were wholly successful, for no U-boat even reported the sailing of the convoy until it was well on its way to the west.

Crew members of *U 427* and the Canadian frigate HMCS *Monnow* chatting on the bridge of the U-boat while both vessels are lying alongside at Loch Eriboll on 16 May 1945 before onward transfer to the assembly port for surrendered U-boats at Lisahally just outside Londonderry in Northern Ireland. Note the schnorkel installation refitted in early 1945 on the port side of the conning tower and the upper deck.

For the convoy pair JW 66/RA 66 the hunt-and-harass tactic was expanded in such a way that even more escorts were detailed to patrol along the planned convoy route, dropping numerous depth charges at infrequent intervals to hold down and deter any likely attacks from the schnorkel U-boats stationed there.

FdU Nordmeer, however, had anticipated some basic elements of the new Allied tactic. Even before the actual operations had started, he radioed his 'Northern Waters Direction No. 47' to all boats at 2246 on 21 April 1945. Suhren advised the boats:

> 1) Circular saws and deterrent depth charges are meant to intimidate U-boats and drown hydrophone bearings of the convoy. They are a vocal expression of the enemy's anxiety.
> 2) Signal strength is no evidence for speed and distance. Boats must at all costs remain high on top for an all-round look.
> 3) Enemy deafens himself and so facilitates attack for the U-boat. After firing, Schweiger [*U 313* on 20 March 1945] stayed at shallow depth, was not detected although the saw remained suspended on the conning tower and was not hurt by 200 close depth charges as they were set much too deep. In addition, by a frequent all-round look he kept the scene under view and retained the possibility of a further attack.[5]

(German crews called the Allied 'Foxer', a towed acoustic decoy designed to fool their homing torpedoes, '*Kreissäge*' = circular saw; one was caught on the conning tower of *U 313* during the incident described.)

Unknown to the FdU Nordmeer, the Royal Navy also laid deep anti-U-boat minefields off the entrance of the Kola Inlet (Operation 'Trammel') on the very next day. After concerns about increasing losses of both merchant ships and escorts from convoys bringing supplies to Murmansk during the first months of 1945, at the end of March 1945 the Admiralty had asked the Naval Mission in Moscow to obtain the agreement of the Soviet authorities to the laying of moored mines inside their operational zone. By 15 April 1945 all outstanding problems had been solved, and on the following day the C-in-C Home Fleet issued orders about the way that the mines were to be laid before the arrival of convoy JW 66. Force 5, consisting of the fast minelayer

HMS *Apollo* (Capt J. A. Grindle, SO), the destroyers HMS *Obedient* (Lt-Cdr H. Kirkwood), HMS *Orwell* (Lt-Cdr J. R. Gower) and HMS *Opportune* (Cdr R. E. D. Ryder), all fitted as minelayers, and the cruiser HMS *Dido* (Capt R. F. Elkins) for AA defence, sailed from Scapa Flow at 0000 on 18 April 1945 to carry out the mine-laying operation. (All operational times are given here in German Summer Time [GMT + 2], which corresponds to B-Zone Time kept aboard British naval vessels throughout the operations in the Northern Theatre.) At 1300 on 21 April 1945 the ships reached Kola Inlet for refuelling, anchoring in Vaenga Bay. In the afternoon of the next day Force 5 left port to carry out the task. On 17 April 1945 the 19th EG, comprising the frigates HMS *Loch Shin* (Temp. Lt-Cdr P. F. Broadhead), HMS *Loch Insh* (Temp. Lt-Cdr E. W. C. Dempster), HMS *Cotton* (Lt-Cdr I. W. T. Beloe), HMS *Goodall* (Lt-Cdr J. V. Fulton) and HMS *Anguilla* (Temp. Lt-Cdr C. Morrison-Payne), left Scapa Flow to operate off the Kola Inlet from 22 April 1945 until the arrival of JW 66. The frigates arrived just in time to carry out an A/S sweep ahead of *Apollo* and *Obedient* before they laid their mines in the eastern area, and then gave close escort to *Orwell* and *Opportune* during their lay in the western area two hours later. Air cover was provided by Soviet aircraft during the whole operation. Between 1832 and 2135 on 22 April 1945 a total of 276 Mk XVII mines were laid, at a depth of 60 feet, in six lines numbered A1–A4 and B1–B2.[6] On completion, the ships of Force 5 returned to the Kola Inlet for refuelling before leaving again at 1245 on 23 April 1945 to return to Scapa, where they arrived on 26 April 1945. The whole operation was carried out without incident.

Build-up of U-boat Group Faust

In the first half of April 1945 only a few U-boats were at sea in Arctic waters; the majority of boats had been ordered back to base after the battle around convoy RA 65 at the end of March 1945. The period until the forthcoming operation against the next Allied supply convoy to Murmansk was used for repairs and rest for the U-boat crews. So, during the first ten days of April, just three boats (*U 668*, *U 312* and *U 716*) were operational, patrolling individually along the coast between Petsamo and the area east of Kola Inlet. On 7 April, *U 716*

(ObltzS Jürgen Thimme) reported its main periscope damaged after being rammed by a destroyer two days before during an abortive attack on a large inbound steamer north-east of the Fischer peninsula, forcing the boat to return.[7] At the same time *U 668* (Kptlt Wolfgang von Eickstedt) started its return to Norway after almost forty days at sea with provisions run down to a minimum. Until mid-April 1945 the remaining boat, *U 312* (ObltzS Jürgen von Gaza), was reinforced by *U 294* (ObltzS der Res Heinz Schütt), *U 295* (Kptlt Günter Wieboldt) and *U 997* (ObltzS der Res Hans Lehmann) sailing from the U-boat bases at Narvik and Harstad in Northern Norway. Two more boats, *U 278* (Kptlt Joachim Franze) and *U 711* (Kptlt Hans-Günther Lange), leaving on patrol in mid-April 1945, were also designated for operations off Murmansk after the completion of reconnaissance missions near the northern Norwegian coast. When reconnaissance by a Ju 88 from 1./Aufklärungsgruppe 124 from Bardufoss during the night of 15/16 April revealed the presence of 41 merchant ships of about 280,000 gross tons at Kola Inlet and Vaenga Bay, this was taken as a strong indication of the passage of a return convoy to Britain in the near future.[8]

By 17 April, FdU Nordmeer still had no specific knowledge about imminent Allied operations. However, from previous experience of convoy cycles, he correctly assumed that an eastbound convoy was already at sea, expecting its arrival in the Bear Island Strait on about 21 April. Therefore, the next four U-boats, *U 286* (ObltzS (K.O.) Willi Dietrich), *U 307* (ObltzS der Res Erich Krüger), *U 313* (Kptlt Friedhelm Schweiger) and *U 363* (Kptlt Werner Nees), sailing from Norwegian bases between 16 and 18 April, were ordered to establish a patrol line south of Bear Island.[9] Over the next two days, these boats, now designated Group Faust, were reinforced by *U 295* and *U 481* (Kptlt Klaus Andersen), the last coming fresh from Narvik. The patrol line of Group Faust was to extend between naval grid squares AC 1988 and AC 4385. The five boats then already off the Murmansk coast were moved right in front of Kola Inlet into the following naval grid squares: *U 711* AC 8864, *U 997* AC 8856, *U 312* AC 8855, *U 278* AC 8865 and *U 294* AC 8853.[10] Although the radio order by FdU Nordmeer for the movement read 'at once', the boats took their stations probably no earlier than 23 April. *U 294* and *U 997* at least were still operating

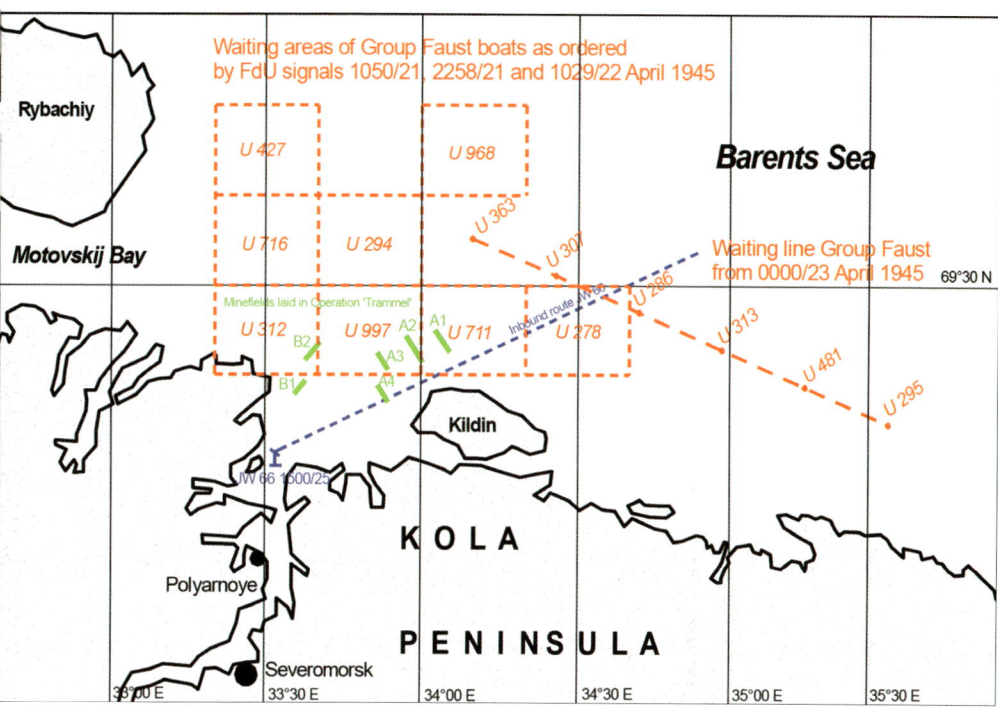

Fig. 17: Waiting positions of Group Faust off Kola Inlet from 21 April 1945.

against Soviet coastal traffic further west on 22 April. The absence of U-boats off Kola Inlet on that day would explain the fact that no reports about Operation 'Trammel' reached FdU headquarters at Narvik.

The Luftwaffe was unable to respond to repeated requests from FdU Nordmeer for reconnaissance along the convoy track on 21 April and the days thereafter owing to its acute shortage of fuel in Northern Norway.[11] Group Faust was therefore directed to leave the patrol line by 0000 on 22 April at high speed on the surface towards the coast off Murmansk to build a new patrol line between naval grid squares AC 8861 and AC 8948 by early morning on the next day.[12] In the meantime, three more boats, *U 427* (ObltzS Karl-Gabriel Graf von Gudenus), *U 716* and *U 968* (ObltzS Otto Westphalen), had sailed from Norway directly towards Kola Inlet to further reinforce the boats already stationed there. They were allocated to the following areas: *U 968* AC 8837, *U 716* AC 8852 and *U 427* AC 8828. Now all boats operating off Murmansk were designated Group Faust. In his usual fanatical manner, FdU Nordmeer ended his radio signal to the boats with the exhortation: 'We are fighting the Battle of Berlin right here. Outfox the Briton and kill the Soviets dead.'[13] In a further message on 23 April he reminded all boats of Group Faust to take care in smooth seas, as radio monitoring had revealed repeated reports from Soviet aircraft about submerged or schnorkelling U-boats. The B-Dienst intelligence service had also noticed the presence of British A/S vessels and consequently the boats were warned accordingly. At the same time FdU Nordmeer ordered them to 'exploit every chance of firing'. From radio monitoring he was also aware that British naval units were then operating east of 25°E.[14] On the following day Group Faust was told to reckon on the arrival of the convoy on the same day or the morning thereafter, as radio reports had revealed the convoy position at 1800 on 22 April 1945 near Bear Island. All boats were accordingly ordered to assemble in the entrance of Kola Inlet. Again, FdU Nordmeer advised them to maintain a survey by periscope, if possible, and to use every opportunity of firing to the full, even firing by hydrophone bearing if necessary.[15] When naval intelligence reported the presence of eight Soviet destroyers at sea on the evening of 24 April, FdU Nordmeer correctly interpreted this as an operation to take up the convoy and informed the boats about this.[16]

However, at 0700 on 23 April 1945 *U 294* reported its return to base due to several technical failures following an unsuccessful attack at 0255 on the day before against the Soviet coastal convoy PK 9 in naval grid square AC 8499 off the eastern coast of the Fischer peninsula.[17] At 1937 on the same day the 19th Escort Group located *U 716* while carrying out an A/S-sweep off Kola Inlet following several U-boat sightings reports and attacks by Soviet aircraft in the area during the previous night. Subjected to several depth-charge attacks by *Loch Insh* and *Cotton*, *U 716* again suffered damage to both its periscopes, sounding gear and all reserve torpedoes, forcing its immediate return to base.[18] According to the British report on the attack, the depth-charge attacks brought boots and emergency food packages floating to the surface. There is a possibility that some of the depth charges were directed against the wreck of *U 425* sunk on 17 February 1945 in a position close to the original contact. The attack left only twelve boats on station off Murmansk. To keep all positions right in front of Kola Inlet occupied, FdU Nordmeer directed *U 968* by radio signal timed 1218/23 to move at once into naval grid square AC 8853, formerly occupied by *U 294*.[19]

Operation 'Roundel' – Part 1

As usual, operation 'Roundel' included running an outbound convoy (JW 66), sailing with supplies for the Soviet Union from the United Kingdom to Murmansk, and a return convoy (RA 66) in the opposite direction. The outbound convoy, JW 66, consisting of 26 merchant ships, left the Clyde just before midnight on 16 April 1945. Close escort was rendered by the destroyers HMS *Zephyr* (Capt J. H. Allison [SO]), HNoMS *Stord* (Kapteinløytnant Helge Øi), and HMCS *Huron* (Lt-Cdr H. V. W. Groos) of the 2nd Destroyer Flotilla. They were reinforced by the 7th Escort Group, including the sloop HMS *Cygnet* (Lt-Cdr P. J. Cowell [SO]) and the corvettes HMS *Lotus* (Temp. Lt T. S. Cox), HMS *Oxlip* (Lt R. M. Sinclair), HMS *Bamborough Castle* (Temp. Lt-Cdr H. Vernon), HMS *Alnwick Castle* (Lt-Cdr H. A. Stonehouse), HMS *Allington Castle* (Acting Lt-Cdr P. A. Read), HMS *Farnham Castle* (Lt-Cdr W. E. Warwick), HMS *Honeysuckle* (Temp. Lt J. A. Wright) and HMS *Rhododendron* (Temp. Lt R. S. Mortimer). The next afternoon *Allington Castle* reported defective steering gear and was ordered to return to harbour for repairs. A covering force commanded by Rear Admiral A. B. Cunninghame Graham, RN, comprising the escort carriers HMS *Vindex* (Capt H. T. T. Bayliss) and HMS *Premier* (Capt R. J. Gardner), the light A/A-cruiser HMS *Bellona* (Capt G. S. Tuck) and the destroyers HMS *Zealous* (Cdr R. F. Jessel), HMS *Zodiac* (Lt-Cdr H. R. Rycroft), HMS *Zest* (Lt-Cdr R. B. N. Hicks) and HMS *Offa* (Lt-Cdr E. M. Thorpe), that was intended to protect against possible German air attacks, left the Clyde on the following day. This group met the convoy at sea on 18 April, while two more escorts as well as sixteen submarine chasers designated for the Soviet Navy under Lend/Lease joined on the following day. This last group, made up of the destroyers HMCS *Haida* (Lt-Cdr R. P. Welland) and *Iroquois* (Cdr K. F. Adams) and the Soviet-manned sub-chasers *SC 1478*, *SC 1479*, *SC 1482*, *SC 1483*, *SC 1486*, *SC 1487*, *SC 1491*, *SC 1493*, *SC 1497*,

Convoy Cruising Order of JW 66 on 17 April 1945

14 *Stevenson Taylor* (US) Kola Inlet	13 *Renald Fernald* (US) Kola Inlet	12 *Woodbridge N. Ferris* (US) Kola Inlet	11 *Keith Palmer* (US) Kola Inlet
24 *Copeland* (Br) Kola Inlet?	23 *Empire Garrick* (Br) Molotovsk	22 *Linn Boyd* (US) Kola Inlet	21 *Park Benjamin* (US) Kola Inlet
34 *Albert C. Ritchie* (US) Kola Inlet	33 *August Belmont* (US) Kola Inlet	32 *British Respect* (Br) Molotovsk	31 *John Gibbon* (US) Molotovsk
	43 *David B. Johnson* (US) Molotovsk	42 *Black Ranger* (Br) Kola Inlet	41 *Samaritan* (Br) Kola Inlet
54 *William D. Byron* (US) Kola Inlet	53 *Laurelwood* (Br) Kola Inlet	52 *Joshua Thomas* (US) Kola Inlet	51 *William Tyler Page* (US) Molotovsk
64 *Owen Wister* (US) Kola Inlet	63 *Cecil N. Bean* (US) Molotovsk	62 *Nelson W. Aldrich* (US) Kola Inlet	61 *Benjamin H. Hill* (US) Kola Inlet
	73 *Kong Haakon VII* (Nor) Kirkenes	72 *Kronprinsen* (Nor) Kirkenes	71 *Lord Delaware* (US) Kola Inlet

Ownership and destination of each vessel shown. General direction of travel. →

SC 1499, SC 1503, SC 1505, SC 1506, SC 1508, SC 1511 and SC 1512, had left Thorshaven on the Faroes on 19 April 1945.

The 26 merchant ships in convoy JW 66 were arranged in seven columns with up to four ships. The convoy commodore, Acting Commodore Sir Roy Gill, sailed in position 41 on the British steamer *Samaritan*, while the masters of the American Liberty ships *Park Benjamin* in No. 21 and *Linn Boyd* in No. 22 served as vice commodore and rear commodore. Among the ships in convoy was also the small British steamer *Copeland*, sailing in position 24 on its thirty-fifth voyage as rescue vessel. The British steam tankers *Black Ranger* and *Laurelwood* were detailed as escort oilers. The necessity for two escort oilers arose from the fact that the convoy included 16 short-legged sub-chasers as well as three Tribal-class destroyers and four old Flower-class corvettes with limited endurance.

The convoy voyage from Britain to Northern Russia was largely uneventful. At 2130 on 19 April *Oxlip* attacked a non-sub contact, while *Zodiac* made a radar contact at 2142 later judged to be a whale. At 1010 on the next day an aircraft was detected on radar at a range of 19 miles, but it disappeared after nine minutes. On 21 April another plane was picked up by radar on *Huron* bearing 146° at a range of 32 miles. *Vindex* vectored in three Wildcats to intercept, but the contact was lost at 0752. However, as it is now known that no German Air Force (GAF) aircraft were sent against JW 66 throughout the whole convoy operation, it is evident that all radar location reports were bogus.

At 0950 on 21 April refuelling of the Russian submarine chasers by the *Black Ranger* and *Laurelwood* started, and was completed by 1300 the next day. The destroyers *Iroquois*, *Zodiac* and *Huron*, as well as the corvette *Oxlip*, were also refuelled that day. On 22 April aircraft from *Premier* and *Vindex* flew numerous patrols around the convoy. During this operation a Swordfish aircraft was lost at 1955 when its rocket-assisted take-off gear failed. The crew bailed out and were picked up by one of the escorts. By 1200 on 23 April, convoy JW 66 had reached the position 73°27'N, 18°57'E, in the Bear Island Passage north of Norway.

On 24 April the convoy turned south-east towards Kola Inlet. At 0026, *Zodiac* obtained an HF/DF bearing at 126° on a U-boat radio transmission. An aircraft was dispatched but found nothing. Throughout 24 April visibility was poor and the convoy was escorted as well by Russian anti-submarine aircraft. Between 1600 and 1700 several HF/DF bearings indicated a number of U-boats about 25 miles ahead of the convoy; these were probably false sky-wave signals.

At 0600 on 25 April Lt-Cdr Cowell in *Cygnet* took over as SO of the advanced screen from Cdr Jessel in *Zealous*. The advanced screen then comprised *Farnham Castle*, *Alnwick Castle*, *Stord*, *Cygnet*, *Offa* and *Bamborough Castle*. At about the same time the Soviet destroyers *Uritski*, *Karl Libknekht*, *Kujbyshev*, *Zarkij*, *Zostkij*, *Derzkij* and *Dostoinyi*, the minesweeper *T-113* and five BO-type sub-chasers from Murmansk reinforced the escort of JW 66 on its final leg. The close convoy screen was then made up mainly by the Flower-class corvettes plus some of the Soviet sub-chasers. The two escort carriers, screened by three fleet destroyers and *Bellona* stood off to the north-east, and their aircraft joined the hunt and harass activities in the waters ahead of the convoy. Lines of sono-buoys dropped by Swordfish aircraft, however, failed to give any contacts.

During the morning scare depth charges were dropped frequently. At 1011 *Rhododendron* obtained a submerged contact and attacked

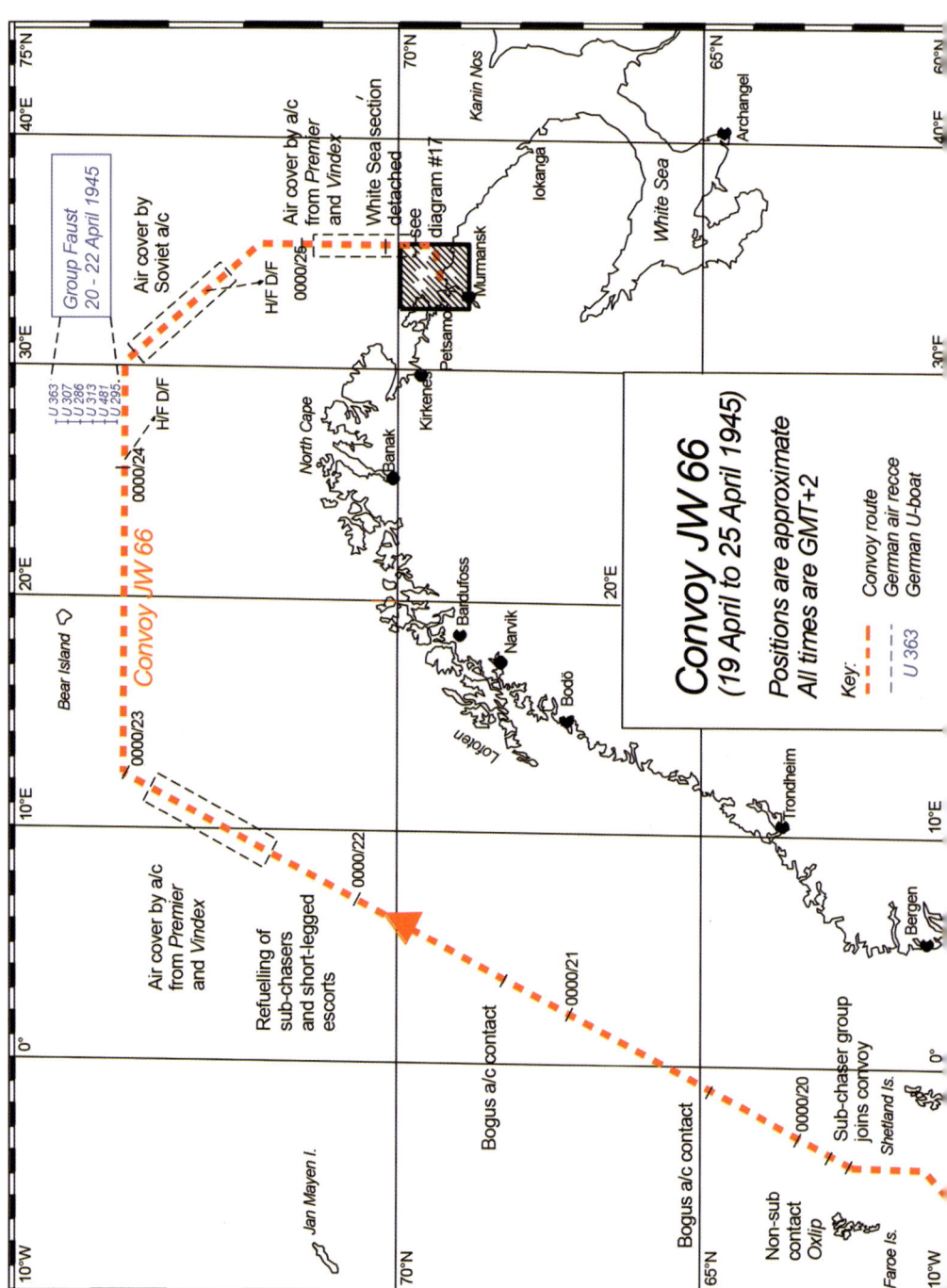

Fig. 18: Convoy operation JW 66 in April 1945.

with depth charges, but results were inconclusive. No U-boat reported being attacked at that time. Around 1130 the five ships of the 19th Escort Group joined the van north of Kola Inlet and took station to the eastward until convoy JW 66 had passed Toros Island at the entrance to Kola Inlet. At 1231 *Alnwick Castle* attacked a possible U-boat with its Squid launcher and *Farnham Castle* was sent in support. However, by 1300 both ships had reported the contact as non-sub. Shortly afterwards the anti-homing torpedo devices (Foxers) were recovered on order of Captain 2nd Destroyer Flotilla to avoid contact with the newly laid anti-U-boat minefields and speed was reduced to 8 knots.

After some more alarms due to contacts subsequently classified as non-sub, the first merchant ships of the convoy entered Kola Inlet at 1433. This was the main group of 13 merchant ships and all 16 sub-chasers destined for Kola Inlet, while 11 ships destined for Molotovsk on the White Sea coast had been detached from the main convoy earlier and reached the ice edge eastwards on the next day to be taken over by Soviet ice-breakers, finally arriving on 28 April 1945. The Norwegian steamships *Kronprinsen* and *Kong Haakon VII*, carrying military and civil relief stores, had been already detached en route to sail directly to the Soviet-controlled port at Kirkenes in northern Norway, where they arrived early on 26 April.[20] After the merchant ships had safely entered Kola Inlet, the escorts of the close and advanced screen turned and proceeded seaward to form various patrol lines off the entrance. Eventually, all escorts entered Kola Inlet shortly after 2100.

The new swamping tactics worked as planned and the convoy suffered no losses. Some twenty-six sonar contacts were attacked, including several mistaken assaults on fish, and more than 400 depth charges were expended by Allied warships. Indeed, only Kptlt Lange in *U 711* sighted convoy JW 66, at 1200 on 25 April in grid square AC 8864 on its inbound course. Counting nine steamers, Lange attacked at once. A fan of probably three LUT pattern-running torpedoes fired at the steamers missed, while a T-V acoustic homing torpedo fired at one of the escorts was believed to have sunk a destroyer after *U 711* heard a torpedo explosion.[21] In fact, no ship was hit and the torpedo must have detonated harmlessly at the end of its running time. The attack was not noticed by any Allied vessel.

Waiting for Convoy RA 66

FdU Nordmeer eventually received news about the arrival of convoy JW 66 at Kola Inlet by the radio signal from *U 711* timed 2311/25.[22] Expecting the return convoy to leave in the evening of 27 April 1945, FdU Nordmeer accordingly instructed his twelve available schnorkel boats of Group Faust at 0936 on 26 April 1945 to occupy the following naval grid squares off the Kola Inlet:

U 427	AC 8828	U 313	AC 8829	U 481	AC 8837
U 286	AC 8852	U 968	AC 8853	U 278	AC 8861
U 312	AC 8855	U 307	AC 8856	U 711	AC 8864
U 997	AC 8858	U 363	AC 8859	U 295	AC 8868[23]

Theoretically, this effectively blocked all exit routes from the Kola Inlet, but thanks to speedy Ultra information from intercepted and decoded U-boat radio transmissions, the U-boat Tracking Room of the Operational Intelligence Centre at the British Admiralty knew the distribution of the U-boats less than six hours later.

During the waiting period for Group Faust off the Kola Inlet until the departure of the return convoy RA 66, two of its U-boats dropped out. At 1426/26 *U 363* reported that it had suffered damage of various sorts through enemy action two days earlier, impairing its operational readiness for a patrol right under the coast off Murmansk.[24] The damage was probably caused by an encounter with a Soviet Boston A-20 bomber, which had attacked a diving U-boat at 0350 on 24 April 1945 in position 69°30′N, 35°00′E. At 1624 on the 26th FdU Nordmeer therefore ordered *U 363* to return to base for repairs.[25] In the meantime, *U 997* had also informed FdU at 1607/26 that it was going to return after having expended all torpedoes in a series of attacks against a Soviet coastal convoy, actually PK 9, four days earlier.[26] Thus, FdU Nordmeer repositioned the remaining ten boats in a signal timed 1915/26 in such a way that *U 711* took over the waiting position AC 8859, formerly assigned to *U 363*, while *U 295* moved into *U 711*'s old position AC 8864. The former operational area of *U 997*, being right next to the exit of the Kola Inlet, was left free. Boats were given freedom to move off to the north to charge their batteries on the surface, if necessary, but were

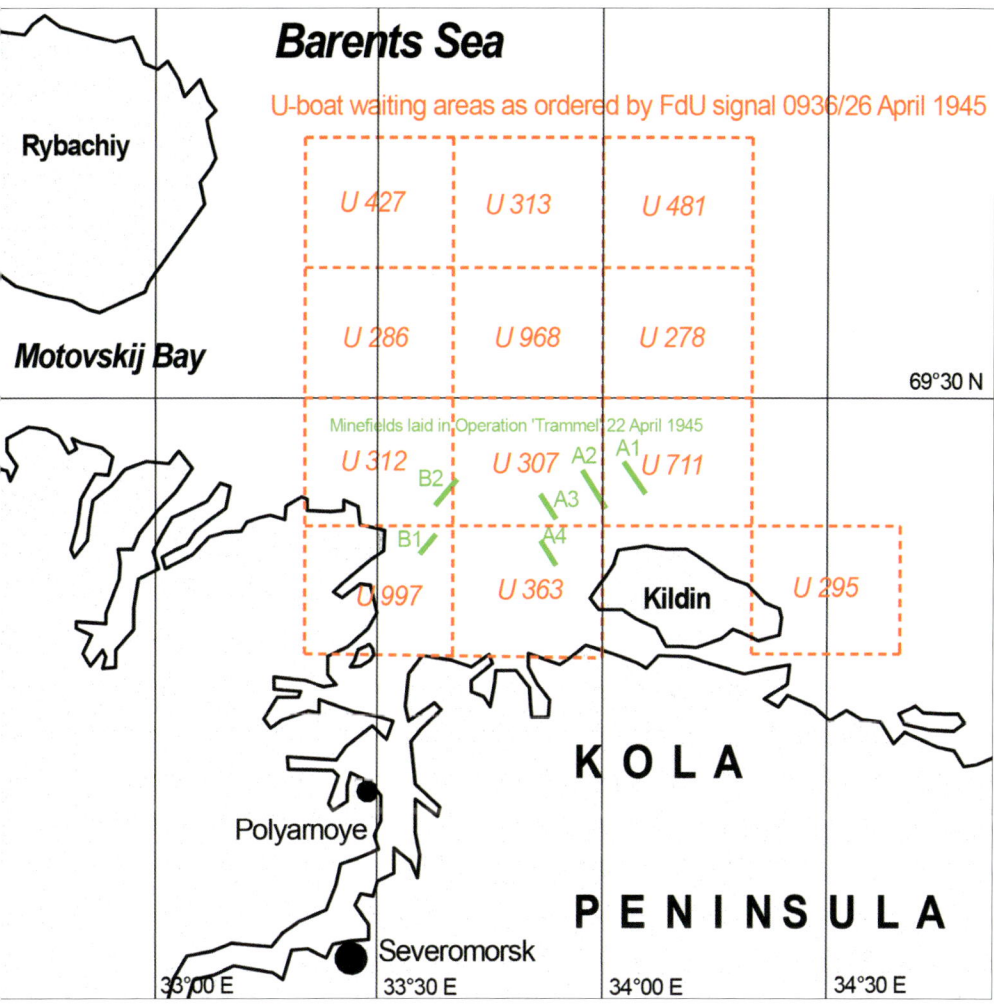

Fig. 19: Waiting positions of Group Faust off Kola Inlet from 26 April 1945

instructed to stay close to the Kola Inlet without fail on the evening of 27 April 1945. FdU Nordmeer also reminded them of the importance of making quick reports about any convoy sailings. Once a convoy had passed through the stationary U-boat positions, all boats were to move away immediately at top speed to naval grid square AB 66 to form a new reconnaissance line.[27] When radio monitoring during 27 April 1945 showed no signs of the imminent departure of a convoy, FdU Nordmeer told the boats about a possible delay in the return convoy at 2314/27, indicating his intention to ask the GAF to carry out an air recce of Murmansk the next day.[28] However, the Luftwaffe was again unable to stage any operations to help the U-boats on 28 April and the next two days.[29]

A British attempt to trick the Germans into thinking that RA 66 was departing on the night of 27/28 April by using dummy radio messages and increased A/S activity off the Kola Inlet failed. In order to mislead the Germans, the Commander-in-Chief of the Soviet Northern Fleet, Admiral Arseni Grigorievic Golovko, even agreed to a suggestion from Rear Admiral Cunninghame Graham to switch on all lights and radio beacons along the coast to simulate the departure of the convoy. Instead, FdU Nordmeer informed the Faust Group boats at 1438/28 about signs of departure of a convoy, but urged them to remain unobserved until there was a worthwhile shot.[30] However, by 2118 on the next day FdU Nordmeer felt sure enough to inform Group Faust that the return convoy had apparently sailed, for there had been a striking amount of radio traffic from Polyarnoye (a Soviet naval base on the Kola Peninsula north of Murmansk) that evening.[31] To get confirmation, the Faust Group was ordered to report any clues forthwith. Boats were also once more reminded to leave at top speed for grid square AB 66 after the convoy had passed.

On 26 April Admiral Golovko issued orders to various naval and air commands to provide support during the departure of RA 66, planned for 0000 on 30 April 1945. This included intensive air patrols in a 60–80 mile zone off the coast between 32° and 36° E on the day before the convoy was to leave. Although Soviet air crews were inexperienced, the aircraft were able to keep the U-boats down. At 0518 on 28 April a Catalina flying boat of No. 118 Reconnaissance Air Regiment unsuccessfully attacked *U 427* with eight depth charges in position 69°50'N, 33°34'E. At noon on the next day, the Soviet minesweeper *T-119*, assisted by the submarine chasers *BO 209*, *BO 225*, *MO 430* and *MO 433*, carried out an unsuccessful search for mines along the designated track of the convoy from the entrance of the Kola Inlet to 69°30'N. Simultaneously, Soviet naval aircraft flew ten anti-submarine patrols off the Kola Inlet. At 1703 a Catalina flying boat spotted a surfaced U-boat north of Teriberka in position 69°43'N, 34°55'E which opened fire on the attacking aircraft. All ten depth charges dropped in the approach missed and the U-boat crash-dived soon afterwards. The attack was directed in all probability against *U 711*, which apparently had moved off temporarily to the north from its attack position to charge on the surface. The boat reported driving off an attack by a Catalina, which caused damage to its starboard blower coupling.[32] Although *U 711* gave no exact date or time for the attack, no other Allied air attack matches the description.

Operation 'Roundel' – Part 2

Late in the afternoon on 29 April, the final convoy battle of the Second World War started around convoy RA 66. Rear Admiral Cunninghame Graham had decided to delay the convoy sailing to this day to give an extra day's rest to escorts and put extra strain on the waiting U-boats. Further, the corvette *Rhododendron* had suffered a dynamo defect which might not have been fixed before 29 April. The British plan was to clear a free passage through the known U-boat concentration off the Kola Inlet by sending a strong force of escorts into this area before the convoy sailed. The five frigates of 19th Escort Group, which left Kola Inlet at 1820 on 29 April, encountered the U-boats first. While proceeding due north in line abreast formation, 3,000 yards apart, at 1856 *Loch Insh* obtained a sonar contact at a range of 780 yards, bearing 65°. This was *U 307* under the command of ObltzS der Res Erich Krüger. The frigate turned towards the contact and at 1900 attacked with a Squid salvo. Thirty seconds later the badly damaged *U 307* surfaced and was fired on by *Loch Insh* and *Loch Shin* plus the sloop *Cygnet* of 7th Escort Group. This group trailed about two miles behind 19th Escort Group in its search for U-boats. At 1903, *U 307* sank stern first, scuttled by the crew. *Cygnet* and *Lotus* covered *Loch Insh*, while it lowered a whaler to pick up survivors from the U-boat; 14 crewmen including the severely wounded commander were picked up by *Loch Insh*, while 37 others were either killed by gunfire or drowned in the icy water. After rescue work had been completed at 1928, the two escort groups continued their sweep. While 19th Escort Group went to the north, 7th Escort Group turned on course 30°, speed 8 knots, again in line abreast 3,000 yards apart. The group was formed into two divisions

U 307 arriving at the U-boat base at Kilbotn near Harstad, probably on 31 March 1945. The photo was taken from the accommodation ship *Black Watch* and shows the stationary AA cruiser *Thetis* in the distance off the western shoreline of Kilbotn Bay.

for this purpose. The first division, consisting of *Cygnet, Honeysuckle, Lotus* and *Farnham Castle*, was ordered to sweep the western half of the assigned area. The second division, led by *Alnwick Castle*, assisted by *Rhododendron, Oxlip* and *Bamborough Castle*, covered the eastern half.[33]

Shortly after the destruction of the first U-boat, *U 286*, whose waiting position was six miles to the north-west of *U 307*, also saw the escorts of 19th EG, and moved in to attack. *U 286*, commanded by ObltzS (K.O.) Willi Dietrich, fired at least one torpedo, which hit *Goodall* at 1935 on the port side under the bridge, causing a huge explosion by detonating its forward magazine. The crippled frigate did not sink immediately and *Honeysuckle* and *Farnham Castle* of 7th EG, then about three miles behind, closed to rescue survivors. While rescue work was in progress, a calcium flare set alight the oil on the water, causing the wreck to burn fiercely for several hours.[34] Despite the intense fire, *Honeysuckle* went alongside the wreck to take on survivors and in doing so was severely scorched by the burning oil on the sea surface and holed above the waterline. *Honeysuckle* and *Farnham Castle* rescued a total of 41 men from *Goodall*.

Just before being torpedoed, *Goodall* had obtained a sonar contact bearing 338° and was preparing to attack. *Loch Shin* immediately turned in this direction. At 1940 *Loch Shin* obtained a sonar contact classified as a submarine at 2,000 yards, and attacked three minutes later with a full Squid salvo without visible results. Following more attacks by *Loch Insh* and *Anguilla*, *Cotton* finally attacked a firm contact at 2017 and reported a patch of oil and wooden wreckage on the surface when closing the position again at 2025. The oil slick, clearly identified as diesel, spread quickly over the next half hour. It marked the loss of *U 286*, sinking in position 69°29′40″N, 33°37′0″E. All 51 crew were lost with the boat. As the SO 19th Escort Group considered it urgent to continue the sweep to ensure the safe sailing of the convoy, no further time was wasted and the group resumed the pre-arranged sweep.

The whole series of actions were observed by the Soviet look-out station at Cape Set-Navolok. To assist in the rescue of *Goodall*'s crew, at 1953 the local Soviet Sea Defence Command directed the submarine chasers *BO 209*, *BO 225*, *MO 430* and *MO 433* together with the motor torpedo boats *215* and *222* to close the damaged escort vessel. Rescue work was completed by 2300 with only 71 men saved. The captain, Lt-Cdr J. V. Fulton, and 97 other crewmen were killed. *Honeysuckle* and *Farnham Castle* subsequently landed 29 hospital cases at Vaenga before re-joining the convoy. The drifting wreck of *Goodall* was finally scuttled by gunfire from *Anguilla* at 0145 on 30 April 1945 in 69°25′N, 33°38′E. The Soviet vessels returned to the Kola Inlet at 0308. The SO 7th Escort Group later wrote that he considered it remarkable after five and a half years of war, that members of *Goodall*'s crew were not wearing life belts or life lines, thereby causing greater loss of life than might have otherwise been the case.

ObltzS Otto Westphalen on *U 968*, stationed in naval grid square AC 8853 immediately to the east of *U 286*, had observed the strong A/S hunt in his vicinity and also moved in to attack, claiming to have sunk two 'destroyers' at 2100 in naval grid square AC 8856. Almost certainly this attack was directed against the escorts of 7th Escort Group trailing behind 19th Escort Group. At 2111 *Rhododendron* reported to *Alnwick Castle* that a torpedo had been fired at the latter in a position 5 miles from the North Kildinsky Lighthouse on a bearing of 317°.[35] *Alnwick Castle* later picked up a definite submarine contact which was attacked with two Squid patterns without evidence of damage.[36] The second torpedo attack by *U 968* was not detected and no ship was actually hit at this time. The Senior Officer 7th Escort Group ordered *Alnwick Castle* and *Rhododendron* to remain in the vicinity until RA 66 had passed. However, *U 968* was not located and slowly moved away submerged to the north-east. In the meantime, the remaining ships of 7th and 19th Escort Groups continued their sweeps for the other U-boats without further incident until they reached the northern limit of the attack area and then turned to join the convoy at the entrance of Kola Inlet at 2334.[37]

In the meantime, *U 427*, stationed in square AC 8828 on the north-western corner of the Group Faust distribution, had observed the column of smoke caused by the burning wreck of *Goodall* at 2013, assuming it to come from a burning tanker. From picking up depth-charge explosions and hydrophone noise in an easterly direction, *U 427*'s commander, ObltzS Carl-Gabriel Graf von Gudenus, concluded that the convoy was trying to pass to the eastward on the former inbound route of JW 66. Since 2055 Gudenus had heard a broad hydrophone band of turbine and piston-engine noises with propeller revolutions corresponding to about 9 knots accompanied by intermittent depth-charge explosions. Some 15 minutes after twilight at 2200, several shadows, bearing 90°, were observed at a distance of 2 to 3 miles. Assuming them to belong to the forward convoy screen, at 2222 Gudenus fired a triple LUT torpedo fan aimed at the convoy ships believed from hydrophone effects to be hidden in the fog behind a destroyer appearing out of the fog. After a runtime of 8.1 and 9.5 minutes respectively he heard a total of three detonations and assumed

From 1943 onwards the US Navy transferred a large number of destroyer escorts built for the USN in American yards to the Royal Navy under the terms of the Lend-Lease Act. Among these was hull number DE-275, which was commissioned on 4 October 1943 as HMS *Goodall*. As part of the 19th Escort Group, the frigate fell victim to a homing torpedo from *U 286* on 29 April 1945 off Kola Bay.

torpedo hits on two targets in the convoy.[38] From the circumstances of the attack, it is virtually certain that it was directed against vessels of the 19th Escort Group still sweeping off the Kola Inlet. However, as none of the group's vessels reported torpedo strikes at that time, it appears that the torpedoes had detonated unobserved in the darkness at the end of their run-time or *U 427* mistook depth-charge explosions for torpedo impacts. Furthermore, it should be noted that the believed presence of convoy RA 66 behind the escort was only wishful thinking on the part of Gudenus, as the convoy had actually not even passed the exit of the Kola Inlet at that time. According to the general narrative of the SOE, the convoy passed Toros Island at the mouth of Kola Inlet only at 0000 on 30 April 1945.[39]

An hour later at 2332 Gudenus, after having gone to periscope depth with *U 427* one minute earlier, observed a corvette-type escort about 200 metres away which turned towards the periscope. After it ran over the boat, a single depth charge exploded above the stern while *U 427* was still at 20 metres, causing widespread damage to the boat's hull and

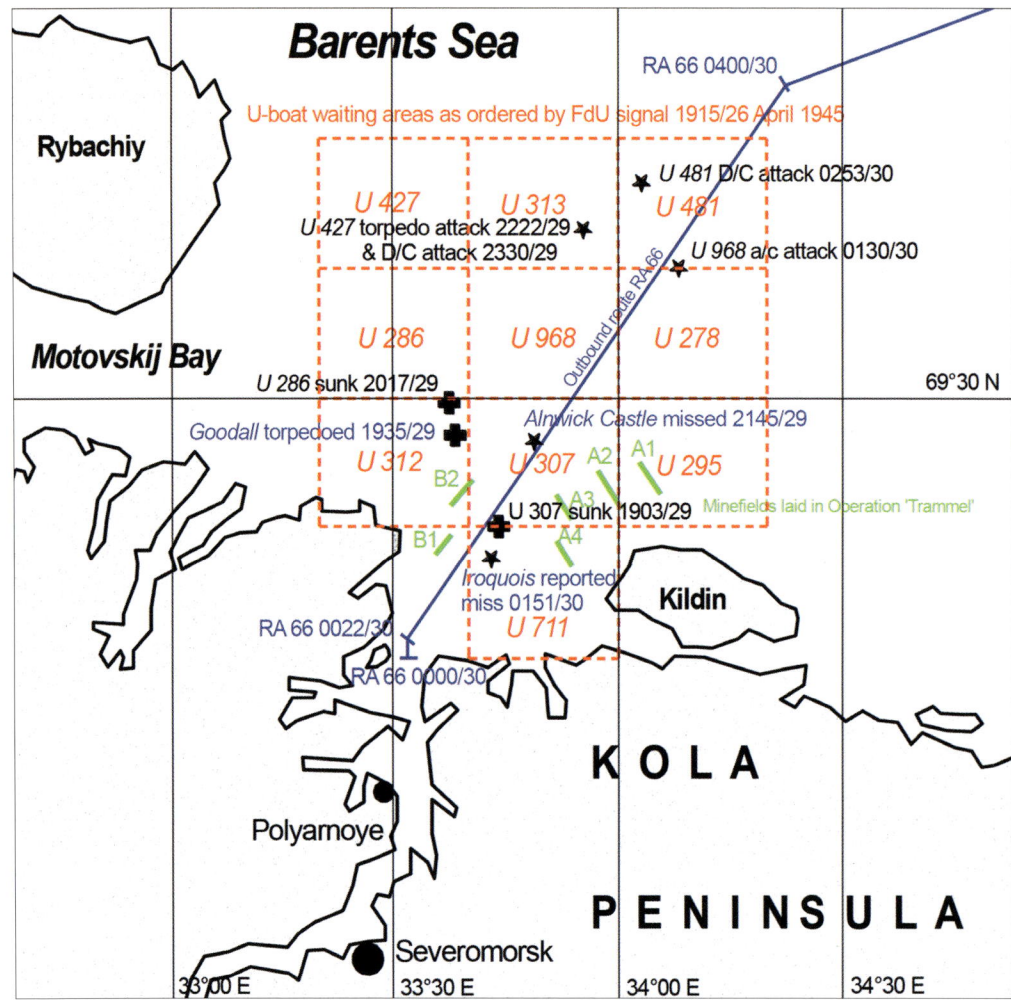

Fig. 20: Operations during the departure of RA 66 on 29/30 April 1945.

other equipment. Gudenus levelled off after a plunge to 180 metres and counted 260 depth charges at medium distance in the following six hours. Curiously, no Allied ship reported making an anti-submarine attack at that time. From the circumstances, it appears that one of the escorts, probably from the 19th EG, had unintentionally placed one of the many scare charges dropped by the escorts during the night right on top of *U 427* without having noticed the presence of the boat. This would also explain the absence of follow-up attacks aimed directly against the boat in the following hours. The reported figure of depth-charge explosions at medium distance can easily be explained by the persistent depth-charge expenditure from escorts to hold down other U-boats known to be in the general area. No evidence can be found in available action reports to support post-war claims about a total number of 678 depth charges dropped on *U 427* in the course of the six-hour action. It will be noted that Gudenus recorded only 260 explosions in his war diary.[40]

Meanwhile, the twenty-six ships of convoy RA 66, including an escort oiler and a rescue ship had left their anchorage inside the Kola Inlet at 1820 on 29 April 1945. Formation of the convoy was going very slowly and it took until 2330 for the four columns of the convoy to proceed at 6.5 knots, finally passing Toros Island at the exit of the Kola Inlet northwards at midnight at a speed of 8 knots. In the absence of the two escort groups, Lt-Cdr Cowell as Captain (D) 2nd Destroyer Flotilla commanding the fleet destroyers *Zephyr*, *Zealous*, *Zodiac*, *Zest*, *Offa*, *Stord*, *Haida*, *Huron* and *Iroquois* screened the merchant ships. At 0022 the course of the convoy was altered to 035°. One minute later six escorts of 7th Escort Group, less *Farnham Castle* and *Honeysuckle*, which were still to land survivors from *Goodall*, joined the close screen. However, encounters with U-boats were far from over. At 0130 a Soviet Catalina flying boat detailed to cover the convoy on its outbound route attacked a periscope with eight depth charges in the reported position 69°36′N, 34°08′E, but could not observe any results due to adverse weather conditions. The attack was seen by the destroyer *Zodiac*, then in the bow screen position of the convoy six miles bearing 225° away from the place of attack. At 0148 *Zodiac* and its sister ship *Zealous* were detached by the SOE to investigate the attack location marked by a white flare from the aircraft. From the summary report of *U 968* on its operation against RA 66 it is obvious that it was this boat being attacked by the Soviet aircraft. Westphalen reported being attacked at 0100 with aircraft bombs while schnorkelling in grid square AC 8837; the bombs knocked out his main periscope and the pressure oil system.[41]

Soviet naval forces also gave support during the departure of RA 66. At 0130 a task group consisting of the destroyers *Zarkij* (Captain 3rd

Convoy Cruising Order of RA 66 on 29 April 1945			
14 *Henry Lomb* (US) Clyde	13 *Leo J. Duster* (US) Clyde	12 *Stage Door Canteen* (US) Clyde	11 *William Wheelwright* (US) Clyde
24 *Byron Darnton* (Br) Clyde	23 *Empire Stalwart* (Br) Loch Ewe	22 *Winfred L. Smith* (US) Clyde	21 *Lawrence J. Brengle* (US) Clyde
34 *Copeland* (Br) Clyde	33 *William Pepper* (US) Clyde	32 *Black Ranger* (Br) Clyde	31 *Grace Abbott* (US) Clyde
44 *Willard Hall* (US) Clyde	43 *W. R. Grace* (US) Loch Ewe	42 *Fort Boise* (Br) Dundee	41 *Nicholas Biddle* (US) Clyde
54 *Fort Massac* (Br) Methil	53 *Dolabella* (Br) Clyde	52 *James M. Gilles* (US) Clyde	51 *Fort Yukon* (Br) Loch Ewe
	63 *Eleazar Lord* (US) Clyde	62 *San Venancio* (Br) Clyde	61 *Charles A. McAllister* (US) Clyde
	73 *John McDonogh* (US) Clyde	72 *Benjamin Schlesinger* (US) Clyde	71 *Eloy Alfaro* (US) Clyde

Ownership and destination of each vessel shown. *General direction of travel.* →

Rank W. G. Bespalov), *Zostkij* (Captain 3rd Rank F. I. Karpenko), *Derzkij* (Captain 3rd Rank S. N. Maksimov) and the submarine chasers *BO 135*, *BO 137*, *BO 219* and *BO 242* left the Kola Inlet to shadow the convoy from a distance of five miles up to the latitude of 70°30′N and to escort possible stragglers or damaged ships back to Murmansk. As RA 66 required no such assistance, the Soviet ships eventually turned for home. On the way back to the Kola Inlet the *Zostkij* gained a sonar contact at 0950 ten miles to the north of Kildin Island, but a subsequent depth-charge attack proved unsuccessful. After breaking off the search, all ships returned to port at 1110.

At 0151 the fleet destroyer *Iroquois* reported a torpedo near-miss. The ship was then acting as part of the close screen at the rear of convoy. At the reported time, RA 66 was still near the mouth of the Kola Inlet. With *U 307* and *U 286* already sunk, none of the other boats of Group Faust reported attacking at this time. Therefore, the incident can only be explained as an erroneous report on the part of the destroyer.

By 0230, the two British destroyers sent out to investigate in the area of the previous aircraft report started their search. However, instead of locating *U 968*, which again had a lucky escape, at 0253 *Zodiac* sighted the periscope of *U 481* inside its turning circle. *U 481* (Kptlt Klaus Andersen) had stayed in its assigned position AC 8837 at the north-eastern corner of the Group Faust waiting area; the crew had recorded hydrophone effects close by and finally observed a destroyer running towards the boat. Correctly assuming it to belong to the forward screen of the outbound convoy, Andersen decided to attack the destroyer with T-V homing torpedoes in order to save the LUT torpedoes for the attack on the convoy ships behind. Just before firing, he realised that the destroyer had spotted his periscope – *U 481* had to use the sky observation periscope for the attack because the main attack periscope had been damaged by a water leak during a deep-diving test on the outbound transit to its operational area. Moments later the torpedoes left the tubes without hitting the targeted escort. Less than a minute later *Zodiac* attacked *U 481* with a shallow ten-charge pattern, causing the failure of all electric systems with the boat falling uncontrolled onto the seabed at 220 metres. Miraculously, the boat took on no water. *Zodiac* was unable to regain contact with the now bottomed boat. At 0258 the frigates *Cotton* and *Loch Shin* of 19th Escort Group, which had joined the convoy screen at 0241 with the group's two other ships, were ordered to take over the hunt from *Zodiac* and *Zealous*. Arriving

The British Z-class destroyer HMS *Zodiac* photographed on 23 March 1945, just one month before the final convoy battle in the Arctic. Early on 30 April *Zodiac* was missed by a homing torpedo from *U 481*.

at the scene at 0335, the two frigates received an order to remain in the vicinity until the escort carrier force, comprising *Vindex* and *Premier* accompanied by the light cruiser *Bellona*, which were scheduled to leave the Kola Inlet at 0400 behind RA 66, were safely past. At the same time the fleet destroyers were released from the escort of RA 66 to rendezvous with the carrier force.

While the crew of *U 481* started repair work down on the seabed, convoy RA 66 left the sea area of the U-boat disposition off the Kola Inlet. At 0300 *U 968*, then still in AC 8837, heard hydrophone effect to the north-east and correctly assumed that the convoy had passed eastwards. RA 66 changed course to 070° True at 0400, now well out of range from the remaining boats of Group Faust.[42] Held down by numerous patrolling Soviet aircraft, the U-boats had to stay submerged for most of the time and were unable to catch up with the convoy. While *U 307*, *U 286*, *U 968*, *U 427* and *U 481* had obviously fallen in with the escorts of 7th and 19th EG, none of the boats had actually made contact with convoy RA 66 itself. With the first two of these boats sunk and the other three more or less damaged, the Allied hold-down tactic had paid off completely.

However, the battle was far from over. While the convoy ploughed on unmolested, the carrier force, now screened by the fleet destroyers *Zealous*, *Zodiac*, *Zest*, *Offa*, *Stord*, *Haida*, *Huron* and *Iroquois* after their release from the close escort of RA 66, once more came into contact with the enemy. This time *U 711* under Kptlt Hans-Günther Lange, which had originally been assigned to the innermost waiting position right in front of the mouth of the Kola Inlet, but apparently was not in that position during the departure of RA 66, was involved. According to a radio report of the boat timed 0930/30, which, however, was intercepted by Allied stations only at 1615, Lange had encountered at least ten destroyers, wide apart on a northerly course in square AC 8596, he made a torpedo attack at 0930 but missed his target.[43] Although the text of the signal merely states that an attack missed, it is likely that no more than one, possibly two torpedoes, very probably T-V acoustic torpedoes, had been fired as the boat had already expended an unknown number of its total equipment of ten torpedoes in its attacks on 19 and 25 April. From the reported

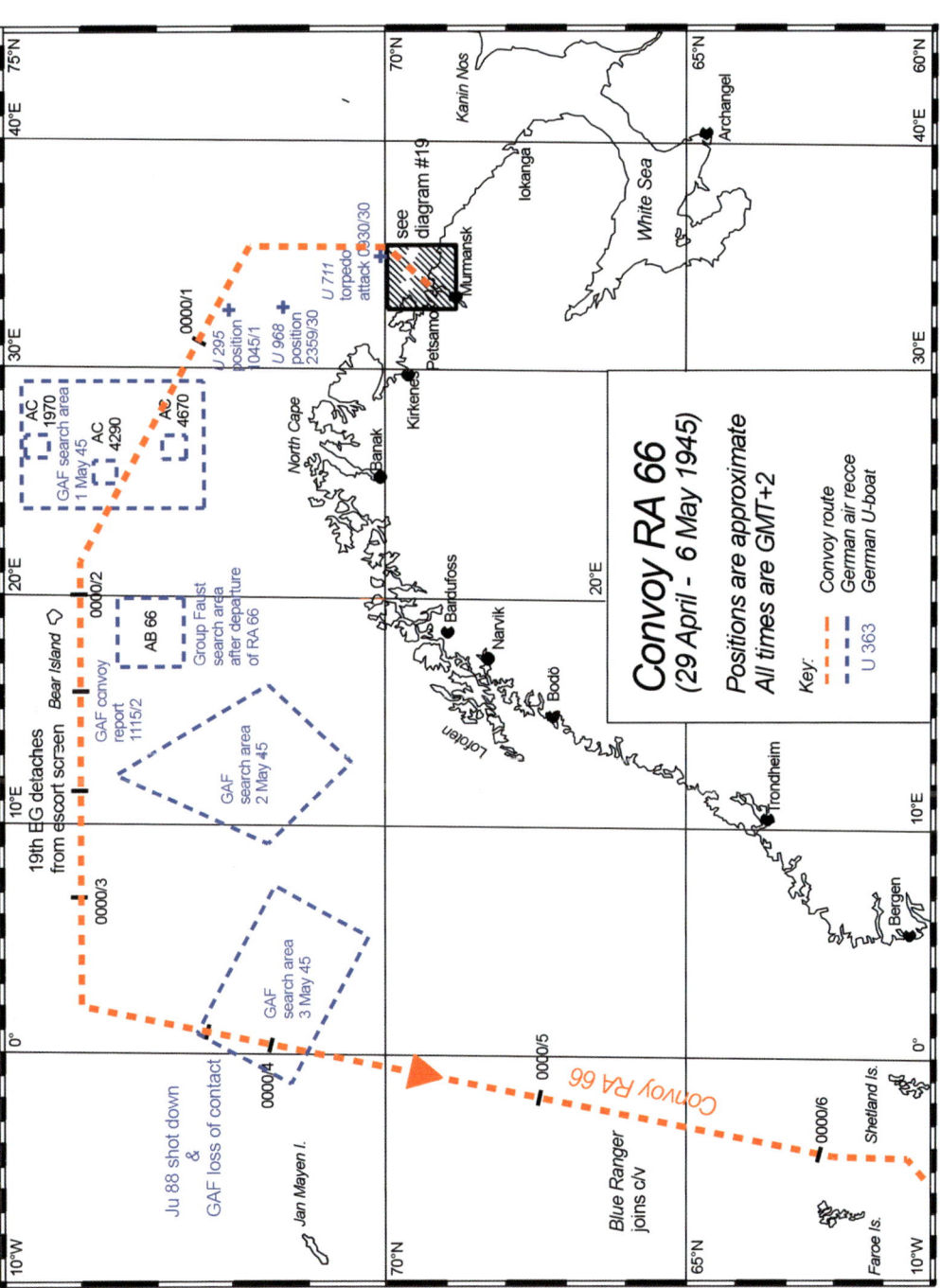

Fig. 21: Convoy operation RA 66 in April/May 1945.

attack position, it appears that *U 711* must have fallen in with the fleet destroyers escorting the carrier group on its way north. However, once again, none of the Allied vessels observed torpedo misses or the attacker itself. With its starboard blower coupling damaged in the air attack the day before, and still inoperable, *U 711* was unable to keep up with the carrier group and moved slowly off to the north.

The crippled *U 427* resurfaced at 0608 in naval grid square AC 8826 and reported one minute later to FdU Nordmeer about being temporarily unable to submerge after having effected emergency repairs. Commencing its return to base, it moved away on the surface at 12 knots on a north-westerly course.[44] Alerted by a series of radio signals sent by the boat in the morning of 30 April, Soviet aircraft were directed to search for it. At 1042, a Catalina of No. 44 Air Regiment spotted *U 427* on the surface and attacked in the face of heavy AA fire with four parachute depth bombs, but they caused no additional damage. Further attempts to attack were frustrated by heavy AA fire and the boat finally submerged unscathed at 1137.[45] Following the first news from *U 427*, at 0648 FdU Nordmeer had already ordered neighbouring boats to render assistance.[46] When at 1107 German radio stations monitored an aircraft report about a damaged U-boat on a westerly course in grid square AC 8547, FdU Nordmeer again asked all boats at 1207 to report and, if in the vicinity, to assist. From plotting evidence, it was correctly assumed that the boat in question must be *U 427*. After a further report from the same aircraft had been intercepted at 1150, wherein it claimed to have sunk the U-boat, FdU Nordmeer at 1233 directed *U 313* (ObltzS Friedhelm Schweiger) to move off at once from its waiting position AC 8829 for rescue as long as no other boats reported their position in the vicinity.[47] In a further signal at 1645, FdU Nordmeer advised *U 313* to be prepared for two Soviet motor torpedo boats in AC 8547 after intercepted radio signals indicated that enemy forces had been dispatched to the scene.[48] After *U 427* had reported again at 0024 on 1 May from AC 8117, FdU Nordmeer eventually instructed *U 313* to re-occupy its former waiting position in AC 8829.[49]

Meanwhile several summary signals from Group Faust boats about encounters with the enemy had arrived at FdU headquarters. From these it was evident that the convoy had passed the U-boat formation

The crew of a Soviet Catalina flying boat in front of their 'ship'. Probably as many as 185 aircraft of this type were delivered to the Soviet Union during World War Two under the Lend-Lease Act. The first batch of 24 aircraft for the Soviet Northern Fleet arrived at Murmansk in June 1944. A lack of trained flying boat pilots and crews caused numerous problems and in 1945 Soviet Catalinas employed in anti-submarine operations in the Arctic were still much less efficient than their British or American counterparts in other theatres.

off the Kola Inlet during the night of 29/30 April. Without any hope of regaining contact with the enemy, the previously ordered movement of all boats towards naval grid square AB 66 was cancelled by a signal timed at 0704/1. Instead, all boats were ordered to move off the coast at economical speed and to report position, stocks, and damage.[50]

The only boats to have energetically moved northwards towards naval grid square AB 66 after it had become obvious that convoy RA 66 had passed the U-boat formation off the Kola Inlet seem to have been *U 295* and *U 968*. *U 295* (Kptlt Günter Wieboldt) reported its position at 1045/1 from AC 5873, whereas U-968 stood even further north-west at that time.⁵¹ All other boats were still reporting from within grid squares AC 8580/90 during the next 36 hours.⁵² GAF aircraft were nevertheless still actively engaged against the convoy. Three Ju 88 reconnaissance aircraft from 1./Aufklärungsgruppe 124 started from Bardufoss during the afternoon of 1 May. Aircraft No. 2 obtained radar contact with the convoy first at 1715 in grid square AC 4670, reporting 35 merchant vessels on course 270°. Shortly thereafter at 1729 No. 3 visually sighted the convoy, reporting 20 merchant ships and one tanker, screened by one aircraft carrier, 8 cruisers and destroyers and 11 other escorts on the same general course in naval grid square AC 4290. Later, the same aircraft crew believed they had found another convoy group with 32 more merchant ships in grid square AC 1970. This misinterpretation may have been the result of poor navigation after the aircraft had come in contact with five fighter aircraft from the escort carrier in the time between. The third Ju 88 failed to locate the convoy.⁵³

The report of Rear Admiral Commanding 10th Cruiser Squadron records the appearance of the first shadowing aircraft at 1722 on 1 May 1945,

Captain (Commodore 2nd Class) Sir Roy Gill, KBE, RD, RNR, sailed as convoy commodore with JW 66 and RA 66. One of the most experienced commodores during the war, he had led numerous convoys since 1940, including SC 19, HX 133, SC 57, ON 176 and HX 237. Of the 1,869 ships reportedly under his control during this period, just 34 did not arrive safely, earning Gill the reputation for being 'the most shot-at commodore in World War II'.

and thereafter mentions groups of three, four and on one occasion five aircraft coming in at about 8-hour intervals. Wildcat fighters from the two escort carriers were sent out to drive them off as soon as they appeared on the Type 277 radar screens. A paucity of radar reports and the very high speed of the reconnaissance Ju 88s made interception difficult. Fighters from *Vindex* fought off two Ju 88. One of the German crews obviously saw the fighters first and escaped, while the second Ju 88 was attacked and damaged. Despite the absence of any more U-boat reports, Rear Admiral Cunninghame Graham expected a renewed attack by aircraft and U-boats in the vicinity of Bear Island. He therefore passed within 20 miles of this island and kept the 19th Escort Group until well clear of this area. The convoy then proceeded along the 74th parallel to the meridian of 2° E before turning south to keep a good distance from the German torpedo-bomber airbase at Bardufoss.[54] GAF planners indeed had intentions for a torpedo aircraft operation against RA 66.[55] Unlike in the second half of April, the fuel situation seems to have been somewhat easier, for on 2 May 1./Aufklärungsgruppe 124 again started three Ju 88 from Bardufoss between 1518 and 1550, though the No. 2 aircraft aborted at 1540.[56] This aircraft could have been Ju 88 D 1 G2+KH of 1.(F)/124, which reportedly crashed during take-off from Bardufoss airfield on 2 May with the crew wounded but otherwise safe, at 1503 local time.[57] The other two aircraft apparently failed to locate the convoy on this day, because RA 66 sailed on a more northerly course than anticipated from previous convoy routes. Plans for an air strike with torpedoes against the convoy therefore had to be given up, although German recce operations continued on the next day. Even worse, at 1812 on 3 May, a Ju 88D-1 of 1.(F)/124 was shot down east of Jan Mayen while shadowing the convoy by two Wildcats of 813 Squadron, FAA, embarked on *Vindex*. Its entire crew (Unteroffizier Karl Kaiser, Fahnenjunker-Unteroffizier Clemens Zimmermann, Unteroffizier Johannes Grabowski, Feldwebel Walter Jahndel) are noted as missing in action.[58] According to British records, the last German reconnaissance aircraft was recorded near the convoy at 1830 on 3 May 1945.[59]

After FdU Nordmeer had cancelled further U-boat operations against RA 66 early on 1 May, he directed *U 427*, *U 481*, and *U 968*, which had all reported damage of various sorts, to commence their return to base by a radio signal timed at 1445 on the same day. *U 312* (ObltzS Jürgen von Gaza) joined them on the next day on account of fuel shortage. The remaining boats were redistributed against Soviet shipping along the coastline between Tanafjord and the northern tip of the Rybachy Peninsula as follows: *U 711* square AC 8170, *U 295* square AC 8430, *U 278* squares AC 8720/30 and *U 313* square AC 8570.[60] In addition to these boats, *U 318* and *U 992* were at sea, carrying special combat forces of Marine-Einsatz-Kommando 35 to be landed near Hopseidet inside the Hopsfjord in a raid against Norwegian resistance groups. However, defects soon also forced *U 711* to begin a return to base, leaving only three boats still in the operational area off the Murman coast by midnight on 2 May. Sadly, the veteran U-boat, operational since March 1943, was sunk shortly after return from its tenth patrol, when the U-boat base at Kilbotn was attacked by British carrier aircraft (Operation 'Judgement') on 4 May; 38 crew members of *U 711* were killed in the attack while aboard the base ship *Black Watch*. When hostilities against the Western Allies were finally stopped on the very next day, all boats at sea headed to Narvik, with the last one arriving on 9 May 1945.

U 711 on 4 May 1945 under attack from British carrier aircraft during Operation 'Judgement' while lying alongside the accommodation ship *Black Watch* at the Kilbotn U-boat base. Both vessels sank shortly thereafter with heavy loss of life among their crews.

The frigate HMS *Anguilla* (ex PF-72 USS *Machias*) took part in the destruction of *U 286* on 29 April 1945 and was later assigned to sink the floating hulk of HMS *Goodall*, previously torpedoed by *U 286*, by artillery fire.

RA 66 sailed unmolested on its final leg towards Britain. On 5 May 1945 the British fleet tanker *Blue Ranger*, which had sailed on 28 April from Scapa Flow under escort from the destroyers *Orwell* and *Obedient* to serve as destroyer oiler during the carrier raid against Kilbotn, joined the convoy, taking station in position 63. On 8 May 1945 the convoy arrived safely in the Clyde. On the same day World War II in Europe ended officially after 69 months of bitter fighting and millions of soldiers and civilians killed.

Defeat of the U-boats

The convoy operations around JW 66 and RA 66 had been a complete success for the Allies. Both convoys had sailed through a concentration of schnorkel boats off Kola Inlet without losses among the merchant ships. With two of the U-boats sunk in exchange for the loss of a single escort, the overall results were more than acceptable. Far more

Victory pennants in the light of defeat. On 30 March 1945 *U 968* enters the U-boat base at Kilbotn as the most successful U-boat in the Northern Theatre in 1945. Under the command of ObltzS Otto Westphalen the boat sank two escort vessels and four merchant ships with one more tanker torpedoed on two patrols in February/March 1945. For this Westphalen was awarded the Knight's Cross of the Iron Cross on 23 March 1945 and has therefore displayed all victory pennants on entering.

important was the fact, that the new aggressive hold-down tactic, using a large number of escorts sweeping the general area in front of the departure port, successfully kept the U-boats underwater and reduced them to static torpedo batteries at best. Ample use of depth charges throughout the preparation and the actual departure of the return convoy RA 66 had a significant deterrent effect on the U-boats in the area, even if they were not actually located by the escorts. Only the most energetic and aggressive U-boat commanders tried in vain to come to grips with the escorts in the hope of getting in contact with the convoy itself. Serving as a textbook action, this final convoy battle in the Arctic waters had shown the path to overcome the threat from old-type U-boats refitted with schnorkel and operating in packs close to the coast.

The reasons for the German failure in the last phase of the U-boat campaign were manifold. Strong surveillance by both naval and air forces in the operational areas and along the transit routes from and to their home bases often led to a somewhat defensive attitude among U-boat commanders. Most were untrained in submerged inshore operations and many lacked even basic combat experience after a generation of watch officers slated for future U-boat commands had been almost wiped out by the heavy U-boat losses since summer 1943. While U-boat training in the Baltic until late 1944 surprisingly still focused on surface pack operations, front-line combat conditions usually called for continuously submerged single operations, static tactics and periscope attacks in adverse tactical situations against a well-organised and efficient opponent. Insufficient and inadequate tactical training in combination with a lack of combat experience caused a heavy toll among U-boats during the inshore campaign. Half of the U-boats lost around Britain during 1944/45 were sunk on their maiden patrols. Although now capable of operating submerged for up to two months thanks to the schnorkel, the refitted old U-boat types were neither designed for nor suited to this sort of operation. Advanced systems for submerged enemy detection and targeting, including automatic fire control and

ObltzS Otto Westphalen, an officer since 1938, began U-boat training in October 1940. After various combat and home-based assignments he commissioned U 968 in 1943. On his first patrol in the Arctic he skilfully survived a depth-charge pursuit by vessels of the 2nd Escort Group under the command of Captain F. J. Walker, CB, DSO**. He was later able to conduct a number of successful attacks against convoys in the waters off Murmansk during 1945.

'blind' shots without periscope use, were not fitted to these types and much had to be improvised or learned the hard way. Therefore, the moderate results achieved by the old U-boat types during this period of the campaign were not surprising, except for the occasional aggressive and able commander.

Allied A/S commands and forces also had to adopt to the new threat from schnorkel U-boats in inshore waters. Search and defence tactics used in the open waters of the Atlantic were often no longer suitable in the shallow and confined waters around Britain. Numerous false Asdic contacts from wrecks and bottom echoes put a heavy strain on escort vessels, especially after it had become known from POW interrogations and Ultra intelligence that U-boats would lie on the bottom when they were waiting for a target or came under attack. Based on a statistical analysis of the swept-path width, the difficult acoustic conditions in coastal waters reduced Asdic performance to less than 20 per cent of its normal efficiency in the open Atlantic. Likewise, despite endless flying hours, patrolling A/S aircraft made few U-boat sightings but did return false reports of schnorkels emitting diesel smoke, which instead were usually natural phenomena like waterspouts or whales. This lack of results produced a growing frustration among aircraft crews, who had played such a prominent role in the fight against the U-boats during the pre-schnorkel period up to mid-1944.

U-boat Command utterly failed to improve the fighting conditions for the U-boats at sea in the steadily deteriorating general situation in the war. Lacking qualified advice from outside its small staff to analyse the tactical situation or technical problems, it simply waited for the new U-boat types to become operational, hoping that these would turn the tide. In the meantime, the Western Allies invested much effort and practical trials to overcome the threat from the old-type schnorkel boats. Thanks to the input from various groups of independent scientists, advisory panels and boards, the British Admiralty and related commands tackled the problem of finding and destroying the schnorkel U-boats off its coasts in a thorough manner. It soon became clear that the best chances for surface ships to locate and attack schnorkel U-boats were in the shipping areas instead of wasting time and effort patrolling the vast stretches along their transit routes. In fact, only a quarter of the 53 U-boats lost to anti-submarine vessels or aircraft in waters around Britain between July 1944 and May 1945 were sunk on transit to their operational areas; the rest were destroyed inside their allocated operational areas. Most losses were inflicted by anti-submarine escorts, sinking a total of 47 U-boats. Aircraft kills against schnorkel U-boats in both areas were rare throughout the period. All six U-boat losses around Britain now attributed to air attack were of U-boats carelessly schnorkelling in daylight, when the schnorkel head was more easily located visually. Interestingly, none of the U-boats ordered to operate around Britain between July 1944 and May 1945 was sunk on its return trip to base. It remains open to question whether this reflected a higher degree of experience among U-boat commanders after some time at sea or was simply caused by increased defensive precautions on the return trip.

ObltzS Karl-Gabriel Graf von Gudenus, captain of *U 427*.

Whether having given away its position by making an attack or after being detected within the confined waters along the coastal shipping lanes, the slow underwater speed of the outdated U-boat types limited their chances of evading destruction from patrolling convoy escorts or support groups. Numerous new and complex tactical operation schemes for Allied anti-submarine vessels and groups had been laid down in the second half of 1944 to ensure swift and sound reaction against any U-boat contact gained in the course of A/S operations. Although U-boats often reduced radio transmissions to no more than two signals during a patrol, signals intelligence from Ultra was still able to provide the Allies with a general picture of U-boat operations thanks to information derived from signals sent out to the boats by U-boat Command. This helped to concentrate escorts and support groups near the focal points, combined with flooding the area with aircraft patrols day and night. The number of escorts engaged in search and destroy operations against U-boats in British coastal waters never exceeded 50–60 ships during 1944/45. But with ever-increasing Allied experience in shallow-water operations, constant training and a steady flow of new search schemes, more sophisticated navigational and detection equipment and a fuller understanding of German intentions and tactics, the number of U-boat losses in the course of the inshore campaign started to rise at the beginning of 1945.

According to postwar analysis, roughly one in four of the U-boats attacked in 1945 was eventually destroyed. Likewise, the large-scale programme of the British Admiralty to lay out defensive anti-submarine minefields inside known U-boat operational areas, starting in November 1944, paid off with at least ten boats eventually falling victim to these traps. U-boat Command remained largely in the dark about the new Allied inventions and the reasons for the upward trend in losses. In spring 1945 German losses reached a record figure of more than 60 per cent of all boats that sailed on patrol during March 1945. With the Operational Intelligence Centre of the British Admiralty usually much better informed about the positions and status of operational U-boats around Britain and elsewhere than U-boat Command itself, the latter realised the change only belatedly by the rising number of boats failing to return from patrol. Eventually, on 30 March 1945, U-boat Command considered the known loss rate in British coastal waters, especially in the heavily patrolled English Channel and the Irish Sea, no longer tolerable and directed the majority of U-boats patrolling in or earmarked for these areas to shift operations to the more distant, deeper waters of the South-West Approaches. Thanks to information gained from Ultra intelligence, Allied search groups followed them and continued to inflict further losses on the U-boats, which were now no longer able to hide on the sea bed while their chances of escape were limited by their slow underwater speed. The situation in the Arctic or distant coastal areas off Canada and the

German inshore U-boat patrols and loss rates September 1944–April 1945				
Month sailed	U-boat type	Boats leaving on patrol	Boats lost on patrol[+]	Loss rate
September 1944	VII C	2 + 5 transfer	0	0%
	IX C	3 + 1 transfer	2	67%
October 1944	VII C	12	2	17%
	IX C	5	1	20%
November 1944	VII C	14	7	50%
	IX C	3	1	33%
December 1944	VII C	18	4	22%
	IX C	2	1	50%
January 1945	VII C	18	10	56%
	IX C	0	0	0%
February 1945	VII C	28	16	50%
	IX C	6	4	67%
March 1945	VII C	24	15[*]	63%[*]
	IX C	9	5[*]	56%[*]
April 1945	VII C	27	7[*]	26%[*]
	IX C	7	2[*]	29%[*]

[+] Excluding patrols terminated prematurely.   [*] Figure incomplete owing to German surrender.

United States mirrored the development in British waters. Because the operations of old-type schnorkel U-boats in the open Atlantic or Arctic waters offered almost no prospects for success against heavily escorted convoys, in May 1945 U-boat Command would have been faced with no alternative other than to recall the old-type U-boats back to base to avoid further horrendous losses. Therefore, the Allies had fully mastered the threat from the old-type schnorkel U-boats by then, although there were still eleven U-boats of these types in their allocated operational areas on 8 May 1945, when the inshore campaign as the last episode of the Battle of the Atlantic finally ended.

Notes to Chapter 3

1. Axel Niestlé, *German U-boat Losses during World War Two*.
2. Jürgen Rohwer, *Axis Submarine Successes*, 209–13.
3. TNA ADM 199/759/3 Convoy: JW 64 and RA 64. Report of Proceedings of Operation Hotbed by Rear Admiral Commanding 1st Cruiser Squadron, on HMS *Campania*, 28 Feb. 45.
4. Ibid., Report of Proceedings – 7th Escort Group covering escort of convoys JW 64 and RA 64, 4 Mar. 45.
5. TNA DEFE 3/743, ZTPGU-38608, TOO 2246/21 Apr. 45, decoded 2055/24 Apr. 45.
6. *Admiralty Staff History on British Minelaying Operations 1939–1945*, Vol. 1, 453–4, unpublished, London, 1973.
7. TNA DEFE 3/743, ZTPGU-38315, TOO 1901/6 Apr. 45, decoded 1601/15 Apr. 45. U 716 probably attacked the Soviet coastal convoy PK 7, but none of the escorts reported a collision.
8. TNA DEFE 3/560, ZTPG 363558, TOO 2322/2338/2359/17 Apr. 1945, decoded 1043/19 Apr. 45; TNA DEFE 3/743, ZTPGU-38450, TOO 1718/17 Apr. 45, decoded 1243/19 Apr. 45.
9. TNA DEFE 3/743, ZTPGU-38443, TOO 2043/17 Apr. 45, decoded 1155/19 Apr. 45.
10. TNA DEFE 3/743, ZTPGU-38558, TOO 1050/21 Apr. 45, decoded 1205/22 Apr. 45.
11. TNA DEFE 3/575, ZTPG 365145, 2141/21 Apr. 45, decoded 0727/24 Apr. 45; DEFE 3/575, ZTPG 365040, 1906/22 Apr. 45, decoded 0204/24 Apr. 45; DEFE 3/575, ZTPG 365499, 2236/23 Apr. 45, decoded 0244/25 Apr. 45; DEFE 3/576, ZTGU-366081, 1952/24 Apr. 45, decoded 0014/27 Apr. 45; DEFE 3/576, ZTPG 366556, 1917/25 Apr. 45, decoded 1440/28 Apr. 45.
12. TNA DEFE 3/743, ZTPGU-38601, TOO 2258/21 Apr. 45, decoded 2029/24 Apr. 45.
13. TNA DEFE 3/743, ZTPGU-38600, TOO 1029/22 Apr. 45, decoded 2035/24 Apr. 45.
14. TNA DEFE 3/743, ZTPGU-38603, TOO 1212/23 Apr. 45, decoded 2054/24 Apr. 45.
15. TNA DEFE 3/743, ZTPGU-38770, TOO 1350/24 Apr. 45, decoded 0711/28 Apr. 45.
16. TNA DEFE 3/743, ZTPGU-38772, TOO 2027/24 Apr. 45, decoded 0711/28 Apr. 45.
17. TNA DEFE 3/743, ZTPGU-38610, TOO 0255/22 Apr. 45, decoded 2207/23 Apr. 45.
18. TNA DEFE 3/743, ZTPGU-38769, TOO 1310/24 Apr. 45, decoded 0604/28 Apr. 45.
19. TNA DEFE 3/743, ZTPGU-38595, TOO 1218/23 Apr. 45, decoded 2000/24 Apr. 45.
20. TNA ADM 199/2316 Admiralty War Diary, 16 Apr. 45–30 Apr. 45, p. 504. There is conflicting information in the sources on the number of ships heading for each Soviet port.
21. TNA DEFE 3/743, ZTPGU-38678, TOO 2311/25 Apr. 45, decoded 0817/26 Apr. 45.
22. Ibid.
23. TNA DEFE 3/743, ZTPGU-38682, TOO 0936/26 Apr. 45, decoded 1250/26 Apr. 45.
24. TNA DEFE 3/743, ZTPGU-38777, TOO 1426/26 Apr. 45, decoded 2005/28 Apr. 45.
25. TNA DEFE 3/743, ZTPGU-38778, TOO 1624/26 Apr. 45, decoded 2005/28 Apr. 45.
26. TNA DEFE 3/743, ZTPGU-38779, TOO 1607/26 Apr. 45, decoded 2002/28 Apr. 45.
27. TNA DEFE 3/743, ZTPGU-38782, TOO 1915/26 Apr. 45, decoded 2047/28 Apr. 45.
28. TNA DEFE 3/743, ZTPGU-38910, TOO 2314/27 Apr. 45, decoded 2312/1 May 45.
29. TNA DEFE 3/576, ZTPG 366899, 1856/28 Apr. 45, decoded 1124/29 Apr. 45; DEFE 3/577,

ZTPG 367266, 2122/29 Apr. 45, decoded 1748/30 Apr. 45; DEFE 3/577, ZTPG 367356, 2051/30 Apr. 45, decoded 2358/30 Apr. 45.
30. TNA DEFE 3/743, ZTPGU-38909, TOO 1438/28 Apr. 45, decoded 2221/1 May 45.
31. TNA DEFE 3/743, ZTPGU-38866, TOO 2118/29 Apr. 45, decoded 0832/1 May 45.
32. TNA DEFE 3/743, ZTPGU-38869, TOO 0930/30 Apr. 45, decoded 0849/1 May 45.
33. TNA, ADM 199/1339, Report of Proceedings 7th Escort Group, 15 April–8 May 1945.
34. Ibid.
35. TNA DEFE 7/743, ZTPGU-38927, TOO 2359/30 Apr. 45, decoded 0222/2 May 45.
36. TNA ADM 199/1339, Report of Proceedings 7th Escort Group, 15 April–8 May 1945.
37. Ibid.
38. BA/MA, RM98/925, KTB *U 427*, 29 Apr. 1945.
39. TNA ADM 199/1339, p. 7.
40. BA/MA, RM98/925, KTB *U 427*, 29 Apr. 1945.
41. DEFE 3/743 ZTPGU 38927, TOO 2359/30.4.45, decoded 0222/2.5.45.
42. TNA DEFE 3/743, ZTPGU, 38927, TOO 2359/30 Apr. 45, decoded 0222/2 May 45; TNA, ADM 199/1339, 7.
43. TNA DEFE 3/743, ZTPGU-38869, TOO 0930/30 Apr. 45, decoded 0849/1 May 45.
44. BA/MA, RM98/925, KTB *U 427*, 30 Apr. 1945, TNA, DEFE 3/743, ZTPGU-38895, TOO 0609/30 Apr. 45, decoded 1354/1 May 45.
45. BA/MA, RM98/925, KTB *U 427*, 30 Apr. 1945.
46. TNA DEFE 3/743, ZTPGU-38868, TOO 0648/30 Apr. 45, decoded 0850/1 May 45.
47. TNA, DEFE 3/743, ZTPGU-38915, TOO 1233/30 Apr. 45, decoded 0007/2 May 45.
48. TNA DEFE 3/743, ZTPGU-38914, TOO 1645/30 Apr. 45, decoded 0010/2 May 45.
49. TNA, DEFE 3/743, ZTPGU-38926, TOO 0024/1 May 45, decoded 0227/2 May 45; DEFE 3/743, ZTPGU-38918, TOO 0434/1 May 45, decoded 0033/2 May 45.
50. TNA DEFE 3/743, ZTPGU-38916, TOO 0704/1 May 45, decoded 0009/2 May 45.
51. TNA DEFE 3/743, ZTPGU-38919, TOO 1045/1 May 45, decoded, 0031/2 May 45.
52. TNA DEFE 3/744, ZTPGU-39008, TOO 2000/2 May 45, decoded 1842/5 May 45; TNA, DEFE 3/744, ZTPGU-39013, TOO 1739/2 May 45, decoded 1105/6 May 45; TNA, DEFE 3/743, ZTPGU-39018, TOO 2051/1 May 45, decoded 0444/7 May 45; TNA, DEFE 3/744, ZTPGU-39025, TOO 0228//2 May 45, decoded 0537/7 May 45.
53. TNA, DEFE 3/578, ZTPG 368993, TOO 0133/4 May 45, decoded 2343/15 May 45.
54. TNA ADM 199/1339, Report of Rear Admiral Commanding Tenth Cruiser Squadron, 9 May 1945.
55. TNA DEFE 3/578, ZTPG 368993, TOO 0133/4 May 45, decoded 2343/15 May 45.
56. TNA DEFE 3/578, ZTPG 368282, TOO 1602/2 May 45, decoded 1650/5 May 45.
57. Personal information kindly supplied to the author by Rune Rautio, Kirkenes (Norway) on 12 Mar. 2020.
58. Ibid.
59. TNA ADM 199/1339, Report of Rear Admiral Commanding Tenth Cruiser Squadron, 9 May 1945.
60. TNA, DEFE 3/744, ZTPGU-39022, TOO 1445/1 May 45, decoded 0507/7 May 45; TNA, DEFE 3/744, ZTPGU-39001, TOO 1313/2 May 45, decoded 1726/5 May 45.

1.
Allied Day and Night Convoy Escort Positions

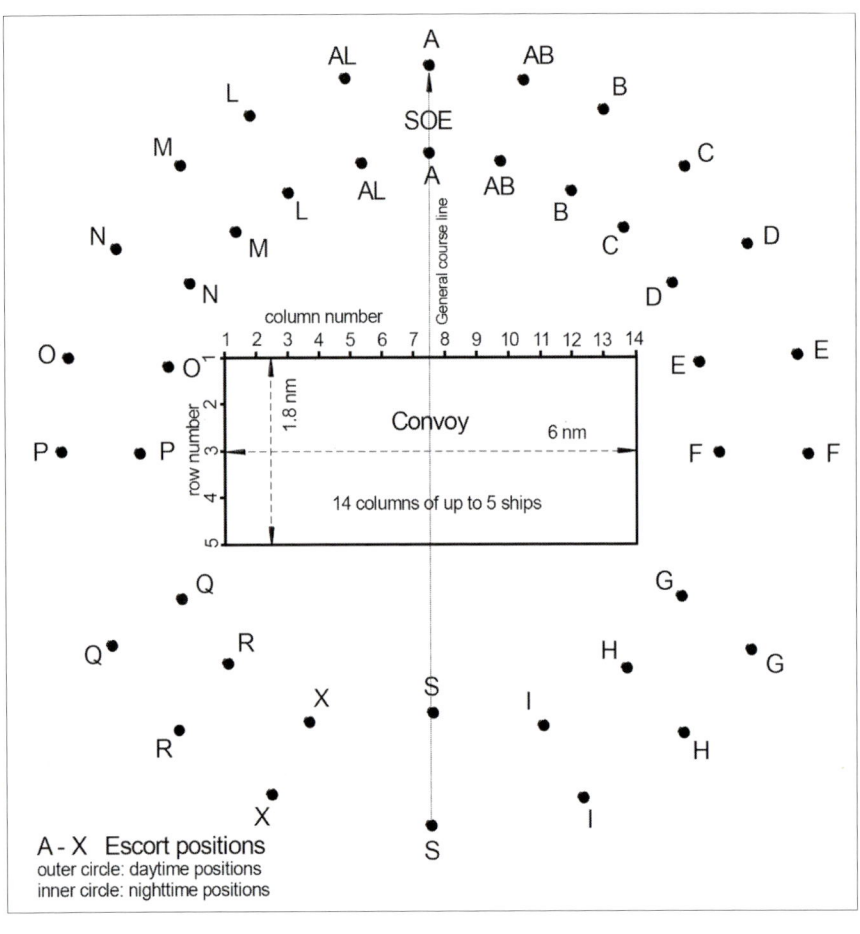

A - X Escort positions
outer circle: daytime positions
inner circle: nighttime positions

APPENDICES

2. U-boat Officers Deployed against Convoy SC 7

	Captain	1st Watch Officer	2nd Watch Officer	Engineer Officer	Supernumeraries
U 28	Kptlt Günter Kuhnke	ObltzS Friedrich Guggenberger	ObltzS Ernst-Ulrich Brüller	Lt Ing Fritz Niewerth	
U 38	Kptlt Heinrich Liebe	ObltzS Heinrich Ratsch	ObltzS Jürgen von Rosenstiel	Kptlt Ing Ludwig Steinmetz	Kptlt Hans-Georg Fischer
U 46	ObltzS Engelbert Endraß	ObltzS Horst Uphoff	ObltzS Hans-Jürgen Hellriegel	Lt Ing Karl Engemann	Kptlt Richard Zapp
U 48	Kptlt Heinrich Bleichrodt	ObltzS Reinhard Suhren	ObltzS Otto Ites	Lt Ing Erich Zürn	Kptlt Hans-Joachim Rahmlow
U 99	Kptlt Otto Kretschmer	ObltzS Klaus Bargsten	ObltzS Horst Elfe	Oblt Ing Gottfried Schröder	Kptlt Siegfried Frhr von Forstner Lt MA Sdf. Herbert Lander
U 100	Kptlt Joachim Schepke	ObltzS Günther Krech	ObtzS Reinhard Böning	Oblt Ing Dietrich Noack	Kptlt Walter Flachsenberg
U 101	Kptlt Fritz Frauenheim	ObltzS Georg-Werner Fraatz	ObltzS Rolf Steinhaus	Oblt Ing Rüdiger Burchards	Kptlt Helmuth Ringelmann
U 123	Kptlt Karl-Heinz Moehle	ObltzS Johann Jebsen	LtzS Ernst Cordes	Kptlt Ing Otto Zschetzsching	
U 124	Kptlt Wilhelm Schulz	ObltzS Heinz Hirsacker	ObltzS Reinhard Hardegen	Oblt Ing Rolf Brinker	Kptlt Wilhelm Kleinschmidt

3. U-boat Officers Deployed against Convoy SC 118

	Captain	1st Watch Officer	2nd Watch Officer	Engineer Officer	Supernumeraries
U 267	Kptlt Otto Tinschert	LtzS Siegfried Breinlinger	LtzS der Res Hans-Dietrich Kaiser	Lt Ing Narziß Schenk	
U 608	Kptlt Rolf Struckmeier	LtzS Karl-Ernst Kaiser	ObltzS Otto Luther	Oblt Ing Emil Walter	
U 187	Kptlt Ralph Münnich	LtzS Rudolf Strait	LtzS Hans-Georg Buschmann	Lt Ing Kurt Meyer	FhrzS Ernst-Jürgen Brehm
U 465	Kptlt Heinz Wolf	LtzS Helmut Wieduwilt	LtzS Alois Renner	Lt Ing Dietrich Warringholz	
U 402	Kptlt Siegfried Frhr. von Forstner	ObltzS Henning Schümann	ObltzS der Res Karl-Wilhelm Pancke	Lt Ing Hermann Hardtke	Obstrm der Res (ROA) Richard Eberlein FhrzS Benno Uter
U 609	Kptlt Klaus Rudloff	LtzS Wolfgang Kazda	LtzS Herbert Mohrbutter	Oblt Ing Rudolf Pieh	
U 262	ObltzS Heinz Franke	LtzS Hans Hellmann	LtzS Horst Hübsch	Lt Ing Heinz Sudholt	FhrzS Hans-Jochen Gustedt
U 454	Kptlt Burkhard Hackländer	LtzS der Res Hans Reimers	LtzS der Res Hans Lehmann	Oblt Ing Wolfgang Fromm	
U 89	Kptlt Dietrich Lohmann	LtzS der Res Dietrich Wilke	LtzS Hans Fischer	Lt Ing Heinrich Kretzschmar	Obstrm der Res (ROA) Hans Pfitzner, Obstrm. der Res (ROA) Johannes Reinhold
U 135	LtzS der Res Heinz Schütt	LtzS der Res Ludwig Cohen-Lade	LtzS Helmut Karstens	Lt Ing der Res Dietrich Stölting	FhrzS Peter Kuhlmann

U 456	Kptlt Max-Martin Teichert	ObltzS Wolfgang Leu	LtzS der Res Adolf Thies	Oblt Ing Lothar Nerlich	FhrzS Hans Gerlach, FhrzS Raimund Lang
U 614	Kptlt Wolfgang Sträter	LtzS Helmut van Norden	LtzS Günter Egidi	Oblt Ing der Res Klaus Hagenmüller	
U 438	Kptlt Rudolf Franzius	LtzS Hans-Eberhard Baumann	LtzS Rolf Hilger	Oblt Ing Ernst Lampe	Obstrm der Res (ROA) Franz Sonnleitner, Obstrm der Res (ROA) Franz Peter Schicke
U 624	Kptlt Ulrich Graf von Soden-Fraunhofen	LtzS Paul-Joachim Bohnstädt	LtzS Alexander Blaha	Lt Ing Walter Meyer	
U 704	Kptlt Horst Keßler	LtzS der Res John Dreyer	LtzS Ernst Hartmann	Oblt Ing Albert Mirwald	
U 613	Kptlt Helmut Köppe	LtzS Eduard Aust	LtzS Fritz Ahnert	Lt Ing Horst Simon	Obstrm der Res (ROA) Eberhard Fulda, Obstrm der Res (ROA) Hans Glatzel
U 752	Kptlt Karl-Ernst Schroeter	ObltzS Günter Pulst	LtzS Peter Hotop	Oblt Ing Eduard Guthmann	Lt Ing Heinz Krey, FhrzS Erich Briegel, FhrzS Hans-Jürgen Mussehl
U 266	Kptlt Ralph von Jessen	LtzS Nikolaus Wayand	LtzS der Res Gerhard Breun	Lt Ing Georg Rowehl	
U 413	Kptlt Gustav Poel	LtzS Dietrich Sachse	LtzS Werner Schwirley	Lt Ing Kurt Bäckert	FhrzS Werner Altstädt, FhrzS Willi Möller
U 594	Kptlt Friedrich Mumm	ObltzS Hartmut Strenger	LtzS Hans Bene	Oblt Ing Herbert Kühne	

4. U-boat Officers Deployed against JW 66 & RA 66

	Captain	1st Watch Officer	2nd Watch Officer	Engineer Officer	Supernumeraries
U 427	ObltzS Karl-Gabriel Graf von Gudenus	ObltzS Hans-Joachim Schult	LtzS Hans-Joachim Schranz	Oblt Ing Karl-Wilhelm Grützemacher	ObltzS der Res Heinrich Kruse
U 313	Kptlt Friedhelm Schweiger	ObltzS Hans-Jürgen Mussehl	LtzS Paul-Gerhard Siebel	Oblt Ing Martin Wefing	ObltzS der Res Karl-Heinz Gerstenberg
U 481	Kptlt Klaus Andersen	ObltzS Herbert Bischoff	LtzS Herbert Weller	Oblt Ing der Res Wolfgang Griebel	LtzS Leberecht Börger
U 286	ObltzS (KO) Willi Dietrich	ObltzS Hans-Günther Bethge	ObLtzS Karl-Heinz Koch	Oblt Ing Ulrich Hemken	ObltzS (KO) Heinrich Scheid
U 968	ObltzS Otto Westphalen	ObltzS Clausdieter Oelschlägel	ObltzS der Res Reinhold Schmidt	Oblt Ing Johann Hirschbrich	ObltzS Hermann Feuerstack
U 278	Kptlt Joachim Franze	ObltzS der Res Gerd Schmidt-Stafford	ObltzS Martin Marhold	Oblt Ing Hans Gillert	Kptlt der Res Herbert Balke
U 312	ObltzS Jürgen von Gaza	ObltzS der Res Ernst Ditzuleit	LtzS der Res Hans-Egon Werle	Lt Ing Werner Rogal	ObltzS der Res Horst Weickmann, Lt Ing der Res Ludwig Häcker
U 307	ObltzS der Res Erich Krüger	ObltzS Edgar Kloock	ObltzS der Res Jürgen Burkhardt	Oblt Ing Wolfgang Vorck	LtzS Hans-Georg Hembd, Ofhr Ing Johann Weiser

APPENDICES

	Commander				
U 711	Kptlt Hans-Günther Lange	LtzS Friedrich Peters	LtzS Eberhard Frank	Oblt Ing Ulrich Bornemann	Kptlt der Res Hartwig Maull, LtzS der Res Paul Frerks
U 997	ObltzS der Res Hans Lehmann	ObltzS Walter-Erich Friederichs	ObltzS Diether Wolffram	Oblt Ing Klaus-Ulrich Sadewasser	ObltzS der Res Theodor Kundt, Lt Ing Helmut Wieduwilt
U 363	Kptlt Werner Nees	ObltzS Kurt Schneider	ObltzS Ludwig Johns	Oblt Ing Hans Kreuzburg	LtzS Karl-Heinrich Kraatz
U 295	Kptlt Günter Wieboldt	ObltzS Hugo Frhr von Seyfertitz	LtzS Burghard de Joncheere	Oblt Ing der Res Fritz Köstler	ObltzS der Res Oleg Todtenhaupt, Lt Ing Helmut Rädel
U 716	ObltzS Jürgen Thimme	ObltzS Johannes Everth	LtzS der Res Werner Menninghaus	Lt Ing Heinz Nobiling	ObltzS Helfried Kramer, Lt Ing der Res Hans-Joachim Röhl
U 668	Kptlt Wolfgang von Eickstedt	LtzS Wolfgang Wüstenberg	ObltzS der Res Hermann-Josef Wethmar	Oblt Ing Helmut Jersch	Lt Ing Fritz Goetz
U 294	ObltzS der Res Heinz Schütt	ObltzS der Res Wilhelm Uhle	ObltzS Jürgen-Paul Schmidt	Lt Ing Manfred Rauch	ObltzS der Res Paul Elbert, LtzS der Res Bernhard Egert, Lt Ing Arthur Schank

5. Torpedo Attacks on SC 7

Key	U-boat	Weather	Observation
	U-boat attacking	1 Wind direction & strength (Beaufort)	1 U-boat unobserved
	Time	2 Sea state	2 U-boat observed optically
	1 Date	3 Visibility (nm)	3 U-boat detected by Asdic/radar
	2 Time of firing	**Convoy**	**Target**
	Grid	1 Convoy number (s = straggler)	1 Ship type
	Naval grid square	2 Escorts present at the time	2 Estimated tonnage

	Time		Grid	Weather			Convoy		Observation			Target	
	1	2		1	2	3	1	2	1	2	3	1	2
U 124	16	0350	AL 2876	S 1–2	1–2	3–4	SC 7 s	–	X			SS	1,813
U 48	17	0553	AL 3388	NNW 1	0	10	SC 7	3	X			T	10,000
	17	0553	AL 3388	NNW 1	0	10	SC 7	3	X			SS	6,000
	17	0553	AL 3388	NNW 1	0	10	SC 7	3	X			SS	5,000
U 38	17	0951	AL 1632	NW 2	1–2	good	SC 7 s	–	X			SS	3,554
	18	0204	AL 1539	SSE 2	1	good	SC 7	2	X			SS	6,000
	18	0227	AL 1539	SSE 2	1	good	SC 7	2	X			SS	6,000
U 123	18	2020	AM 2799	SSE 2	1–2	good	HX 77 s	–	X			SS	11,000
	18	2028	AM 2799	SSE 2	2	good	HX 77 s	–	X			SS	11,000
U 46	18	2046	AM 2799	SSE 2	2	good	HX 77 s	-	X			SS	11,000
	18	2058	AM 2922	SSE 3–4	3	moderate	SC 7	3	X			SS	6,000
	18	2100	AM 2922	SSE 3–4	3	moderate	SC 7	3	X			SS	7,000
	18	2103	AM 2922	SSE 3–4	3	moderate	SC 7	3	X			SS	4,000
U 46	18	2104	AM 2922	SSE 3–4	3	moderate	SC 7	3	X			SS	4,000
U 101	18	2112	AM 2921	SE 2–3	2	2–3	SC 7	3	X			SS	6,000
	18	2112	AM 2921	SE 2–3	2	2–3	SC 7	3	X			SS	5,000
U 99	18	2112	AM 2921	SE 2–3	2	2–3	SC 7	3	X			SS	3,000
	18	2202	AM 2924	SE 4	3	5–7	SC 7	0	X			SS	6,000
	18	2206	AM 2924	SE 4	3	5–7	SC 7	0	X			SS	6,500
U 46	18	2225	AM 2922	SSE 3–4	3	moderate	SC 7	0		X		SS	6,000
U 99	18	2230		SE 4	3	5–7	SC 7	0		X		SS	6,000
U 123	18	2244		SE 2	2	good	SC 7	0	X			SS	9,000
	18	2245		SE 2	2	good	SC 7	0	X			SS	6,000
	18	2246		SE 2	2	good	SC 7	0	X			SS	6,000

APPENDICES

Attack	Distance	Claim
1 Surface attack	1 Distance estimated by U-boat (m)	1 Hit on target
2 Submerged attack	2 Running time (sec)	2 Hit on other target
3 Surfaced *coup de grâce*	3 Actual distance (m)	3 Miss
4 Submerged *coup de grâce*		4 U-boat report: S = sunk, D = damaged
5 Number fired		Result
6 Torpedo type		

Attack						Distance			Claim				Result
1	2	3	4	5	6	1	2	3	1	2	3	4	
	X			1	T1	1,000	48	988	X			S	SS *Trevisa* sunk
X				1	T2	3,000	160	2,469	X			S	MT *Languedoc* sunk
X				1	T2	4,000	265	4,089	X			S	SS *Scoresby* sunk
X				1	T2	4,000	371	5,725	X			D	missed
	X			1	T2	1,000					X	S	SS *Aenos* missed, sunk by gunfire
	X			2	T2	1,700	115	1,774	X			S	SS *Carsbreck* 1 hit, damaged
	X			1	T1	1,000					X	–	missed
	X			1	T2	1,100	72	1,111	X			D	MS *Port Gisborne* hit
	X			1	T1	1,200	52	1,070	X			D	MS *Port Gisborne* hit
	X			1	T2	3,000	181	2,793	X			S	MS *Port Gisborne* sunk
X				1	T2	1,800					X		missed
X				1	T2	1,500			X			D	SS *Convallaria* sunk
X				1	T2	3,600			X			S	missed
X				1	T1	1,800			X			S	missed
X				1	T2	3,750	250	3,858	X			S	missed
X				1	T2	3,650	243	3,749	X			S	missed
X				1	T2	3,650					X	–	missed
X				1	T1	4,000					X	–	SS *Creekirk* missed
X				1	T2	705	47	725	X			S	SS *Creekirk* sunk
X				1	T2	1,500				X		S	SS *Empire Miniver* sunk
X				1	T2	1,500					X	–	missed
X				1	T2	2,000					X	–	missed
X				1	T2	2,000					X	–	missed
X				1	T2	2,000					X	–	missed

	Time		Grid	Weather			Convoy		Observation			Target	
	1	2		1	2	3	1	2	1	2	3	1	2
U 101	18	2308	AM 2952	SE 2–3	2	5	SC 7	0	X			SS	6,000
	18	2308	AM 2952	SE 2–3	2	5	SC 7	0	X			SS	6,000
	18	2309	AM 2952	SE 2–3	2	5	SC 7	0	X			SS	3,500
	18	2309	AM 2952	SE 2–3	2	5	SC 7	0	X			SS	6,000
U 100	18	2317	AM 2921	SSE 3	1	moderate	SC 7	0				SS	5,458
U 123	18	2320		SE 3	2–3	good	SC 7	0	X			SS	5,000
U 99	18	2330	AM 2928	SE 4	3	5–7	SC 7	0	X			SS	7,000
U 100	18	2337	AM 2916	SSE 3	1	moderate	SC 7	0		X		SS	3,500
U 99	18	2355	AM 2928	SE 4	3	5–7	SC 7	0	X			SS	6,000
U 123	19	0021		SE 3	2–3	good	SC 7	0	X			SS	6,000
U 101	19	0122	AM 2958	SE 2–3	2	8	SC 7	0	X			SS	7,000
	19	0122	AM 2958	SE 2–3	2	8	SC 7	0	X			SS	7,000
	19	0122	AM 2958	SE 2–3	2	8	SC 7	0	X			SS	4,000
	19	0124	AM 2958	SE 2–3	2	8	SC 7	0	X			SS	3,000
U 123	19	0131	AM 2951	–	–	–	SC 7 s	–	X			SS	7,000
	19	0135	AM 2951	–	–	–	SC 7 s	–	X			SS	4,000
U 99	19	0138	AM 2955	SE 4	3	5–7	SC 7	0	X			SS	6,000
U 123	19	0155	AM 2927	–	–	good	SC 7 s	–	X			SS	4,000
U 99	19	0155	AM 2957	SE 4	3	5–7	SC 7	0	X			SS	7,000
	19	0240	AM 2981	SE 3–4	3	5–7	SC 7	0	X			SS	9,500
U 100	19	0250	AM 2919	SE 3	1	moderate	SC 7 s	–	X			SS	4,155
U 99	19	0255	AM 2981	SE 3–4	3	5–7	SC 7	0	X			SS	9,500
U 100	19	0300	AM 2919	SE 3	1	moderate	SC 7 s	–	X			SS	4,155
U 99	19	0302	AM 2981	SE 3–4	3	5–7	SC 7	0	X			SS	9,500
U 123	19	0317	AM 2946	SSW 3	2–3	–	SC 7	0	X			SS	5,500
U 99	19	0356	AM 2981	SE 3–4	3	5–7	SC 7	0	X			SS	3,106
	19	0358	AM 2981	SE 3–4	3	5–7	SC 7 s	–	X			SS	3,106

6. Attacks on U-boats near SC 7

Date	German Time	Allied Time	U-boat	Grid Square	German Position
17 Oct.	0918	0818	U 48	AL 3474	59°15'N, 17°24'W
17 Oct.	1015	0910	U 48	AL 3474	59°15'N, 17°24'W

Attack						Distance			Claim				Result
1	2	3	4	5	6	1	2	3	1	2	3	4	
X				1	T1	5,100	255	5,248	X			S	SS *Beatus* sunk
X				1	T2	4,000					X	–	missed
X				1	T2	3,600	238	3,672	X			S	SS *Gunborg* sunk
X				1	T2	3,600	240	3,703	X			D	missed
X				1	T1	1,000	51	1,050	X			D	SS *Shekatika* hit
X				1	T2	800					X	–	missed
X				1	T2	1,740	116	1,790		X		S	SS *Blairspey* hit
X				1	T2	1,000	63	972	X			S	SS *Boekelo* sunk
X				1	T2	750	50	772	X			S	SS *Niritos* hit
X				1	T2	500					X	–	missed
X				1	T1	1,350	66	1,358	X			S	SS *Assyrian* sunk
X				1	T2	870	58	895	X			S	SS *Empire Brigade* sunk
X				1	T2	1,150	77	1,188	X			S	missed
X				1	T2	1,725	115	1,774	X			S	SS *Soesterberg* sunk
		X		1	T1	1,900	95	1,955	X			S	SS *Shekatika* sunk
		X		1	T1						X	–	SS *Niritos* missed
X				1	T2	945	63	972	X			S	SS *Thalia* sunk
		X		1	T2	1,100	73	1,126	X			S	SS *Niritos* sunk
X				1	T2	975	65	1,003	X			S	SS *Fiscus* sunk
X				1	T2	700					X	–	SS *Sedgepool* missed
		X		1	T2	975	65	1,003	X			D	SS *Bairspey* hit
X				1	T2	700					X	–	SS *Sedgepool* missed
			X	1	T2	780	52	802	X			D	SS *Blairspey* hit
X				1	T2	720	48	741	X			S	SS *Sedgepool* sunk
X				1	T2	660	44	679	X			S	SS *Snefjeld* sunk
X				1	T2	750					X	–	SS *Clintonia* missed
X				1	T1	920	46	947	X			D	SS *Clintonia* hit

Allied Position	Weapons Used	Attacking Units	Rating*	Result
59°10'N, 17°50'W	4 D/C	Sunderland H/210	E	no damage
59°10'N, 17°44'W	21 D/C	HMS *Scarborough*	–	no damage

* 'Rating' refers to an Allied system for evaluating attacks on suspected U-boats, ranging from category A 'known sunk', through E 'probably slightly damaged', to J 'insufficient information to assess'. See also Appendices 9 and 10.

7. Torpedo Attacks on SC 118

Key	U-boat	Weather	Observation
	U-boat attacking	1 Wind direction & strength (Beaufort)	1 U-boat unobserved
	Time	2 Sea state	2 U-boat observed optically
	1 Date	3 Visibility (nm)	3 U-boat detected by asdic/radar
	2 Time of firing	**Convoy**	**Target**
	Grid	1 Convoy number (s = straggler)	1 Ship type
	Naval grid square	2 Escorts present at the time	2 Estimated tonnage

		Time	Grid	Weather			Convoy		Observation			Target	
		1	2		1	2	3	1	2	1	2	3	1	2
U 262	5	0555	AK 8443	W 3	2–3	5–6	SC 118 s	–	X			T	12,000
	5	0606	AK 8443	W 3	2–3	5–6	SC 118 s	–	X			SS	9,000
	5	0609	AK 8443	W 3	2–3	5–6	SC 118 s	–	X			SS	9,000
	5	0812	AK 8427	W 3	2–3	5–8	Escort	–	X			DD	1,500
U 413	6	1305	AK 8134	NW 5–6	6	14	SC 118 s	–	X			SS	5,000
	6	1330	AK 8134	NW 5–6	6	14	SC 118 s	–	X			SS	5,000
	6	1421	AK 8134	NW 5–6	6	14	SC 118 s	–	X			SS	5,000
U 266	6	1817	AK 9142	SW 2	1–2	good	SC 118 s	–	X			SS	4,077
	6	1830	AK 9142	SW 2	1–2	good	SC 118 s	–	X			SS	4,077
	6	1832	AK 9142	SW 2	1–2	good	SC 118 s	–	X			SS	4,077
U 262	6	2155	AK 6676	NNW 1	1–2	5–8	SC 118	10	X			T	8,000
	6	2200	AK 6684	NNW 1	1–2	5–8	SC 118	10	X			T	8,000
	6	2205	AK 6684	NNW 1	1–2	5–8	SC 118	10	X			T	9,000
U 402	7	0247	AK 6668	W 3	2	4	SC 118	9	X			SS	6,000
	7	0249	AK 6668	W 3	2	4	SC 118	9	X			T	10,000
	7	0252	AK 6668	W 3	2	4	SC 118	9	X			T	10,000
	7	0302	AK 6668	W 3	3	4	SC 118	8	X			T	10000
U 614	7	0311	AK 6684				SC 118	8				T	8,000
U 402	7	0338	AK 6666	W 3–4	3–4	4	SC 118	8	X			T	12,200
	7	0412	AK 6666	W 3–4	3–4	4	SC 118	8	X			T	12,200
	7	0536	AL 4441	W 4	4	4	SC 118	8	X			SS	8,000
	7	0559	AL 4441	W 4	4	3	SC 118	8	X			SS	6,200

APPENDICES

Attack	Distance	Claim
1 Surface attack	1 Distance estimated by U-boat (m)	1 Hit on target
2 Submerged attack	2 Running time (sec)	2 Hit on other target
3 Surfaced *coup de grâce*	3 Actual distance (m)	3 Miss
4 Submerged *coup de grâce*		4 U-boat report: S = sunk, D = damaged
5 Number fired		Result
6 Torpedo type		

Attack						Distance			Claim				Result
1	2	3	4	5	6	1	2	3	1	2	3	4	
X				3	T2	1,000			X				3 hits observed, SS *Zagloba* sunk
X				1	T2	1,200					X		possibly missed ship of stray column 4
X				1	T2	1,000					X		possibly missed ship of stray column 4
X				2	T2	1,500					X		USCGC *Bibb* missed
X				4	T2	3,500	161	2,400	X				1 hit SS *West Portal*
			X	1		2,000					X		SS *West Portal* missed, torpedo malfunction
			X	1		1,000	84	1,300	X				SS *West Portal* sunk, 53°N, 36°W
	X			1		1,000	24	370	X				SS *Polyktor* hit
			X	1	T2	600	24	370	X				SS *Polyktor* hit
			X	1	T2	600	24	370	X				SS *Polyktor* sunk
X				2	T2	1,200				X			2 hits heard, detonator malfunctioning
X				2	T2	1,200			X				2 explosions heard after 67 sec., damage assumed, no ship hit
X				1	T2	1,000			X				explosion observed after 75 sec., sinking assumed, no ship hit
X				1	T2	1,000	135	2,075	X				SS *Toward* sunk, 55°43'N, 26°40'W
X				2	T2	2,000						X	1 miss, 1 tube runner, against ST *Robert E. Hopkins*
X				1	T2	1,000	140	2,075	X				ST *Robert E. Hopkins* hit
		X		1	T2		130	2,000	X				ST *Robert E. Hopkins* sunk
X				3		1,500				X			heard 3 explosions, 1 hit on SS *Harmala*, sunk 55°14N, 26°37'W
X				1	T2	1,000	90	1,400	X				MT *Daghild* hit
		X		1	T2	2,000					X		MT *Daghild* missed
X				1	T2	1,200	90	1,400	X				SS *Henry R. Mallory*, sunk 55°18'N, 26°39'W
X				1	T2	1,200	53	820	X				SS *Kalliopi*, sunk 55°27'N, 26°08'W

	Time		Grid	Weather			Convoy		Observation			Target	
	1	2		1	2	3	1	2	1	2	3	1	2
U 402	7	0635	AL 4418	W 4	4	3	SC 118	8	X			SS	8,900
	7	0750	AL 4424	W 4	4	3	SC 118	7	X			SS	7,000
U 89	7	1326	AL 4426	W 6	5	3	SC 118 s	–	X			T	8,000
	7	1339	AL 4426	W 6	5	3	SC 118 s	1		X		T	8,000
U 402	8	0042	AL 5134	NW 3	3	1	SC 118	7	X			SS	10,900
U 608	8	0137	AL 5143	W 3	2	7	SC 118 s	2	X			T	12,000
	8	0150	AL 5143	W 3	2	7	SC 118 s	2	X			T	12,000

Key (both tables)	U-boat		Weather		Observation	
	U-boat attacking		1 Wind direction & strength (Beaufort)		1 U-boat unobserved	
	Time		2 Sea state		2 U-boat observed optically	
	1 Date		3 Visibility (nm)		3 U-boat detected by asdic/radar	
	2 Time of firing		Convoy		Target	
	Grid		1 Convoy number (s = straggler)		1 Ship type	
	Naval grid square		2 Escorts present at the time		2 Estimated tonnage	

8. Torpedo Attacks on JW 66 & RA 66

	Time		Grid	Weather			Convoy		Observation			Target	
	1	2		1	2	3	1	2	1	2	3	1	2
U 711	25	1200	AC 8864				JW 66	26	X			SS	7,000
	25	1200	AC 8864				JW 66	26	X			DD	
U 286	29	1934	–				19. EG	–			X	DE	
U 968	29	20xx	AC 8856				7th EG	–	X			DE	
	29	2100	AC 8856				7th EG	–	X			DE	
U 427	29	2222	AC 8829	4	3	1	7th EG?	–	X			SS	
	29	2222	AC 8829	4	3	1	7th EG?	–	X			SS	
U 481	30	0254	AC 8837				2nd D Fl	–		X		DD	
U 711	30	0930	AC 8596				2nd, 7th EG 23rd D Fl	–	X			DD	

APPENDICES

Attack						Distance			Claim				Result
1	2	3	4	5	6	1	2	3	1	2	3	4	
X				1	T2	1,000	48	740	X				SS *Afrika*, sunk 55°16'N, 26°31'W
X				1	T2	1,000				X			surface runner
		X		1					X				MT *Daghild* hit
			X	1						X			MT *Daghild* hit, 55°34'N, 25°52'W, scuttled by FFS *Lobelia*
X				1	T2	1,000	95	1475	X				SS *Newton Ash*, sunk 56°25'N, 22°26'W
X				1	T2						X		SS *Adamas* missed
X				1	T2	2,400	155					X	1 explosion heard, SS *Adamas* missed

Attack	Distance	Claim
1 Surface attack	1 Distance estimated by U-boat (m)	1 Hit on target
2 Submerged attack	2 Running time (sec)	2 Hit on other target
3 Surfaced *coup de grâce*	3 Actual distance (m)	3 Miss
4 Submerged *coup de grâce*		4 U-boat report: S = sunk, D = damaged
5 Number fired		Result
6 Torpedo type		

Attack						Distance			Claim				Result
1	2	3	4	5	6	1	2	3	1	2	3	4	
	X			3	T-2 LUT						X		unknown
	X			1	T-5				X				unknown
	X			1	T-5				X			S	HMS *Goodall*, sunk
	X			3	T-2 LUT				X				HMS *Alnwick Castle*, missed
	X			2	T-5				X				unknown
	X			1	T-2 LUT	1,000	486		X				unknown
	X			2	T-2 LUT	1,000	546		X				unknown
	X			2	T-5						X		HMS *Zodiac*, no hits
	X			1?	T-5?					X			none.

9. Attacks on U-boats near SC 118

Date	German Time	Allied Time	U-boat	Grid Square	German Position
04 Feb.	–	1059	U 187	–	–
04 Feb.	2012	1913	U 608	AK 7966	51°27′N, 35°35′W
04 Feb.	2247	2130	U 267	AK 7969	51°21′N, 35°35′W
04 Feb.	2141	2055	U 454	AK 7963	51°33′N, 35°35′W
04 Feb.	2232	2131	U 402	AK 7965	51°27′N, 35°45′W
04 Feb.	0030	2327	U 465	AK 7925	51°45′N, 36°15′W
04 Feb.	0043	2330	U 262	AK 7697	51°57′N, 35°55′W
05 Feb.	0410	0305	U 609	AK 7664	52°21′N, 35°55′W
05 Feb.	1335	1234	U 465	AK 8165	53°15′N, 34°15′W
05 Feb.	1449	1346	U 267	AK 8518	52°33′N, 33°45′W
06 Feb.	1200	1157	U 465	AK 6757	54°03′N, 30°25′W
06 Feb.	1208	1108	U 454	AK 6769	54°03′N, 29°35′W
06 Feb.	1500	1404	U 624	AK 6489	54°39′N, 30°05′W
06 Feb.	1600	1500	U 608	AK 6578	54°39′N, 29°15′W
06 Feb.	1615	1517	U 614	AK 6528	55°15′N, 28°45′W
06 Feb.	2008	1908	U 267	AK 6919	54°21′N, 27°35′W
06 Feb.	2115	2015	U 456	AK 6568	54°57′N, 28°15′W
06 Feb.	–	2046	U 609	–	–
06 Feb.	2240	2145	U 438	AK 6682	54°51′N, 27°15′W
07 Feb.	0310	0045	U 624	AK 6658	54°57′N, 27°15′W
07 Feb.	0349	0245	U 262	AL 4447	54°57′N, 26°25′W
07 Feb.	0520	0412	U 613	AK 6666	55°03′N, 26°35′W
07 Feb.	0540	0439	U 135	AL 4416	55°21′N, 26°05′W
07 Feb.	1038	0935	U 89	AL 4434	55°21′N, 25°25′W
07 Feb.	1453	1345	U 89	AL 4422	55°27′N, 25°45′W
07 Feb.	1810	1712	U 624	–	–
07 Feb.	2340	2230	U 456	AL 5115	56°15′N, 23°15′W
08 Feb.	0245	0128	U 402	AL 5135	56°15′N, 22°15′W
08 Feb.	1410	1214	U 135	AL 0237	57°03′N, 19°48′W
08 Feb.	1645	1537	U 135	AL 0245	56°51′N, 20°48′W
09 Feb.	1240	1142	U 614	AL 5293	55°45′N, 20°35′W

APPENDICES

* 'Rating' refers to an Allied system for evaluating attacks on suspected U-boats, ranging from category A 'known sunk', through category E 'probably slightly damaged', to category J 'insufficient information to assess'.
An additional category PJS meant 'pending, insufficient information to assess, Soviet'.
These categories are also used in Appendices 5 and 10.

Allied Position	Weapons Used	Attacking Unit(s)	Rating	Result
50°12′N, 36°34′W	30 D/C, H/H, gunfire	HMS *Vimy*, HMS *Beverley*	A	sunk
–	D/C	HMS *Vimy*		no damage
51°14′N, 35°38′W	15 D/C	HMS *Beverley*, HMS *Anemone*	G	no damage
51°54′N, 35°32′W	10 D/C	HMS *Campanula*	G	no damage
52°30′N, 34°04′W	1 D/C	USS *Bibb*	H	no damage
–	D/C	HMS *Beverley*		no damage
51°50′N, 35°50′W	10 D/C, gunfire	HMS *Mignonette*	F	slight damage
52°02′N, 35°17′W	4 D/C	FFS *Lobelia*	G	no damage
52°28′N, 33°20′W	H/H	HMS *Beverley*	F	no damage
52°32′N, 33°15′W	33 D/C, H/H	HMS *Beverley*, HMS *Vimy*	D	no damage
53°50′N, 30°35′W	6 D/C	Liberator W/120, RAF	F	severe damage
53°50′N, 30°20′W	2 D/C	Liberator W/120, RAF	E	medium damage
54°33′N, 29°27′W	6 D/C	Liberator X/120, RAF	D	slight damage
54°10′N, 29°42′W	gunfire	Liberator W/120, RAF		no damage
54°30′N, 28°48′W	4 D/C	Liberator R/120, RAF	D	no damage
53°55′N, 29°02′W	D/C	Liberator R/120, RAF; HMS *Vimy*		severe damage
54°56′N, 28°11′W	11 D/C	FFS *Lobelia*	E	no damage
54°56′N, 28°11′W	10 D/C, H/H	FFS *Lobelia*		sunk
54°55′N, 27°31′W	gunfire, 10 D/C	HMS *Abelia*	H	slight damage
54°53′N, 26°55′W	3 D/C	USS *Babbitt*	F	no damage
54°12′N, 27°28′W	D/C	HMS *Campanula*	D	medium damage
55°17′N, 26°38′W	10 D/C	FFS *Lobelia*	B	no damage
55°21′N, 26°12′W	8 D/C	HMS *Abelia*	F	no damage
55°12′N, 26°31′W	8 D/C, gunfire	HMS *Campanula*, HMS *Mignonette*	F	no damage
55°25′N, 26°06′W	gunfire	FFS *Lobelia*		no damage
55°42′N, 26°17′W	7 D/C	Fortress J/220, RAF	A	sunk
56°31′N, 21°51′W	H/H	HMS *Beverley*	H	no damage
–	gunfire	USS *Bibb*		no damage
56°32′N, 20°06′W	1 D/C	Liberator K/120, RAF	G	medium damage
–	D/C	USS *Bibb*		no damage
56°12′N, 20°59′W	6 D/C	Fortress L/206, RAF	D	severe damage

10. Attacks on U-boats near JW 66 & RA 66

Date	German Time	Allied Time	U-boat	Grid Square	German Position
23 April		0400	U 481	AC 8522	70°45′N, 33°30′E
23 April	1937	1737	U 716	AC 8852	69°33′N, 33°30′E
24 April	0440	250	U 363	AC 8861	69°33′N, 34°10′E
28 April	0518	325	U 427	AC 8827	69°39′N, 33°10′E
29 April	1703	1503	U 711	AC 8864	69°27′N, 34°10′E
29 April	1856	1658	U 307	–	–
29 April	1940	1735	U 286	–	–
29 April		1957	U 968	AC 8856	69°27′N, 33°50′E
30 April	0130	2327	U 968	AC 8837	69°39′N, 34°10′E
30 April	0253		U 481	AC 8837	69°39′N, 34°10′E
30 April	1042		U 427	AC 8541	70°27′N, 32°10′E

APPENDICES

Allied Position	Weapons Used	Attacking Unit(s)	Rating	Result
70°50′N, 33°41′E	6 D/C	Soviet Catalina	PJS	no damage
69°35′N, 33°45′E	D/C	HMS *Loch Insh*, HMS *Cotton*	D	damaged
69°30′N, 35°00′E	4 D/C	Soviet Boston A20	–	damaged
69°55′N, 33°54′E	8 D/C	Soviet Catalina 116th Air Regt.	PJS	no damage
69°43′N, 34°55′E	10 D/C	Soviet Catalina	PJS	slight damage
69°24′N, 33°44′E	Squid	HMS *Loch Insh*, HMS *Loch Shin*, HMS *Cygnet*	A	sunk
69°23′N, 33°37′E	Squid, D/C	HMS *Loch Shin*, HMS *Anguilla*, HMS *Cotton*	B	sunk
69°30′N, 33°34′E	Squid	HMS *Alnwick Castle*	E	no damage
69°36′N, 34°08′E	8 D/C	Soviet Catalina	–	damaged
69°45′N, 33°47′E	10 D/C	HMS *Zodiac*	D	damaged
69°28′N, 34°18′E	4 D/C	Soviet Catalina, 44th Air Regt.	–	no damage

11. Details of Air Cover for SC 118

Date	Aircraft	Up (Base)	Down (Base)	Task	On Task	Remarks
26 Jan.	4 Aircraft			Escort	1039–1307	
					1615–2142	
27 Jan.	1 Aircraft			Escort	1633–2052	
28 Jan.	4 Aircraft			Escort	1211–2138	
30 Jan.	Ven P-12/93 USN	0800/30 (Ar)	1240/30 (Ar)	Escort	0900–1135	
	Ven P-7/93 USN	1322/30 (Ar)	1754/30 (Ar)	Escort	1522–1645	
31 Jan.	Ven P-2/82 USN	0800/31 (Ar)	1233/31 (Ar)	Escort	1010–1125	
	Cat P-8/31 USN	0845/31 (Ar)	1737/31 (Ar)	Escort	1430–1535	
	Ven P-8/82 USN	1312/31 (Ar)	1752/31 (Ar)	Escort	1415–1620	
	Ven P-5/93 USN	2100/31 (Ar)	0130/1 (Ar)	A/S sweep		
1 Feb.	Ven P-6/82 USN	0814/1 (Ar)	1347/1 (Ar)	Escort	1105–1150	
	Ven P-10/82 USN	1113/1 (Ar)	1651/1 (Ar)	Escort	1251–1450	
6 Feb.	Lib X/120	0323/6 (A)	2123/6 (B)	Escort	1154–1459	1043 sighted *U 413*, 1405 attacked *U 624*
	Lib W/120	0538/6 (R)	2136/6 (R)	Escort	1000–1704	1056 attacked *U 465*, 1108 attacked *U 454*, 1500 attacked *U 608*
	Lib O/120	1142/6 (A)	0039/7 (R)	Escort	1829–2009	1720 sighted *U 267*
	Lib R/120	1156/6 (R)	0129/7 (R)	Escort	1923–2032	1516 attacked *U 614*, 1835 sighted *U 267*
07 Feb.	Cat P/84 USN	0256/7 (R)	1235/7 (R)	Escort	c/v not met	Recalled due to weather
	Cat O/84 USN	0407/7 (R)	0715/7 (R)	Escort	Broke off	Recalled due to weather
	Cat B/84 USN	0430/7 (R)	0709/7 (R)	Escort	Broke off	Recalled due to weather
	Cat I/84 USN	0511/7 (R)	1431/7 (R)	Escort	Recalled	Recalled due to weather
	Cat G/84 USN	0603/7 (R)	1155/7 (R)	Escort	Broke off	Recalled due to weather
	Lib C/120	0730/7 (A)	2220/7 (B)	Escort	c/v not met	Searched for convoy 1222 till 1800
	Lib S/120	1023/7 (B)	0015/8 (B)	Escort	1737–1950	
	For G/206	0644/7 (Be)	1615/7 (Be)	A/S sweep	0907–1435	
	For B/206	0658/7 (Be)	1641/7 (Be)	A/S sweep	0912–1435	
	For L/206	0934/7 (Be)	2002/7 (Be)	A/S sweep	1225–1752	
	For R/220	1227/7 (B)	2240/7 (B)	A/S sweep	1511–2014	
	For N/220	1228/7 (B)	2315/7 (B)	A/S sweep	1520–2044	
	For J/220	1230/7 (B)	2308/7 (B)	A/S sweep	1512–2000	1707 sank *U 624*
08 Feb.	For D/206	0520/8 (Be)	1513/8 (Be)	Escort	1149–1226	
	For L/206	0837/8 (Be)	1810/8 (Be)	Escort	1244–1524	
	Lib N/120	1112/8 (A)	2245/9 (B)	Escort	1505–2210	
	For B/206	1208/8 (Be)	2204/8 (Be)	Escort	1542–1929	
	Sun T/228	1420/8 (Ca)	1955/8 (Ca)	Escort	Broke off	Recalled due to weather 1655
	For G/206	1425/8 (Be)	2259/8 (Be)	Escort	1740–2029	
	For R/220	0513/8 (B)	1644/8 (B)	A/S sweep	0922–1333	1152 sighted *U 89*
	For H/220	0532/8 (B)	1638/8 (B)	A/S sweep	0943–1317	
	For J/220	0634/8 (B)	1715/8 (B)	A/S sweep	1053–1407	
	Lib K/120	1043/8 (R)	0003/9 (R)	A/S sweep	1427–1925	1315 attacked *U 135*
09 Feb.	For B/220	0702/9 (B)	1723/9 (B)	Escort	1125–1551	
	For L/206	0655/9 (Be)	1720/9 (Be)	A/S sweep	0816–1600	1142 attacked *U 614*
	For G/206	0700/9 (Be)	1821/9 (Be)	A/S sweep	0834–1710	
	For D/206	0705/9 (Be)	1844/9 (Be)	A/S sweep	0833–1723	

Aircraft: Cat = Consolidated Catalina; For = Boeing Flying Fortress; Lib = Consolidated Liberator; Sun = Short Sunderland; Ven= Lockheed Ventura.
Bases: A = Aldergrove, Northern Ireland; Ar + Argentia, Newfoundland; B = Ballykelly, Northern Ireland; Be = Benbecula, Outer Hebrides; Ca = Castle Archdale, Northern Ireland; R = Reykjavik, Iceland.

Ranks and Abbreviations

The following ranks and abbreviations are used in the main pages of this book. Exact equivalents in other navies cannot always be given and designations of senior non-commissioned personnel in particular included a wide variety of ranks and job titles in both German and Allied services, far more than can be mentioned here.

Selected Officer Ranks		
Kriegsmarine	*Royal Navy*	*Royal Air Force*
Fähnrich zur See (FhrzS) Oberfähnrich zur See (OfhrzS)	Midshipman	Pilot Officer
Leutnant zur See (LtzS)	Sub-Lieutenant	Flying Officer
Oberleutnant zur See (ObltzS)	Lieutenant	Flight Lieutenant
Kapitänleutnant (Kplt)	Lieutenant-Commander	Squadron Leader
Korvettenkapitän (KKpt)	Commander	Wing Commander
Fregattenkapitän Kapitän zur See	Captain	Group Captain

British officers might be designated as RN, RNR or RNVR: Royal Navy (i.e. regulars); Royal Naval Reserve (men with naval training whose pre-war jobs were usually as merchant navy officers); Royal Naval Volunteer Reserve (men with little or no direct seagoing experience).

German personnel similarly included officers 'der Reserve' (der Res); there was also the rank of Reserveoffizieranwärter (ROA) – reserve officer candidate; a senior petty officer given a wartime commission might be designated a Kriegsoffizier (KO); designations for officers of the engineering branch included 'Ing' for Ingenieuroffizier.

Marine-Artillerie Sonderführer (MA Sdf, translated as Naval Artillery Special Duties Officer) was a rank often given to propaganda photographers or journalists serving on U-boats in order to to provide them with appropriate status among the crew.

Non-commissioned roles mentioned in the text are Steuermann/Obersteuermann (Strm/Obrstrm; translatable as helmsman/chief helmsman) roughly equivalent to the RN positions of coxswain or boatswain – in RN service often the senior non-commissioned man aboard a ship, likely a chief petty officer in rank.

Maschinenobergefreiter, mentioned in a caption, is roughly equivalent to the RN rank of leading stoker, a junior NCO of the engineering branch.

Index

Abelia 11, 87, 112, 123, 125, 146, 151, 161, 163–4, 177, 185–6, 192
Adamas 86, 169, 176–9, 181–2, 255
Adams, Kenneth Frederick 209
Aenos 19, 25–6, 35, 249
African Prince 86–7, 112
Afrika 86, 163, 166–7, 255
Allen, Roland Charlton 36, 55, 59
Allington Castle 209
Allison, John Hamilton 209
Alnwick Castle 198, 209, 211, 213, 218, 220, 255, 259
Andersen, Klaus 16, 206, 225, 246
Anemone 87, 101, 104, 107, 109–11, 114, 175, 186, 257
Anguilla 205, 219, 233, 259
Annik 86, 96
Apollo 205
Assyrian 19, 43, 49, 51, 55, 62, 351
Athelprince 86–7

Babbitt 99, 129, 151, 176–7, 179, 181, 192, 257
Baker, Ernst Reginald 31
Bamborough Castle 209, 211, 218
Bass, Kenneth Burdett 182
Baudoux, Everett Large 79
Bayliss, Horace Temple Taylor 209
Beatus 19, 36, 48, 51, 53, 55, 251
Bellona 209, 211, 226
Beloe, Isaac William Trant 205
Bespalow, W. G. 224
Beverley 87, 96–7, 99–101, 104, 107–11, 114, 119–21, 127, 175, 177, 181–2, 257
Bibb 90–1, 107, 118, 121, 127–8, 133, 142, 154, 157, 165, 168, 171, 177–8, 181, 184, 186, 253, 257
Bingham, Leslie 93
Bismarck 9
Black Ranger 210–11, 224
Black Watch 218, 232
Blairspey 19, 36, 55, 62–3, 65, 251
Blanc, Rene 156
Bleichrodt, Heinrich 27–8, 31, 70, 243
Blue Ranger 233
Bluebell 3, 27–9, 31, 37, 41, 44, 47, 52–3, 59, 61, 63
BO 135 224
BO 137 224
BO 209 216, 219
BO 219 224

BO 225 216, 219
BO 242 224
Boekelo 19, 51, 55, 58–9, 251
Brown, Harold Hinksman 111, 155–6

Campanula 87, 95, 106, 147, 153, 167–8, 171, 177, 186, 192, 257
Carsbreck 19, 32, 35, 37, 249
Clintonia 19, 68, 70, 72, 251
Convallaria 19, 42–5, 68, 249
Copeland 210, 224
Cordelia 93–4, 185
Cotton 205
Cowell, Patrick James 209, 211, 223
Cowey, Robert Leonard 172
Cowichan 87
Cox, Thomas Spencer 209
Creekirk 2, 19, 47, 49, 249
Cunninghame Graham, Angus Edward Malise Bontine 209, 216–17, 231
Cunningham, Robert Dickinson 182, 184
Cygnet 209, 211, 217–18, 259

Daghild 86, 148–9, 158, 162, 170–1, 182, 253, 255
Debnam, Herbert John Harry 182
Deido 86, 148
de Lisle Bush, Christopher Godfrey 26
Dempster, Edward Welstead Charles 205
Derzkij 211, 224
Deyczakowski, Zbigniew 117
Dickinson, Norman Vincent 23, 36
Dido 205
Dietrich, Willi 17, 206, 218, 243, 246
Dönitz, Karl 1–4, 8–9, 12–13, 19, 75–6, 82, 85, 97, 135, 163, 171, 176, 191
Dostoinyi 211
Drummond, Roderick Patrick 182
Dunbar-Naismith, Martin Eric 60
Dunvegan 87

Eaglescliffe Hall 19, 25–6
Eagleston, Norman Fountain 182
Edser, Walter Edwin 172
Egidius, Olaf Kristian 159
Eickstedt, Wolfgang 206, 247
Elkins, Robert Francis 205
Empire Brigade 19, 62, 251
Empire Miniver 19, 47, 51–2, 249
Empire Spey 65

Endraß, Engelbert 30, 33, 41, 51–2, 243
Estabrook, William Sears 141

Farnham Castle 209, 211, 213, 218–19, 233
Faust, U-Boat group 16, 205–8, 214–16, 220, 224–6, 228
Fennel 87
Fiscus 19, 65, 77
Flemming-Williams, Donald Charles 135–6
Forstner, Siegfried Freiherr von 100, 107, 121, 154, 158, 162–3, 165–7, 171, 177–8, 182, 185–6, 243–4
Forsyth, Hugh Caldwell Codrington 87
Fowey 26, 29, 31, 37, 41, 47, 51–2, 55, 59, 61, 63
Franke, Heinz 101, 103, 110–11, 117–18, 146–7, 149, 153, 186, 244
Franze, Joachim 206, 246
Franzius, Rudolf 145–7, 176, 245
Frauenheim, Fritz 33, 42, 50, 53, 62, 67, 73, 243
Frewen, Jerome Hugh 130, 133–4
Fulton, James Vandalle 205, 209

Gardner, Robert James 209
Gaza, Jürgen von 206, 232, 246
Gill, Roy 230
Golovko, Arseni Grigorevic 216
Goodall 205, 218–21, 223, 233, 255
Goodfellow, Robin 136–7
Gower, John Ronald 205
Grabowski, Johannes 231
Griffin, Oswald Joseph 123
Grindle, John Annesley 205
Groos, Harold Victor William 209
Gudenus, Karl-Gabriel Graf von 207, 220–3, 237, 246
Gunborg 19, 49, 53, 251

Hackländer, Burkhard 105–7, 129, 133, 167, 185, 244
Hagen, U-Boat group 202
Haida 209, 223, 226
Hanson, Ronald John 25
Harmala 86, 127, 156–7, 159–60, 189, 253
Haudegen, U-Boat group 84–5, 90, 92, 97, 121
Heartsease 36–7
Henry R. Mallory 6, 84, 86, 114–15, 118–19, 127, 160, 163–4, 167–8, 178, 253

INDEX

Hesperus 87
HG 76 9
Hicks, Roger Bertram Nettleton 209
Hill, Philip Michael 182
Hitler, Adolf 9
Honeysuckle 209, 218–19, 223
Horton, Max 99
Hudson, Gordon K. 155
Hübsch, Horst 146
Huron 209, 211, 223, 226
HX 72 8
HX 77 40–1, 248
HX 78 23
HX 79 75
HX 219 87
HX 223 85
HX 224 85, 91, 93, 97, 136, 161, 181, 185

Ingham 6, 91, 99, 128, 133, 142, 151, 168, 171, 178, 186, 191
Iroquois 209, 211, 223–4, 226
Isted, Desmond James 130, 133

Jaguar, U-Boat group 85, 92, 97
Jahndel, Walter 231
Jensen, Emanuel Broholm 167
Jeremiah van Rensselaer 160
Jessel, Richard Frederick 209, 211
Jessen, Ralf von 123, 140, 245
JW 64 201
JW 65 202

Kaiser, Karl-Ernst 169
Kalliopi 86, 165, 253
Karl Libknekht 211
Karpenko, F. I. 224
Keppel 25
Kessler, Horst-Wilhelm 122
King, E. S. 77
King, Patrick George Alexander 104
Kirkwood, Henry 205
Kong Haakon VII 210, 213
Kontisas, Nikos 140
Köppe, Helmut 158–9, 245
Kretschmer, Otto 4, 33, 47, 55, 61, 63, 65, 70, 73, 166, 243
Kronprinsen 210, 213
Krüger, Erich 206, 217, 246
Kuhnke, Günter 33, 243
Kujbyshev 211

Lange, Hans-Günther 206, 213, 226, 247
Languedoc 19, 27, 29, 31, 249
Lapwing 202
Laurelwood 210–11
LCT 2335 159
Leary 91
Lehmann, Hans 206, 244, 247
Leith 35–7, 41–3, 45, 47, 52, 55, 59–63
Liebe, Heinrich 5, 26, 34, 37, 243

Linn Boyd 210
Lobelia 91, 111–12, 114–15, 118, 142–6, 154, 156–7, 159–62, 164, 167, 171, 181, 185–6, 192, 255, 257
Loch Insh 205, 208, 217, 219, 259
Loch Shin 15, 205, 217, 219, 225, 259
Lohmann, Dietrich 125, 153, 170, 182, 244
Lotus 209, 217–18

MacIntyre, Donald George Frederick Wyville 87
Mackinnon, Lachlan Donald Ian 43
Maksimow, S. N. 224
Marshall, Edward 93
Martinson, Albert Mathias 128, 151, 178
Maudsley, Arthur Terence 79
Mayflower 87
McGrigor, Rhoderick Robert 201
Mignonette 87, 111, 114, 143–4, 155–6, 159, 164, 167–8, 171, 177, 186, 257
MO 430 216, 219
MO 433 216, 219
Moehle, Heinz 31, 33, 38, 40, 52, 63, 70, 243
Moffat, John Knox 172
Morrison-Payne, Christopher 205
Morsier, Pierre de 114–15, 143–4
Mortimer, Ralph Smith 209
MTK 215 219
MTK 222 219
Mumm, Friedrich 123, 140, 245

Nees, Werner 206, 247
Nelson, Lawrence Macauley 172
Newton Ash 86, 177–9, 255
Niritos 19, 25, 52, 60–1, 63, 251
North, Edward John Robert 36

OA 228 27
OB 228 32
Obedient 205, 233
Offa 209, 211, 223, 226
Øi, Helge 209
OL 7 25
ON 160 85
ON 161 85
Opportune 205
Orwell 205, 233
Oxlip 209–11, 218

Park Benjamin 210
Patrick, Richard Cecil 185
Pfeil, U-Boat group 84, 91–4, 97, 103, 105, 113, 115, 121, 124, 126, 141, 145, 149, 167–8, 174–6, 186–7
PK 9 208, 214
Plaep, Friedrich Hermann 79
Poel, Gustav 122, 245
Polyktor 86, 127, 129–31, 140, 149, 253

Pontikos, Nikos 165
Port Gisborne 40–1, 47, 52, 73, 249
Premier 209, 211, 226
Price, Rodney Athelstan 97, 110, 127, 182
Proudfoot, Francis Babington 87, 91, 97, 99, 103, 107, 112, 117, 119, 123, 127, 130, 136, 138, 143, 151, 154, 156–7, 164–5, 171, 178, 185–6, 191–2
Purvis, James 178

Quarles, Samuel Frank 129, 151, 179

RA 64 201
RA 65 202, 205
Radport 149
Raney, Roy Livingston 107–8, 168, 178, 184
Read, Phillips Almond 209
Rhododendron 209, 211, 217–18, 220
Roberson, George Peter 172–3
Robert E. Hopkins 86, 148–9, 155–6, 253
Roberts, J. 87
Robinson, George Moorhead Melville 65
Römer, Bernhard 187
Rogers, Benjamin Andrew 106, 153
Roxburgh, William 172, 182
Rudloff, Klaus 101, 112–15, 118–19, 124, 129, 135, 141–2, 145
Rycroft, Henry Richard 209
Ryder, Robert Edward Dudley 205

Salvonia 62, 65, 72
Samaritan 210
Samuel Huntington 86, 177
SC 2 8
SC 117 85
SC 130 193
SC 1478 209
SC 1479 209
SC 1482 209
SC 1483 209
SC 1486 209
SC 1487 209
SC 1491 209
SC 1493 209
SC 1497 209
SC 1499 210
SC 1503 210
SC 1505 210
SC 1506 210
SC 1508 210
SC 1511 210
SC 1512 210
Scarborough 23, 28–9, 31, 36, 41, 251
Schenck 91, 141, 147, 153–4, 167, 186, 191–2
Schepke, Joachim 1, 33, 54–5, 58, 63, 65, 243
Schroeter, Karl-Ernst 139, 141, 245

INDEX

Schulz, Wilhelm 24–5, 243
Schütt, Heinz 121, 161, 190, 206, 244, 247
Schweiger, Friedhelm 204, 228, 246
Scoresby 19, 27, 29, 249
Sedgepool 19, 56, 65
Sgourdaios, Fragkopoulos 181
Shekatika 23, 54–5, 59, 63, 251
Sherwood, Robert Evan 27
Shikari 72
Sinclair, Roy McEwen 209
Skrzipek, Heinrich 187
Snefield 19, 65
Soden-Allmendingen, Ulrich Graf von 133, 135, 144–5, 151, 173, 245
Soesterberg 19, 51, 62
Sommerstad 86, 149
Stannard, Richard Been 8
Stonehouse, Herbert Arthur 8, 99, 103, 136, 185
Stord 209, 211, 223, 226
Sträter, Wolfgang 135, 186, 188, 245
Struckmeier, Rolf 102–3, 126, 135, 167, 169, 178–9, 244

T-113 211
T-119 216
Teichert, Max-Martin 136, 142–4, 175, 181, 245
Thalia 19, 61, 64–5
Thimme, Jürgen 206, 247
Thorpe, Ernest Michael 209
Tinschert, Otto 103–4, 119–20, 136–8, 244
Toward 86–7, 91, 97, 100, 103, 107, 117–18, 122–3, 130, 142, 145, 149, 154–7, 161, 191, 253
Trevisa 19, 25, 249
Truro 87
Tuck, Gerald Seymour 209
Turnbull, Bryan Walker 182, 184
Turner, Reginald Thomas Frederick 172

U 28 33, 38
U 32 76
U 38 5, 25–6, 32–38, 54, 74, 243
U 46 22, 30, 32–3, 40–2, 47, 49, 51, 73, 78–9, 243
U 48 26–9, 31–3, 35, 37, 40–1, 67–8, 70, 72, 243
U 89 92, 97, 125, 129, 145, 153, 168, 170–1, 174, 181, 184–5, 244
U 99 2, 4, 18, 29, 32–3, 38, 40, 45, 47, 49, 52, 55–6, 60–1, 63–5, 68, 70, 72–3, 77, 166, 243, 248, 250
U 100 1, 32–3, 38, 51, 53–5, 58–63, 65, 243, 248, 250
U 101 32–3, 38, 40, 42–3, 45, 47–50, 52–3, 55, 61–2, 67, 73, 74, 243, 248, 250
U 123 31–3, 38, 40–1, 46–7, 52, 61–3, 65, 70, 72–3, 243, 248, 250
U 124 24–25, 243, 248
U 135 92, 97, 121, 125–6, 155, 161, 173, 176, 184, 190, 244, 256, 260
U 187 8, 12, 92, 96–7, 99–100, 108, 183, 187, 244, 256
U 262 92, 103, 105, 107, 111, 113, 115, 117–18, 120, 125, 127, 142, 146–9, 151, 153, 174, 244, 252, 256
U 265 97
U 266 97, 122–3, 131, 139–40, 245, 252
U 267 92, 97, 103–4, 107–9, 119–21, 125, 130, 136–7, 139, 167, 244, 256, 260
U 278 206, 214, 232, 246
U 286 15, 17, 206, 214, 219–21, 224, 226, 233, 246, 254, 258
U 294 206, 208–9, 247
U 295 206, 214, 229, 232, 247
U 307 15, 206, 214, 217–18, 224, 226, 246, 258
U 312 205–6, 214, 232, 246
U 313 204, 206, 214, 228, 232, 246
U 318 232
U 357 87
U 363 206, 214, 247, 258
U 402 92, 96, 100, 103, 107–8, 113, 119, 121, 123, 145, 152, 154, 158, 160, 162–5, 167, 173, 176–9, 180–4, 186–7, 244, 252, 254, 256
U 413 92, 97, 120, 122–3, 131, 139, 179, 245, 252
U 425 208
U 427 203, 207, 214, 216, 220–3, 226, 228, 231, 237, 246, 254
U 438 97, 121, 145–7, 175–6, 245
U 454 92, 105–7, 125, 129, 133, 139, 167–8, 171, 174, 184–5, 244, 256, 260
U 456 91, 97, 136, 142–4, 146, 160, 167, 171, 175–7, 181, 192, 245, 246
U 465 92, 99, 110, 118–21, 125, 131, 133, 139, 166, 170, 244, 256, 260
U 466 97
U 481 16, 206, 214, 225–6, 231, 246, 254, 256, 258
U 594 92, 97, 122–3, 139–40, 245
U 608 92, 102–3, 115, 125–6, 135, 167, 169, 173, 176, 178–9, 181, 187, 244, 254, 256
U 609 92, 101, 112–15, 117–21, 123–5, 127, 129, 135–6, 138, 141–2, 144–5, 154, 156, 160, 167, 192, 244, 252, 256
U 613 97, 121, 133, 157–62, 173–4, 184, 245, 256
U 614 97, 135–6, 156–7, 167, 176, 184–5, 188–9, 245, 252, 256, 260
U 624 97, 121, 127, 133–5, 144–5, 149, 151, 172–4, 183, 192, 245, 256, 260
U 632 93–5
U 668 205–6, 247
U 704 97, 121–3, 139, 245
U 706 97
U 711 206, 213–14, 217, 226, 228, 232, 247, 254, 258
U 716 205, 207–8, 247, 258
U 752 97, 121, 139, 141, 245
U 968 198, 207, 209, 214, 220, 223–4, 226, 229, 231, 234–5, 246, 254, 258
U 992 232
U 997 206, 214, 247
UB 68 2
Uritski 211

Vanessa 87–8, 117, 127, 151, 156–7, 166, 186, 192
Vernon, Henry 4, 209
Vimy 8, 87–8, 99–100, 103, 119–21, 127, 136–8, 157, 161, 185–7, 257
Vindex 209, 211, 226, 231

Walker, Frederic John 192–3, 235
Walker, Harry Chessman 159
Warwick, William Eldon 209
Weaver, Horace Rudolph 168
Weir, Robert Stanley 182
Welland, Robert Philip 209
West Portal 86, 120, 122–3, 130, 140, 253
Westphalen, Otto 207, 220, 223, 234–5, 246
Wieboldt, Günter 206, 209, 247
Wilson, Henry John 182
Winona 19, 23
Witch 91, 99
Wolf, Heinz 99–100, 110, 118, 131, 133, 166, 244
Woods, Sidney Richard James 99
Wright, John 172
Wright, James Alfred 209

Zagloba 86, 117–18, 130, 140, 253
Zarkij 211, 223
Zealous 209, 211, 223, 225–6
Zephyr 209, 223
Zest 209, 223, 226
Zimmermann, Clemens 231
Zodiac 209–11, 223–6, 255, 259
Zostkij 211, 224